DATELINE '79:
Heretical Concepts for the Community College

Arthur M. Cohen

Graduate School of Education
University of California, Los Angeles

with a Foreword by Alvin C. Eurich

GLENCOE PRESS
A Division of The Macmillan Company
Beverly Hills, California
Collier-Macmillan Ltd., London

First printing, 1969

Library of Congress catalog card number: 70-77486

The Glencoe Press
A Division of The Macmillan Company

Collier-Macmillan Canada, Ltd., Toronto, Canada

Printed in the United States of America

To my wife, Barbara

Foreword

"And God said, 'Let there be light'; and there was light . . . .

> "And God said, 'Let there be lights to separate the day from the night.' And God made the two great lights, the greater light to rule the day, and the lesser light to rule the night; he made the stars also . . . .

> > "Then God said, 'Let us make man in our image.' . . . So God created man in his own image."

> > And man said, "Let there be horseless carriages," and he made the automobile.

> And man said, "Let there be flying ships that will carry hundreds of people through the air at 2000 miles per hour," and he made the supersonic jet.

Then man said, "Let us go to the moon," and he went there.

These words from the first chapter of Genesis and the few samples of man's enormous achievements reveal that God and man have not been content to predict the future: they have invented it. For as Dennis Gabor has said, "the future cannot be predicted, but it can be invented." How man will shape it, Gabor adds, "is largely a matter of free human choice, not the business of machines, nor of scientists, not even psychologists; but the prerogative of inspired humanists, of poets and writers. . . . It was man's ability to invent which has made human society what it is."

And it was man's ability to invent which made our schools, colleges, and universities what they are today — what they will be ten, twenty-five, and a hundred years from now.

In this book, Professor Arthur Cohen adds significantly to a rapidly growing, impressive, and most useful futuristic literature. He invents the community college of 1979. His book is a blockbuster. Few readers, I venture a guess, will agree with all the elements of his plan. Most thoughtful and knowledgeable readers will concur in the general direction in which he leads.

The need for such a book is urgent. Community colleges are now being established at the rate of more than one each week. Are they merely physical plants? Merely shells with no inner substance or adequate facilities for learning? Or are they founded with a carefully thought-out educational philosophy, sound plans, and realistic financial projections? By setting up the guide lines to be thought through, by stimulating the imagination needed to formulate plans, the author has rendered a genuine service to all who have responsibility for on-going colleges and those who feel impelled by circumstances to start new ones.

The author makes abundantly clear that we know more about how a college should be related to the community and about learning than we generally apply.

With the tremendous increases in college enrollments, with costs skyrocketing, with employment opportunities for college-age youth disappearing, time is fast running out. Of necessity, changes will come. Those projected in this book call for rethinking entire programs and the means of support.

The author's general prescriptions, if they are followed, will obviously not usher in the millennium — nor does he assume they will. Our community colleges will, however, offer more fully the educational opportunities that enable students to achieve the goal so well expressed in the seal of the State University of New York: "Let each become all he is capable of being."

ALVIN C. EURICH

Academy for Educational Development
New York, New York
January, 1969

Preface

In the course of my work, I speak with junior college faculty members and administrators in most areas of the United States. On occasion, I find fault with their practices and, when I do, I am met invariably with the accusation, "You are another!" Not until they are satisfied that I recognize the shortcomings in my own teaching and the inadequacies of the university with which I am affiliated will they attend to my arguments.

Let it be said, then, at the beginning, that all criticisms of junior college curriculum and instruction included in this book may be applied with equal validity to my efforts and to those of the university. Most institutions of higher education, including my own, are at least as guilty — perhaps more so — on all counts.

But, having made this disclaimer, let me hasten to add that I am not apologizing for the tenor of this work. As a glance at the literature of the field will show, internal criticism is one of the scarcest commodities in American education. The junior college segment of that field suffers particularly from this lack: instead of genuine self-appraisal, most of its writings contain a curious mixture of defensiveness and self-congratulation. I consider myself a member of the community college family, so to speak, by virtue of the thrust of my work at UCLA, and hope this volume will be received as an authentic attempt to redress the imbalance at least partially.

The reader should bear in mind that I am attempting to answer certain special questions. As Collingwood (1939) said, before one can criticize answers, it is essential that he know what the questions are. The point deserves elaboration.

Not long ago, I received a query from the president of a new junior college in a small southern town. He wanted the names of people "with Ph.D.'s" whom he might be able to entice to serve on his staff. My reply was to send a few names along with the admonition that it might be possible for him to build a good program with non-doctoral people. Only later, when I received a set of public relations releases from the college, did I realize I had misinterpreted his question. I thought he had been asking, "How can I find people to help me create a viable post-secondary educational program in an area where there was none before?" But his question had actually been, "How can I gain prestige in my district most rapidly?" The matter became clear when I saw that, regardless of its topic, each release was careful to note that the college "had nine Ph.D.'s on the staff — more than any other junior college in the state!"

Another example of the importance of knowing the questions before criticizing the answers is apparent in the junior colleges' current pattern of curricular revision. Regularly, like the swing of a pendulum, many colleges go from multi-level grouping of freshman composition students on the basis of "ability" to single courses mandated for all, and back again. They start with single required courses and soon begin to build honors sections "above" and remedial sections "below" what has by then become the "regular" or "transfer" course. In time, as many as seven tracks — including "sub–sub-remedial" — may be created. Eventually the staff realizes that it has no valid way of sorting students into the courses, or that all the courses are essentially the same anyway, and it shifts back to the single-course pattern.

There is a similar periodic introduction and rejection of writing laboratories and many other special instructional programs. Ostensibly, college staffs are asking the question, "How can we organize our curriculum and our instructional procedures so that more students learn to write effectively?" The vacillation seems to relate to the fact that no one knows whether or not students learn more or better when they are grouped according to "ability," given material at "their level," and "taught" by this method or that.

But the heart of the problem is in the question, which is currently unanswerable because the faculty possesses no definition of what it means by "effective" writing. It has neglected to ask an essential pre-liminary question: "What (in terms that have clear and common refer-rent) must our students be able to do in order to satisfy our requirement that they 'write effectively'?" Not until the staff answers that question can reliable measures be developed to let students in and out of the courses ("They must be able to do *this* upon entrance and *that* upon exit"). And unless such devices are built, there is no way to tell what instructional pattern is best. The fluctuations themselves are clearly the result of constant dissatisfaction; one curriculum paradigm is followed until, as Veblen (1931, p. 178) said in speaking of a similar phenomenon in women's fashions, "aesthetic nausea" sets in, whereupon another is adopted.

It is possible that I have misinterpreted the purpose of the ever-changing modes of curriculum and instruction. They may actually be in answer to the question, "How can we innovate often enough so that we maintain an excitement in our work or so that our confreres do not consider us stodgy?" In that case, the response is correct: shift back and forth with such frequency that the staff is continually titillated and the onlooker perceives a state of "educational ferment."

Several instances where I have deliberately misinterpreted ques-tions may be found in these pages. For example, I am critical of the cur-rent state of research in the community college (Chapter Twelve) largely because I refuse to acknowledge the fact that research offices are pri-marily concerned with gathering information for use in public relations activities or data on which to base proposals for augmented funding. Junior college leaders seldom admit it, even to themselves, but the ques-tion from which almost all their research stems is, "How can we aggran-dize the institution?" I don't think self-perpetuation should be the sole — or even the overriding — purpose of an educational structure. My criticism, then, is directed not so much as the research itself as at the fact that researchers are addressing themselves to the wrong issues. If they were asking, "Are we in fact educating the masses of people who come through our doors?" their responses (the methods they currently employ) would be wrong. As it is, they are obtaining the correct answers to *their* question but I cannot reconcile their question with my view of what a college or its research effort should be about.

The college of 1979 as sketched in this book is an answer to a question I posed to myself. I had been in the field of education only a short time when I reached the conclusion that any educational structure, to be worthy of the name, must define and bring about learning along particular dimensions. Thus, my question: What form would a community junior college take if it were organized deliberately to cause learning?

The paradigm college was created by applying a defined-outcomes rationale to a composite of current institutional forms and then extrapolating. I picked the year 1979 because I felt it would take ten years to build such an institution. The college of 1979 differs from many projections into the future in that it is not a showcase for randomly selected educational novelties. I was not trying to answer anyone else's questions.

Whether or not any single college will look like this model ten years from now depends on many things: the relative affluence of its parent community, the pattern of evolution in neighboring educational institutions, and the caliber of people attracted to the college staff, to name only a few. More than anything else, it depends on whether any of the current generation of leaders *want* their institutions to look like this one, because the college of '79 will be shaped by decisions that are being made now. My guess is that the mechanical aspects of the college — class scheduling by computer, multi-media instructional devices, etc. — will be adopted by many institutions and the ethos by few; it is much easier to change hardware than guiding concepts.

It is difficult to trace ideas to their sources. Most of the concepts outlined in this book have been iterated by educators for decades. In fact many of the issues are brought together by Alvin C. Eurich in *Campus 1980* (1968), a book I read after this work was substantially complete.

My contribution is the synthesis of many notions in the context of the community junior college. I picked the two-year college not because I think it particularly more open to change than any other educational structure (none of them change much until the rocks start coming through the windows) but because the need is especially urgent. In their speeches and pronouncements, junior college leaders have indicated an acceptance of the charge to teach all. Now it is up to them to deliver.

In the course of preparing this work, I received help from many people. The university allowed me to take a quarter on sabbatical leave. The staff of the ERIC Clearinghouse for Junior College Information, headed by Barbara Willis, provided typing and clerical support. The manuscript was read and criticized by several colleagues and friends including B. Lamar Johnson and C. Robert Pace, senior professors in the Area of Higher Education, and Florence B. Brawer, Assistant Research

Educationist. Martin J. Cohen contributed ideas in his inimitable way. In addition, I discussed these thoughts with many groups of graduate students and junior college faculty members. I thank them all and hope they learned as much from me as I did from them.

A.M.C.

Graduate School of Education
University of California, Los Angeles
January, 1969

(NOTE: — The parenthetical citations in the text refer to the bibliography preceding the index. Page numbers are specified only when it is necessary to pinpoint a reference in a book-length work.)

Contents

PART TWO: MEANS, ENDS, AND ANOMALIES

PART THREE: THE CONCEPTUAL BRIDGE

PART FOUR: DEFINED OUTCOMES

Introduction

Why has America become conscious that its education is not good enough? Why now and not twenty years ago?
— A. S. Neill (1968.)

The wonder is, when you think about it, how long our schools have managed to stay the same.
— George B. Leonard (1968, p. 213.)

The community junior college today represents one of the few unique accomplishments of American education in the twentieth century — expanded educational opportunity for all citizens. It is viewed variously as democracy's college, as an inexpensive, close-to-home alternative to the lower division of a prestigious university; as a place to await marriage, a job, or the draft; and as a high school with ash trays. For many of its enrollees, it is a stepping stone to the higher learning; for most, it is the last formal, graded, public education in which they will be involved. The community college is — or attempts to be — all things to all people, trying valiantly to serve simultaneously as custodian, trainer, stimulant, behavior-shaper, counselor, adviser, and caretaker to both young and old. To a greater or lesser degree, it succeeds in most of its many endeavors.

The junior college is not a basic research institution, nor is it a home for a "community of scholars"; to conceive of it as a truncated university is thoroughly inappropriate. Similarly, despite its roots, the community college should not be considered an extension of secondary school; it has broader purposes and a different student population. The college is, however, becoming the vehicle by means of which the nation is accelerating the pursuit of its educational ideal — providing all youth an opportunity to obtain an education and training to the limit of their capabilities. (National Science Foundation, 1967, p. 23.) That is its unique mission. As responsible groups have phrased it:

> The goal of universal education beyond the high school is no more utopian than the goal of full citizenship for all Americans . . . . If a person is adjudged incapable of growth toward a free mind today, he has been adjudged incapable of the dignity of full citizenship in a free society. That is a judgment which no American conscious of his ideals and traditions can rightly make. (Educational Policies Commission, 1964, p. 360.)

In that context, to bar the ignorant is as undemocratic as it would be to refuse admission to the poor. These are the ideals which have given rise to community colleges.

THE CHALLENGE OF CHANGE

What next, then, for this new, fast-growing offspring of American higher education? The first experiment, begun at the turn of the century, is now over. The nearly two million students enrolled in more than 900 American junior colleges indicate the nation has been sold on the idea that post-secondary education is necessary and desirable for all young people — various commissions and agencies have done that job quite well over the past twenty years. (Gardner, 1960, p. 91.)

It is time now to plan for a further stage of community college development. It is unreasonable to expect that the institutions will continue to be supported indefinitely without clearer definition of their effects on students and their contributions to community life. Proliferation of colleges at the current rate cannot continue forever. Some form of publicly supported higher education will be made available for all but it will not necessarily be housed in institutions like the community college of the 1960's.

A second reason for taking fresh views of the community college is based on the fact that the college, charged as it is with unique educational tasks, must develop unique curricular and instructional forms — however, it has not yet done so. In a classic of understatement, Reynolds (1966, p. 110) has said of the junior college, "The relationship between the implications of stated purposes for the educational program and the program itself is not always consistent." Most practices currently in vogue were designed by and for universities or secondary schools, but community colleges must eventually develop their own procedures if they are to achieve their purposes.

Another fundamental concern is apparent. Despite its size, growth rate, and multiplicity of functions, the junior college has not yet succeeded in gaining a position as a genuinely respected force in American education. A sense of self is lacking, an unease reflected in the defensive character of much of the writing by leaders in the field. (Gleazer, 1968b.) Can the movement achieve direction, focus, emphasis, and withal the identity so long desired but so futilely sought?

The lack of an established educational role makes it increasingly difficult for community colleges to attract qualified staff members, and greatly intensifies the problems of those who make plans and set policies for these institutions. Junior colleges cannot measure up to the demands placed upon them by aping the practices of the secondary schools or the universities, which were designed in other times to provide other services to different populations. Nor can identity be gained by instructors' saying repeatedly, "We are professionals!" and administrators' claiming, "We are part of higher education and deserve respect accordingly!" A distinct and unique rationale — a new focus — is required. The community colleges' sense of self can arise only from such a definition of purpose and a clear demonstration of their value.

Internal matters need resolution as well. Certain problems cannot indefinitely be swept under the rug: student unrest (especially the noiseless type); conflicts over curriculum; the tendency to innovate first and ask questions later (if at all) that is in fact a cover for insidious institutional ossification; faculty members' incessant, desperate attempts to plant sprigs of ivy at the gates so that the barbarians will be dissuaded from entering (as if by incantation); and growing community disaffection that is leading to the withdrawal of financial underpinning. Each issue affects*and is affected by the others; attempts to solve them in piece-meal fashion are not likely to succeed.

HISTORICAL CONTEXTS

Educational institutions take shape in response to needs, pressures, and forms in the community which constructs them. Five hundred years ago, Western society was based on inherited class distinctions. The roles and functions of its members derived from rigid tradition; there was little vertical movement between classes. In that society, business and trade were conducted by a merchant group, vocations were pursued by informally trained artisans, and the intrigues of government were sepa-rate from and had little effect upon the lives of the masses of people. The society's store of abstract knowledge was in the keeping of a small group who by choice resided in isolation from the rest of the populace. Advancement of the frontiers of their knowledge was undertaken by discourse among members of that select group. Communication among members of the elite was through word of mouth or with the aid of laboriously handmade books. The isolate company perpetuated itself by inducting novitiates into the tight circle; the processes of their learning were thoroughly mysterious. Society in general was little concerned with, and even less affected by, the dialogues in which the group engaged.

Educational institutions within that society had as their overriding purpose the provision of an environment in which scholars might pursue their discourses and pass on their knowledge to the young who had been selected to join their ranks. The campus was isolated from the community, the faculty set apart from society, and the curriculum concerned primarily with preserving among a few a spiritual and intellectual heritage from the great minds of the past. That was the college which developed in Western Europe between the thirteenth and the eighteenth centuries.

A contemporary society dedicated to technological progress and free movement between classes requires a different educational form. In our society, status is closely linked to occupational role, and the barriers between role distinctions are so pliable that people frequently transfer positions. Merchants, artisans, and governmental leaders are interlocked; the actions of each are known to affect the others. There exists more abstract knowledge than any one group of people anywhere can possess. The store of information expands exponentially through the efforts of tens of thousands of empiricists. Bits of new data can be instantly retrieved and transmitted around the world. Information must often be provided to all of society because all its members are immediately affected by, and intimately involved in, its consequences. If society is to function effectively, all members must understand and be able to deal in abstractions. More than *people* to be learned from, there is a body of *knowledge* and codes of behavior which must be learned.

Such a society requires educational institutions in which *all* the young are brought to a minimum degree of competence in handling abstract knowledge — places where they learn to react flexibly to many kinds of situations and to communicate with their fellows. Virtually all of society's pool of information will soon be instantaneously retrievable, time and distance quickly ceasing to operate as limiting factors. Ours is becoming a society whose "business" is "learning." (McLuhan, 1964.) Many types of educational institutions are needed — publicly and privately supported, formally and informally organized. All of the population must be involved to some degree.

Within each of their communities, junior colleges can help contemporary society — not by perpetuating the forms of the past, but by designing and implementing new thrusts in education. Certain limitations in educational planning are apparent. We do not yet know enough about the effects of release from work and of electronic media on the individual. We do not know how instant communication, total information retrieval, and the other results of advanced technology can best fit into the design of a teaching institution. We do know, however, that present instructional forms are so archaic their purposes, functions, and practices seem hardly to belong to modern America.

DATELINE '79

In this book, a direction is proposed for the community junior college, one whereby the college may better serve its students and its community by employing current knowledge of effective instruction. The text challenges many traditions and favored assumptions on which current practices are based. Those assumptions must be questioned because until they are, perception of problems is limited and lasting changes are unlikely. The most pervasive barriers to change are not limitations in money or staff time, as often suggested. The real barriers are subtle limitations in vision, attitudes, and expectations, conditioned as they are by present-day practices.

This book deals particularly with curriculum and instruction because, throughout the history of the movement, the junior college has taken pride in being a "teaching institution." Modes of financial support, architecture, and administration are described only minimally and as they relate to the process of instruction. The history and current status of teaching and learning are treated more fully because it is necessary to consider how they evolved if one is to attempt to change them.

The text is divided into four sections. Part One presents a paradigmatic picture of a community college as it might look in 1979. The model presented is that of a "self-renewing institution" (Gardner, 1963) offering a flexible curriculum built on a firm instructional base. The design is an outgrowth of the presumed effect of many current forces — student unrest and community disaffection, for example, to name but two. It considers that student unrest flooding from the university will splash over the junior college in the early 1970's (Lombardi, 1969), and there meet a groundswell of desire for curriculum control arising from the local community. Together, the waves will break and recede, leaving a residue of change possibly along the lines presented here. Lay citizens will sit on general-education advisory committees as they now participate on trades advisory committees. Students will find curricular relevance in a range of community involvements—from tutoring elementary school pupils to serving in Peace Corps type endeavors — all under the auspices of the college. (Mayhew, 1968.)

At the core of the college's processes will be the deliberate practice of instruction. It will be built on a definitive teaching–learning paradigm and employ a built-in system of evaluation. Student learning — predictable, measurable, definable — will be the college's raison d'etre. The college will predict and accept accountability for its effects. No longer slavishly following the university, it will take a lead in experimenting with instructional forms — not by innovating for the sake of innovation, but by setting hypotheses, introducing changes, and assessing their impact. The community in which the college is located will look to it to provide particular services, seeing it no longer as a symbol, but as a force for shaping the life of the community.

And what of 1969? "Change, innovate, experiment!" call the educators. (Johnson, 1964, 1969.) But in what directions? And why is there such continuing interest in instructional innovation? Why the many calls for curricular experimentation? Part Two attempts to answer these questions by tracing some backgrounds of practices in junior college curriculum and instruction. It considers current forms as they relate to stated purposes and points out several anomalies and incongruities. As a way of helping the colleges organize to predict and assess effects, this section examines some of the concepts on which current forms are based, discussing particularly archaisms and inconsistencies.

Part Three relates the model college of 1979 to its current counterpart, suggesting and extending arguments for making the transition. The charge is made that junior college leaders can best serve their communities by cutting away irrelevant practices — by turning their institutions into places where learning happens, through which their communities are transformed.

For decades, educators have cried out for schools and instructors to specify the directions they are taking. Twenty years ago, Paul Klapper (1949) visited numerous college classrooms and concluded, "Aimlessness is the most important single cause of ineffectiveness in teaching and of frustration of educational effort. Again and again one looks in vain for evidence of purpose in classroom, lecture hall and laboratory." It is futile to attempt to design instruction or even examine the process of learning itself unless specific ends are stipulated. What does "learning" — presumably the end of all educational effort — mean? How is it exhibited?

Part Four examines a defined-outcomes approach to teaching and learning. Any instructor may incorporate the ideas presented in this section in his own work, whether or not others in his institution follow along — and indeed whether he is in a high school or in the graduate division of a university. Much work in defined learning needs to be done. The use of specified objectives, the effects of the process on teacher and student, and the theories on which defined outcomes are based are so important to education that they cannot long be ignored by anyone in the junior college.

Of course a publicly supported institution is taking a risk when it displays its precise goals to the public (one of the features of the college of '79) but the alternatives — clandestine ends, or no clear goals at all (only processes) — seem more dangerous. In large measure, the college's success depends on the good will and intelligence of the community in which it is located and to which it is accountable. This bespeaks a risk similar to that taken by the founders of the United States when they determined that an informed electorate should vote on issues that affect it. Democratic government is dangerous but its alternatives are more so; the same goes for democratic education.

How will change be triggered? Intensified civil disorder would be more likely to lead to retrogression within the schools than to new forms of education. Similarly, a lessening of community financial support would bring about a type of change but not necessarily in the direction proposed in this volume. Direct competition from private corporations, a possibility discussed in the Epilogue, may lead to beneficial revisions. Whatever it takes to move the junior colleges off dead-center, let it be soon!

Part One

The College— 1979

Chapter One

Conceptual Bases
and
Physical Structure

The college of 1979 serves a medium-sized city and several suburbs. For the past fifteen years, the district's population has been 300,000, but, although the size of the population has remained the same, its composition has changed. The wealthier members of the population have moved to the suburbs, many of which are out of the district, and their places have been taken by the less affluent.The center of the district is an urban area characterized by an old city core, declining residential sections, and a few large retailing centers. Urban renewal programs, sponsored by a combination of public and private funds, are beginning to slow the advance of decay. Some heavy industry remains in the city, but the major part of industrial production is in new, technologically advanced factories on the periphery. Job retraining is a continuing necessity for a large portion of the work force.

THE EDUCATIONAL CONTEXT

Opportunities for education are many and varied. In addition to the information disseminated through the efforts of the mass media, several types of formal educational institutions are available. A humanist center conducts an continuing dialogue on issues of social import. A liberal arts college in the vicinity offers a program not very different from that provided by its nineteenth century predecessor. The state university has abandoned the pretext that it affords an opportunity for general education; it devotes its energies to research and to the training of researchers. Industries have expanded their training programs to the point where they no longer ask the public schools to prepare their workers and technicians. The citizens of the community, acting alone or in small groups, offer specialty courses in modern foreign languages, cottage trades, and uses for leisure time. The variety of education in the city has expanded tremendously.

The community college itself is a public, two-year institution supported by a combination of state and local efforts. Organized in 1929 as part of a high-school district, it separated thirty years later and now operates as an independent institution. Although the college looks different now, vestiges of its origins remained for more than a decade after the separation. For a long time there was little staff turnover and only minimal changes in the curriculum and instruction methods. Until the early 1970's, the college's forms and procedures were much as they had been prior to the redistricting arrangement.

For example, in 1969 the college offered transfer or college parallel courses, technical and vocational training programs, and a conglomerate of community-service and "non-credit" classes. In many respects, it seemed to be a service center for the university rather than a community college. The college sought the university's approval for its curriculum and instructional forms, screened students and referred them to "transfer" and "non-transfer" tracks, sent the most capable students on, flunked out the less competent, and generally, enabled four-year institutions to maintain a tight set of entrance requirements. Because it and similar community colleges in the state had become well developed, the publicly supported universities were able to raise standards for admission so high that they accepted only those students who placed in the upper quintile on intelligence tests or achieved a similarly high record in prior academic work.

Remedial education was the focus of a growing set of problems occasioned by two factors: the percentage of the district's young people who sought to take advantage of the college's services was becoming steadily larger, and the percentage of students from families with traditionally high aspirations for the education of their children was becoming steadily smaller. Other issues also claimed attention. Demands that the college serve more and different types of people were growing, but its financial support was not increasing at a rate commensurate with its efforts to provide the expanded services. The curriculum, originally modeled on that of the university, was outmoded and, despite repeated attempts at innovation, instructional forms were archaic. The college depended on outside sources for the solutions to these problems — that is, it consumed rather than produced knowledge about methods of instruction. The college characterized itself as a "teaching institution" even though the question of whether or not anyone was learning anything was rarely put to the test.

The college had no way of determining the extent to which its efforts were effective, because the studies in which it participated were devised solely to compare it quantitatively with similar institutions. Its student dropout rate — the difference between the number of students who enrolled and those who completed any program — was well over 50 per cent. In short, in 1969 it was a typical urban community college: It reacted to pressures from various segments of the population it purported to serve, resisted change because of its reliance on perceived tradition, and was beset by misunderstanding and lack of communication among students, faculty, and administration. Yet it had persevered and represented what was then viewed as a triumph of democratic educational opportunity.

The changes of the last decade surpassed any of those that occurred during the previous forty years. Now, in 1979, the outward forms of the college look familiar, but the structure behind the facade is different. There are many differences in the purpose, function, philosophical and conceptual bases and in effect on students and the larger community. The district contributes approximately the same financial support, but the college does more with the money. The curriculum is founded upon core courses; course proliferation is a thing of the past. Remedial education is no longer offered as such. All distinctions between "transfer" and "terminal" programs have broken down. The relevance of the curriculum is carefully guarded — students no longer view their college experience as an abstraction outside the reality of their lives. The institution is a medium for change in the community.

By deliberate intent, the modes of instruction at the college are extremely varied. The sections of the courses are different in design and emphasis. The roles of the faculty and the administration have been specialized and clarified. *Student achievement of specific learning objec-*

tives is the focus — the acknowledged, sanctioned, overriding purpose of the institution. The college has gained direction, status, and a unique form. In daring to meet the challenges of the process of becoming, it has found its own self, its own identity.

CONCEPTUAL BASES

Among the major changes in modes of conceptualizing the college that have occurred over the past ten years is a different way of considering time. Curriculum and instruction are now geared exclusively to student achievement. The significance of the number of hours spent in class by a student has changed; the time is not considered indicative of the student's commitment to or the value of, his learning. The student's time is his own; he may spend it on campus or off; in class or at work; reading or listening. The college seeks only student achievement in the form of a tangible product.

The semester and unit blocks of time have been completely abandoned; previously they had been the basic measuring devices because *what* was to be learned was poorly defined, and *how* learning occurred was largely unknown. In 1979, the knowledge of *what* and *how* has eliminated the use of time as the measure of student attainment.

A second basic difference in the college of '79 is its concept of space, both the life space of the instructor and the spatial boundaries of the campus. In addition to the earlier evaluation of time spent by a student in class, there was a parallel view of the value of an instructor's presence. The person of an instructor was curiously seen as having worth in itself. This concept was reflected in the untoward difficulty of introducing replicable media into instruction at the college and in the fact that instructors resisted all attempts to be separated physically from the students — as, for example, in large group or televised instruction. (When one is sprinkling drops of wisdom, one wants the recipients to stand close!) The present role differentiation allows a few instructors to continue as full-time media, but most perform other tasks — tasks which may or may not bring them into contact with students.

A view of the value of the campus itself is another difference in space conceptualization. As they are presently organized, the college's curriculum and instruction utilize many parts of the city; the community is used as a social laboratory. The core social science sequence employs students in jobs as data collectors, poll takers, field workers in a variety of public campaigns, and in similar capacities. Students do not remain on a campus to learn about society; they learn by participating in the community's activities, being involved in field projects, and attempting to manipulate small segments of the community in laboratory-type experiments. These experiences are not adjuncts to courses, they are forms of cooperative study that indicate the distinct conceptual break away from the campus as a closed community.

By another change, the college is seen as a learning laboratory. Although some progress has been made, even now in 1979, knowledge of how people learn is still sketchy. The study of learning as a phenomenon of living organisms was previously confined to universities and research laboratories. The results of their studies were translated and disseminated to the community colleges, but diffusion was incredibly slow. Now, the community college itself studies learning among its own students with investigations conducted by its own staff. By experimentalists' standards the studies may seem crude, but they result in changed practices in the college, and that is the objective.

Although the universities to which many of the college's students eventually transfer continue to maintain their own student-screenings, the college no longer designs its programs on the basis of the university's requirements. Disciplinary action, such as probation and/or suspension, because of a student's "academic difficulties" is no longer practiced. Tracking (placing students into transfer and non-transfer courses) is passé. The college of '79 exists to serve its students and its community; it is not a sorting mechanism operated for the benefit of the university.

Through a variety of community involvements such as student tutoring of elementary-school pupils, service projects, and the use of the city as a social and technical laboratory, the college exerts direct influence on its parent city. Students who intend to transfer are not injured, the university accepts them as before and the community itself is helped. This represents a change in conceptualization of the college's purposes for, although its staff had always spoken of serving the students and the community, institutional practices that too closely followed university dictates tended to belie the point.

The definition of learning within which the college functions points to one more major conceptual change: *Learning is now defined as the changed capability for, or tendency toward, acting in particular ways.* Inferences of learning at the college are made by assessing students' capabilities prior to and after instruction. If no change can be observed, no inference of learning is made.

The adherence to this definition influences practices in a most pervasive fashion. Specific, measurable objectives are devised for all units in all sections of all courses; that which is to be learned by the students is clearly defined and communicated. Information regarding the students' achievement of objectives is gathered routinely, and changes in media frequently are made on the basis of these data. The college is focused on defined outcomes — the specific ends toward which all instruction is designed to lead. Each objective set by the college meets three criteria. These are a task or action to be performed by the student that will demonstrate his learning; a set of conditions under which the task will be performed; and the minimum acceptable performance level.

The specification of such objectives has brought about several practices that are different from those employed by earlier generations of instructors, who sorted students on a scale that pitted one against another. Students were "marked" on the basis of how well they performed in comparison with their fellows; the "less able" were screened out. Now, each objective must be mastered at the level specified. In no sense does the college encourage students to compete with one another for "marks"; instead, they compete with and attempt to achieve the stated ends — the objectives themselves. When the students attain the pre-set objectives, they have "learned" and concretely demonstrated their capabilities.

For a long time, writers in the field have spoken of the junior college from the viewpoint of *function* — transfer, terminal, remedial, and adult education, and community service — as though its function was a charge permanently assigned to the institution by society at large. In many instances, community colleges were "sold" to prospective parent communities by zealots who alleged that unemployment would be reduced, the problems of the ghetto would be alleviated, and the material and spiritual well-being of the people would be measurably enhanced almost as soon as the institution opened its doors. Colleges were organized and financed. They accepted functions not previously filled, such as offering vocational retraining, localized college-parallel training, and certain community-service courses. To the extent that they provided an opportunity for the community's young to attend an institution at which they might be counseled, retrained, and exposed to college courses, they filled an existing void. But in most instances, the college provided an opportunity for learning without accepting the accountability for that learning. There is a marked difference between *allowing* a student to learn and taking responsibility for the direction and extent of that learning.

The college of 1979 has blocked out an area of competence and is accountable for the learning achieved by its students; in the broadest sense, this reflects its new concept of education. Setting the objectives and leading students to their attainment are the institution's main purpose, but it is also a medium of change in the city. In this sense, the college may be seen as using *processes* on *people* for definitive *ends*. The staff does not merely examine its processes or its people when it attempts to define its own operation. It accounts for the *effects* of those processes upon the students who attend the institution, and upon the larger community. Similarly, the college does not pretend to do all things for its students and the community. It attempts only to cause its students, and through them, its community, to develop specified minimal skills and attitudes.

PHYSICAL PLANT

The college is of the city; the campus on the hill outside the town is no more. The image of higher education as a retreat from life stemmed from a time when all knowledge was carried in the minds of elders, when knowledge was advanced by those elders conversing with each other, and when students were sent from the "base distractions" of pedestrian society to a "place of knowledge." Now, because knowledge can be transmitted instantly to and from any point in space, the college functions as a direct and deliberate agent of social change. Conceptually, the community college is not a place apart from the "evil influences" of the city, but is actually a part of the community. It appears to be a decentralized college; actually its campus has expanded to include the confines of the entire community.

The college of '79 operates in nine branch centers, each of which offers a full program of core courses. Each center is autonomous: it determines its own hours of operation, course scheduling, and personnel employment policies. Each one feeds data about students into a central computer storage bank and determines what courses it will offer.

Each center enrolls between 900 and 1,500 students. They are located in rented stores, in spaces that formerly were office buildings, and in old mansions that had outlived their original purposes. Easy access by numbers of students and economy of physical-plant operations are the chief criteria by which locations are determined. Because "college" as a symbol of an elitist era dies hard, some efforts are made to have the centers appear like traditional campuses. Consequently, when possible, a park or greensward is made a part of the college center. However, the college seeks primarily to buy or lease existing buildings so that each center is disposable at little expense to the institution. Most students enroll at the center nearest their home, even though they may "stop in" and take a unit of a course anywhere in the city if they wish.

The internal appearance of the college is somewhat different, too, from that of the college of an earlier time. There are no science laboratories. Computer-simulated laboratories, the most fruitful development in computer-assisted learning in the past several years, are available in all centers. Remote terminals permit students to participate in laboratory exercises and allow the core science course to be offered in all locations. There are few classrooms as such; large lecture halls are used for some sections, and carrels for others. Comfortably furnished, small meeting rooms are available for participants in discussion sections.

In each center there is a library where media of all sorts are arranged in kits according to units of the core courses. There are many media patterns; the kit for a unit of a course may be a box in which are enclosed a closed-loop, single-concept film, a tape, and several reprints from books. As new media are developed, the contents of the kits are changed and made available immediately. There are no hardcover books in the library; paperbacks are used exclusively because of their demonstrated effect on students' reading habits. (Fader and McNeil, 1968.) A bookstore is operated along with the library. Any paperback in the collection is available not only for check-out, but also for purchase; the book carries a return date *and* a purchase price. The overall library collection is minimal; students use branches of the public library for general readings.

As a part of the community, the center is subject to the same regulations as other public buildings and streets. There are no fraternities or intercollegiate athletics; the city's clubs and professional sports have taken over these functions of entertaining the young. No student newspaper is sponsored by the college, but some students edit a college section for the city paper. Several groups of students publish and distribute papers of their own; these sheets are sold at the centers' newsstands along with the community's newspapers. The college yearbook is a "house organ" similar in format to a combination of a corporation's annual report and employee newsletter.

Each center operates on a year-round schedule. Core courses are offered in ten-week segments. With the addition of a week of testing and a two-week vacation period, the cores make a cycle which is repeated four times a year. Once every three years, on a rotating basis, each center is closed for three months for plant maintenance and staff sabbaticals. If students wish to pursue studies during the quarter in which a center is closed, they do so at any of the other eight centers in the city.

The branch centers are specialized only to the extent that they avoid duplication of expensive equipment. All data processing for the college is done at the center that has the computer installation; thus industrial concerns teach certain specialty courses in programming and data processing there. Another center has a large media-production facility. Although faculty and students may make simple tapes and strips at any of the centers, they must go to the media facility for elaborate productions. The administrative offices are located at another center. This branch is the location of courses requiring "committee service." The college owns no industrial equipment; it makes no space available for machinery on which vocations may be learned. Students go to the community's factories, shops, and laboratories for their technical training.

The college resists all pressures to make the centers "total campuses" with resident students and isolation from the community in spirit if not in fact. The relevance of the students' studies to their lives is kept in the foreground, through the courses that are offered and through the "part-of-the-city" appearance of the college centers. To a considerable degree, the college has blended into the city; the community flows through it — physically and spiritually.

Chapter Two

Curriculum

The curriculum in the college of '79 is built on the unifying theme of general education. This theme stems from the acknowledged purpose of the college as a member of a broad system of American higher education and from an awareness of the needs of the student body. For many students, especially those coming from middle- and high-income families, there is no necessity to earn money. The college charges no tuition, they live at home, and their financial needs are met by the family income. To a degree never before realized, the expanded programs of Social Security, medical insurance, and various other forms of social legislation have insured a future free from want for them and their families. Because the pressures to enter the work force are delayed, students have been freed to search more deeply and deliberately for the meaning of life. They have also been enabled to help their community upgrade itself. In turn, to help students individually and as a community service, the college offers a core curriculum that combines elements of sequences formerly designated as "college-parallel" and "remedial" education.

The college serves another segment of the population in a different way. For more than a third of the city's youth, employment cannot be delayed indefinitely; governmental social legislation provides a standard of living that is not much above bare subsistence. These students must work; yet there are few jobs for high-school graduates, few points at which they can enter the work force without further training. In addition to the young who seek first-time employment, a substantial number of older workers need retraining. Technological advances have made their skills obsolete; they must be upgraded in their own trades or prepared for other types of work. For these two groups, then, vocational and technical training programs are offered by commercial establishments that operate under the college's supervision.

The college does not limit its services to a small group of the population, however. The ease of entry to, and exit from, units of the core curriculum encourages *all* young people of the community to attend from time to time. And, because the college refuses to accept an artificial distinction between "education" and "training," many units in the core curriculum include "vocational" elements, with objectives similar to those found previously only in "trades programs." The greatest single difference among groups of students is the time it takes for each one to complete the core course. Some individuals, especially those from families in which the pressure is for "academic achievement," complete the program in less than two years. Others who must work at full-time jobs and train at the same time often do not complete the course for many years.

The core curriculum is based on the idea, old in education, that there are basic principles that must be learned by all members of a community if it is to function effectively and with a minimum of disorder. Problems in various domains of human living, viewed through various subject areas, are its organizing center. The curriculum is constructed so that interrelationships among bits of knowledge are clarified. It is not designed particularly as a preparation for university specialization; it stands alone as a contribution to the students' knowledge, and it helps them understand their world. Thus the students receive something of value even if they never take another formal course in school.

The general-education curriculum at the college includes four core courses, in the traditional areas of communications, humanities, sciences, and social sciences. The survival of these four areas as separate foci of curricular organization is not surprising because historically scholars working in these broad fields have taken quite distinct approaches to knowledge. There is overlap in content and approach, but not to the earlier extent of offering hundreds of varied courses, whose relation to one another was hardly considered.

A defined-outcomes approach to curriculum and instruction is manifested in the core courses, each of which is organized in units that run for periods of time varying from one to four weeks. The units are discrete and, although some are prerequisite for others, many may be taken out of numbered sequence. Each unit includes its own entrance requirements, its own instructional media, and its own end-of-unit objectives. In a sense, each core course is a sequence of short courses, all of which form a cohesive program.

No attempt will be made here to examine any of the core courses in depth, but an examination of some of the course goals and plans for units may illuminate the concepts on which the college is built.

THE COMMUNICATIONS COURSE

The *Communications* course combines elements of old courses in English, composition, speech, journalism, radio-television and basic mathematics with material formerly not presented in formal junior-college courses. It is designed to lead students to communicate by using writing, speech, and other symbolic media and to understand effects of all types of communications media on their lives. The course's forty units include titles such as *Reference Materials in Communications; Paragraph Structures; Television as a Communications Form;* and *Mathematics as Symbolic Language.*

The following are sample end-of-unit objectives.

Persuasive Writing and Propaganda:

        Task: The student will write an essay of 400 to 750 words in which he uses considered argument and other linguistic means deliberately to move his reader toward a particular point of view.

  Conditions: Fifty minutes in exam situation; dictionary and thesaurus allowed.

    Criterion: No gross grammatical errors.

The Tutorial as a Medium of Communication:

        Task: The student will tutor two or more elementary-school pupils in one of their areas of study for a period of not less than ten hours.

  Conditions: Mandatory.

    Criterion: Evidence of pupil gain to be submitted by elementary school teacher.

Each concise unit includes one or more specific objectives of the type indicated. The sequence of units in the course is such that mastery of earlier units may be required before a student is allowed to enter a later unit. For example, because the unit on *Persuasive Writing and Propaganda* demands a written essay with "no gross grammatical errors," the units *Spelling, Punctuation, Sentence Structure,* and *Paragraph Structure* are listed as prerequisites. On the other hand, the unit *The Tutorial as a Medium of Communication* requires only that the student have mastered *Principles of Communication* and *Styles of Speaking* before he becomes a tutor.

In addition to the rather typical objectives cited, students receive credit for participating in committees on revision of curricula and other school affairs. The *Committee Service* unit includes the following objective that demands "participation" for its own sake:

> Task: The student will meet with a standing college committee and contribute ideas in a free discussion. Upon completion of the meetings, he will discuss the deliberations with his section leader, demonstrating an understanding of the purposes and practices of the committee to the instructor's satisfaction.
>
> Conditions: Mandatory.
>
> Criterion: At least four hours in committee meetings.

This unit objective insures that all students have an opportunity to participate in the planning and policy decisions of the college.

THE SOCIAL SCIENCE COURSE

The *Social Science* course introduces students to the various fields of study in the social sciences and to the methodology of each one. The course is designed for the purpose of encouraging the students to become "responsible citizens," a term defined as "people applying reasoned thought to social issues." Through its student-follow-up program, the college continually collects data on the activities of its alumni, especially on their attitudes and actions concerning community problems.

The goal of leading students to the designated ability is in no way inconsistent with another underlying purpose of all courses in the core curriculum—that of helping students choose fields for further study. The student who "acts" as a sociologist, for example, is not only being trained in the patterns of thought associated with that discipline, he is also becoming better able to decide if he wants to pursue sociological scholarship or social work as a profession. In addition to helping the student gain an ability to apply (or at least to understand) sociological reasoning and methodology to community problems, the units in which he designs and conducts simple sociological studies help him select other areas that he is interested in pursuing. Thus, he is in a position to make a career choice more accurately than the student who merely reads or talks to a counselor about sociology.

Like the other core courses, the *Social Science* course is composed of discrete units, some of which act as prerequisites for others. These units include the terminology, methodology, and concepts in the fields of anthropology, sociology, history, economics, geography, political science, and psychology. Each unit in the course includes its own set of specific, measurable objectives, some samples of which are the following:

The Terminology of Anthropology:

> Task: Given a paragraph from any of the written works on a provided list, the student will define each of the underlined terms as it is used in context. No definitions will exceed fifty words.
> Conditions: Dictionary permitted; time: forty minutes.
> Criterion: Ninety per cent accuracy.

Methods Used by the Sociologist:

> Task: Given a written case study of a community problem, the student will select from a given list the methods most likely to be employed by a sociologist who would study the problem further. He will support each of his choices in a statement that will not exceed fifty words.
> Conditions: Any reference work permitted; time: sixty minutes.
> Criterion: Ninety per cent accuracy.

The Social Scientist and Urban Problems:

> Task: In a written paper of from 250 to 1,000 words, the student will take and defend a position on "Ways of Providing Equal Medical Care to All Citizens of Our City." The paper will include:
> (1) historical rationale for student's position;
> (2) quotations from medical and political leaders that both support and refute the student's position;

> (3) supporting arguments from the student's own experience;
>
> (4) cohesion of structure and argument.
>
> Conditions: Any reference source permitted; time: three hours.
>
> Criterion: One hundred per cent accuracy in assigning supporting positions and in presenting historical rationale.

The content of the latter objective is changed often because different community problems are studied in the unit; however, the general task remains the same.

The "terminology" units run for one week each; the "methodology" units for two weeks each; and the "concepts" units for four weeks each. The sectioning and time patterns used at the college generally allow students to tailor their educational programs to their own interests and desires. Some students complete all of the "terminology" units first, as a way of learning and comparing terms used in the entire *Social Science* course; others prefer to follow one discipline, such as anthropology, from the "terminology" unit through the "methodology" and "concepts" units before studying the other fields in the course. In either case, the end-of-unit objectives must be completed successfully.

THE HUMANITIES COURSE

The *Humanities* course is a compromise between attempts to teach students about broad historical movements in music, art, and literature as they relate to other aspects of human history and, on the other hand, to encourage a firm understanding of particular works, approaches, and styles. The course stands somewhere between what has been called "intellectual tourism" and the idea of "the work as its own 'world.' " (D. Bell, 1966). The stated goals are: (1) the student will understand the ideas and feelings which great works can evoke, and (2) he will tend to seek art as a means of contributing to his own life.

Because the local secondary schools teach some historical perspective in art and literature, the college can concentrate on exploring individual works in depth. However, history is included in the *Humanities* course because, although it is "taught" in the secondary school, the college faculty cannot assume it was "learned" by all students.

Discrete units in the *Humanities* course deal with literature, art, music, history, and drama in the ancient and contemporary Eastern and Western worlds. History in the *Humanities* course differs from history in the *Social Science* course to the extent that one considers the chronological setting for the artistic endeavor while the other is concerned more with the methods and trends in the study of history as a field of inquiry.

The following are sample end-of-unit objectives.

Early Eastern Art:

Task: The student will write an essay of from 350 to 750 words in which he outlines the historical context at the time bronze casting began in Japan; names the early artists working in bronze and gives examples of their works; and explains the stylistic conventions used.

Conditions: Time: two hours; no reference books permitted.

Criterion: One hundred per cent content accuracy.

Contemporary American Music:

Task: The student will discuss verbally three contemporary musical selections chosen by the instructor, identifying the style of music and explaining his own subjective, emotional response.

Conditions: During or within ten minutes after hearing each selection.

Criterion: Accuracy and pertinence of comments, to be assessed by instructors.

Contemporary European Drama:

Task: The student will participate in an informally staged scene from a play. He will take an acting role or otherwise help in the production.

Conditions: Under direction of the instructor.

Criterion: One hundred per cent (automatically given for the student's mere participation).

Although a student may attempt to exempt a unit by examination (a procedure explained more fully in Chapter Three), he cannot enter the instructional sequence for that unit until he has demonstrated appropriate competency by passing the prerequisite unit. This procedure allows instructors to make useful assumptions about their students — assumptions based on demonstrated achievement.

In the *Humanities* course, as in the *Social Science* course, sequencing is, to a great extent, left to the students. Some of them prefer to study literature through the ages, followed by art, then music, and finally history; others prefer to spend eight weeks studying the literature, art, music, drama, and history of one era and then to progress to another one. The flexibility of the curricular and instructional processes at the college allows any student to block out the pattern that suits him best and to change the pattern at will. The integration of the humanities as they relate to each other and to human life is stressed in the units' objectives.

THE SCIENCE COURSE

The *Science* course is also composed of discrete units, each of which has its own set of objectives. However, because of the nature of the discipline, more of the units are prearranged in series or sequences of prerequisites. And, although units are discrete, they attempt to integrate concepts from natural and physical science with mathematics and other disciplines.

The primary purpose of the *Science* course is to give the students an understanding of the fundamentals of science so that they can adjust to and improve their environment. Students learn how to use basic mathematical and mechanical skills and how to apply a "scientific" method to the solution of problems. The course functions as a background prerequisite for many advanced university courses in the sciences. In addition, many of the *Science* course's units are required in the trades curricula that are supervised by the college.

Units in the *Science* course include terminology, methodology, and concepts in the life sciences, the physical sciences and higher mathematics, along with much of what was formerly included in health-education courses.

General Scientific Methodology:

> Task: Given ten one-paragraph descriptions of problems, the student will select from accompanying lists of choices: the best methodology to employ in solving each problem; an appropriate hypothesis to test; the types of data to collect; and a statistic or formula to apply.
>
> Conditions: Ninety minutes; any reference works permitted.
> Criterion: Eighty per cent accuracy.

Gases:

> Task: Given a list of twenty statements about gases, the student will select those that are contained in kinetic molecular theory and note which statements are fact and which are assumptions.

Conditions: Time: one hour; no reference works permitted.
Criterion: Eighty per cent accuracy.

In addition to selecting the units within the courses that he wishes to pursue at a given time, a student may elect to study *Humanities, Science, Social Science,* or *Communications* exclusively for several months. He may enroll simultaneously in several units of any one of the courses. Many students prefer to do this rather than to approach each of the conceptual areas separately at different times of the day. However, although he may choose to study one core course at a time and units in sequences that fit his preferences, a student who wishes to obtain an Associate in Arts degree must complete all of the units in each of the core courses.

SPECIAL-PURPOSE COURSES

The college of '79 provides specialty courses that operate in a fashion similar to the college-sponsored technical training programs; that is, the college helps other groups in the community organize and operate the courses but maintains the right of certification of the students upon their completion of the programs. In some cases, the college administers examinations to insure satisfactory learning achievement.

The specialty courses include most of those formerly offered as "electives" and courses that were rather narrowly designed as prerequisites to specialized university curricula. Modern foreign-language courses fall in this special-purpose category along with a number of courses that do not fit into the core curricula but which are offered for "community enrichment."

The college faculty helps the community's experts in particular fields arrange instructional sequences appropriate to the material to be learned. In the case of modern foreign languages, persons who wish to teach the course negotiate with the college to have their qualifications and offerings certified. The faculty works with the outsiders in designing courses, in a sense acting as a resident instructional consultant agency. The college pays the off-campus instructors at a rate based on their students' achievement.

Each specialty course includes its own set of objectives and, in most cases, credit is not offered to students who have merely been in attendance. Many specialty courses are offered for four to six weeks; others are of longer duration. But the concept of defined outcomes is used throughout. In many of the vocational and other special-purpose sequences, the faculty may require that students pass several units of one or more of the core courses before they can receive a certificate of satisfactory achievement.

Vocational education takes place in factories which serve during off-hours as training centers for students who may later work there or elsewhere. The college helps the industrial concerns organize the vocational training programs in their own facilities by providing its instructional expertise, media production centers, and evaluation techniques. Only in cases when such facilities are not available, as in data processing, does instruction take place at the college. This method is not so much a return to the apprenticeship concept of learning trades as it is a deliberate step toward insuring curricular relevance and a refusal to spend money to construct what must become, at best, an artificial campus environment. The training programs are operated by the industries and are not a part of the college's core curriculum. Specialized industrial training is the responsibility of the industries, but assistance is provided by the college. The archaic practice of collecting taxes from local industries to finance the local junior college so that it can prepare young people to work in the factories has been mitigated. Industries receive local tax relief based on the number of students they train.

The junior college sets up, supervises, and accredits vocational programs. It certifies students when they complete the courses. Instructors serve as consultants to plant managers and aid them in designing and conducting technical programs. Workers and managers *in the plants* receive "released time" to teach. Young people of the community, all of whom are "students" because they possess enrollment identity cards, can attend any class and learn segments of work in any industrial training center. The processes of working and learning are approaching a merger.

Chapter Three

Instruction

Instructional methods at the college are a necessary compromise between the old college's single mode of instruction that resulted in ill-defined objectives and the ideal of a totally receptive, omniscient environment that can help any learner at any time determine a goal and then lead him to attain it. The concept of "defined outcomes" pervades instructional processes; it is manifest in the specific objectives set by the faculty for all units of all courses. Instruction is seen as a set of sequences that move learners deliberately, actively, and overtly toward the objectives.

The college's basic instructional aim is to engender minimum, fundamental achievement. It says, in effect, "*These* objectives will be achieved at the level of competence specified." All of the instructional processes are then directed toward bringing students to the goal. Students are not sorted on the basis of "how well" they did in a particular program, course, or course unit. They do not flounder in a climate of unknown effect but are clearly aware of their progress at all times.

Instruction is built on the assumption that people have varying cognitive and emotional styles in their approach to learning of which they may or may not be aware. Many classification schemes have attempted to order these differences among people. Some individuals tend to be concerned with details and to neglect general ideas until the pieces form a comprehensive whole for them; others prefer to consider generalizations and often overlook the specific details which support the broader principles. Some people proceed inductively; others, deductively; some are divergent, others convergent, thinkers. Whatever the classification, these different preferences or tendencies may be found among students who employ varying strategies in their approaches to different subjects. Some students seem able to do better under a particular teacher or instructional form; some glumly refuse to learn unless conditions are drastically changed.

One of the striking ironies of education is that no one style or approach to learning, even when laboriously identified, has proved sufficiently powerful to warrant the classification of students into useful instructional groups. Arguments about instructional methods soon lead to similar dead ends. Critics of programming and other replicable media aver that "the good teacher" can "turn on" the student. He can stimulate and motivate in mysterious ways. However, these skeptics fail to account for the fact that some students are turned *off* by live instructors. In the past, how many students came to the junior college seeking direction, found instead instructors fulfilling themselves in incomprehensible ways, and then became "failures" or "dropouts"? A live instructor can stimulate some students in a fashion that a replicable medium cannot; a replicable medium may teach other students much better than certain instructors can.

Linear programming's greatest single drawback is that it attempts to force all students onto one path. The greatest problem with "homogeneous groupings" is that any criterion used to group individuals ignores other differences that may exercise a powerful effect.

In the past, junior colleges sorted students on the basis of general ability tests or their declared intent to transfer to a university. But these sorting methods proved little more relevant to the students' patterns of learning than if the sorting had been done on the basis of the students' heights or on the color of their eyes. No single approach to grouping students or to teaching has ever been demonstrated to produce uniform results.

In its attempt to resolve many such problems, the college offers six distinctly different types of instructional sections in each course (though not for each unit). Each section has its own reason and style; each one is based on a specific instructional form—yet all sections lead to similar course goals.

The six types of sections offered in each course are categorized by the different media employed. These varied media are not simply different reading lists or types of lectures given by different people; each one is a distinct design for instruction that is built on a distinct rationale. Most units in each core course are offered in lecture, discussion, independent-study, tutorial, audio-tutorial, and computer-assisted sections. The sections run concurrently throughout the year in staggered time sequences.

In the *Social Science* course, for example, each of the six sections begins at the end of the first unit in the numbered section preceding. Section One begins on the first day of the year; the first unit within that section is taught for two weeks. At the end of that time, Section One begins the second unit but Section Two starts work on Unit One—in effect a repeat of Unit One in Section One. Similarly, two weeks later, Section One begins Unit Three, Section Two begins Unit Two, and Section Three begins Unit One. At the end of twelve weeks, the cycle starts again. The course includes forty units and runs for two years in all, but a student may, at almost any point in time, find a section offering a unit he needs.

The units in each of the sections carry the same objectives. A student may enroll in Section One of a course and if, at the end of the two- or three-week period, he finds he cannot achieve the objectives as they are specified, he may repeat the unit in Section Two. Thus, in a course with six sections, the student may attempt to achieve the unit's objectives six times. Because of careful instructional planning and sequencing, however, a majority of the students pass the course without repeating units.

By taking the examination or performing other required tasks, a student may exempt (test out of) any or all of the units in any course. There are test days at the end of each ten-week period for this purpose. Nearly half of the entering students exempt one or more units of each course; then they participate in instructional sections for those units that they have not successfully exempted. Proceeding through the course, they pick units in sequences of their choice and sections in which the pattern of instruction fits their own styles or approaches.

Each unit's objectives are held constant in all sections. The test items for each section are drawn from a common pool. At one time, there was concern lest the students know which items were to be used on the tests and thus could study the examination questions only and ignore most of the instruction. However, this concern evaporated because successful mastery on the part of the student is the chief concern of the community

Schedule, First Quarter, 1979, College Center 1

SOCIAL SCIENCE

Section	Jan 1-14	Jan 15-28	Jan 29-Feb 11	Feb 12-25	Feb 26-Mar 10	Mar 11-16	Mar 17-31
Section I Lecture	Unit I / Title / Prerequisites / Objectives / 1__ 2__ 3__	Unit II / Title / Prerequisites / Objectives / 1__ 2__ 3__	Unit III / Title / Prerequisites / Objectives / 1__ 2__ 3__	Open (c)	Unit V	Test days	Vacation Period for Students / Interim Period for Staff
Section II Discussion	Unit XX	Unit I	Unit II	Unit III	Unit IV	Test days	
Section III Independent Study and Service	Unit XIX (a)	Unit XX	Unit I	Unit II	Unit III	Test days	
Section IV Tutorial and Programmed Instruction	Unit XVIII	Unit XIX (a)	Unit XX	Unit I	Unit II	Test days	
Section V Audio-Tutorial Instruction	Open (b)	Unit XVIII	Unit XIX (a)	Unit XX	Unit I	Test days	
Section VI Computer-Assisted Instruction	Unit XVI	Open (b)	Unit XVIII	Unit XIX (a)	Unit XX	Test days	

NOTES: (a) Unit XIX is a three-week unit; Unit XX is a one-week unit.
(b) Objectives for Unit XVII involve a community service project; the unit is taught in Section III only.
(c) The objective for Unit IV is "Participation in Discussion . . ."; the unit is taught in Section II only.

college of 1979, not the way in which mastery is achieved. The pools of test questions are so large that if a student successfully memorizes the correct responses to all items, he has learned much more than ordinarily would be required of him. This method is in contrast to that of earlier times when students could anticipate test items by obtaining old examinations. The college has released its students from such haphazard and wasteful exercises by offering exemption by examination; it has no desire to keep students in classrooms for specified periods of time.

COURSE SECTIONS

The organization of *lecture* sections in the college of '79 is much like the format used in colleges for several centuries past. Students typically sit in a large hall and watch and listen to a person speak for forty minutes or so. They take notes or otherwise attempt to absorb the information. In many of the units at the community college, closed-circuit television is used for lecture–demonstration presentations. Most lecturers make use of a modern student-response system; at frequent intervals, the lecturer flashes a question on a screen behind him to which students respond by pressing a key on their chairs. At the lectern is a device by means of which the lecturer can determine how many of the students have been following and understand the presentation. Obtaining this feedback allows him to change his speed or to repeat points that students have failed to grasp.

The lecture format especially appeals to students who have just enrolled, perhaps because it allows them to feel as though they are in an "old-time" college; their sense of tradition is thus upheld. This is particularly true for students who attend college for the image-value it holds for them and their families. Other students savor the lectures for their entertainment components; they like to watch the lecturers perform and to listen to the reactions of their fellow students. Several of the lecturers are charismatic figures and, because of their compelling pull, lectures are often attended even by students who have already passed the unit's exams or who are attending other sections.

Discussion sections are small groups of from eight to ten students who prefer to learn through verbal interplay. Although many topics arise, a proctor is present to guide the conversations. Gaming or Simulation-gaming is employed in some of these sections when it is appropriate. This technique, which derives from the old concept of role-playing as an aid to learning, is particularly useful in certain units in the *Social Science* and the *Humanities* courses. Students who learn best in such sections appear to be those who enjoy having their thoughts stimulated by peers and those who must see all of the topical relationships before any become clear. The make-up of the discussion sections varies from unit to unit. A student will often shift to another section if the proctor or some of his fellow students annoy or distract him.

Independent study sections are arrangements whereby students who prefer (and are able) to proceed on their own can report periodically at their will to faculty members and take unit exams. The fact that the independent-study sections are offered by units in time sequences simply means that a faculty member who is especially qualified to guide the study in a particular area of inquiry is on call during that time. Each center has a dial-access information retrieval facility which is tied to a central file. Students who are skilled in tracking down and assimilating information independently use this system and other more conventional media to gain the knowledge they use to achieve unit objectives.

Independent study enables students to proceed at their own paces. Many of the faster learners, those who could probably learn well under any instructional form, choose this mode almost exclusively. They are the ones who find that many types of media interrupt their own ways of proceeding; thus they choose to read and examine on their own. The independent-study student seldom has to repeat unit exams. It is apparent that with these students, the specification and communication of objectives, along with their previously learned skills, stimulates them to apportion their time satisfactorily and encourages them to structure their own learnings.

The *service* component of the independent-study section is the coordinating device for students who participate in social-service projects in their own communities or abroad. Each of the core courses includes at least one unit for which the objectives can be fulfilled only by the students' working in an "off-campus" environment. Students may obtain credit through volunteer service in hospitals and social-service agencies or they may be employed in a variety of paid positions. The field coordination is arranged by the faculty of the independent-study sections.

The *tutorial and programmed* sections in each of the core courses are based on a one-to-one question–answer format. In these sections, students report regularly to tutors—usually fellow students—who help them learn by asking questions and by providing immediate feedback to their responses. The step-by-step learners—those who proceed best by assimilating small amounts of data at a time—are especially aided by the tutorial sections. Because the concepts on which they are based are similar to this tutorial mode, printed auto-instructional programs are also used in the tutorial sections. Although the college's instructors write some of the single-concept programs in use at the institution, most of them are purchased from outside agencies.

Even though programs are available for most units, the college retains the live tutorial because it serves as a learning device for the tutors as well as for the tutees. Tutors are selected from students who have achieved the unit's objectives for which they are tutoring others. By serving as tutors, students are forced to employ different procedures to attempt to draw out learners through the use of varied devices. The student–tutor who has learned a concept in his own way must be adaptable enough to restructure his knowledge so that the tutee can learn in *his* way. This type of effort broadens the tutor's own understanding and may help him to learn other units faster because he has grasped different strategies.

Another fundamental reason for employing students as tutors (especially as tutors to younger children in other schools) is that tutoring helps satisfy the students' needs for active, relevant participation in community life. The *Communications* course requires students to tutor elementary school children; this puts them in direct contact with the community, and by tutoring they help pupils who might otherwise become dropouts. Thus, the college serves the community directly, the students learn by teaching, and their needs to be "involved" are at least partially fulfilled. In previous years, students often organized tutorial and summer-camp projects on their own; in the college of 1979, these activities are a part of the regular curriculum.

Audio-tutorial sections are employed in many units of all core courses. This mode of instruction combines elements of independent study with advantages derived from tutorials and allows multi-sensory input teaching. Simultaneously, students can listen to directions, review demonstrations, and manipulate equipment. In the audio-tutorial mode, students sit in carrels with workbooks, tapes, slides, film strips, and similar materials at hand. The audio-tutorial method is an integrated learning process; the students pick up their kits of materials for the unit, go to the carrels, start the tapes, and receive complete directions for proceeding. Those students who need much guidance find this method useful because they are led through all of the procedures by the information in the workbooks and on the tapes. The test that determines whether or not the unit objective has been mastered is effected by a proctor in a one-to-one situation.

A final form of instruction—one that in 1979 is not yet fully developed in more than a few units—is the *computer-assisted* laboratory and the computer-assisted tutorial. Computer-assisted instruction is an area in which the college is participating in direct liaison with industry. The college uses the computer-simulated lab in some of the *Science* course's units and the computer-assisted tutorial in *Communications;* local software firms employ college instructors to write and to validate programs which they market nationally. It is a symbiotic relationship: The companies gain expertise and a laboratory in which to test materials, and the college gains the use of expensive equipment and programmers who are paid by the companies.

Computer-simulated labs have many varied uses at the college. For example, in the business-management unit of the *Social Science* course, the student asks the computer for data on fashion trends and market characteristics, orders materials, borrows money, employs a staff, and otherwise runs a business for "months." The computer then provides information on the extent to which the student has "succeeded" in business. In every unit of the *Science* course that calls for laboratory manipulation, students use the computer to simulate a chemical and physical laboratory. They "mix chemicals" and conduct experiments with the use of the computer.

The computer also aids students in selecting occupations. Through the use of computer simulation, more students are enabled to "try out" different "trades" without large investments of time. In an hour, a student can practice a trade to an extent that would take weeks on an actual job. The student is better able to choose an occupation because he has actually "been" a journeyman in several trades.

It should be repeated that not all units of all courses are taught with the use of all forms of instruction and that, regardless of the form used in a particular section, the comparable units carry the same objectives. Exceptions to the rule of common objectives occur only in units in which the instructional experience is its own end (as in computer-simulated employment) and in units in which objectives can be attained only by participation (as in units calling for the demonstration of verbal skills).

Students sort themselves into the sections that best fit not only their cognitive preferences but also their emotional and developmental demands. The following example illustrates this fact. For a long time, educators felt it was important for teachers to "know" their students. Acting on the advice of a few vocal youngsters who demeaned the impersonality of large classes and the dehumanizing influence of replicable media, they often sought to arrange small-group and individualized instruction for all. These educators failed to realize that for many students, instructors were intrusive forces standing between them and the knowledge to be gained — the material and behaviors to be learned. These students, busy with peer relationships, really did not care to associate closely with teachers. By defining clear-cut unit objectives, the college allows students with such attitudes to remain free of personal contact with instructors.

The selection of his preferred instructional form is based on the student's own preference or feeling for a particular form and on the basis of his own success in achieving the objectives.

Chapter Four

Managing the College

CREDITS AND DEGREES

Upon completing the cycle in the four core courses, a student gains the equivalent of forty-eight credits. With the credits he has gained in certain special-purpose courses or projects, these credits qualify him for an Associate in Arts degree (A.A.). The special projects for which a student may receive credit include service in the Peace Corps, campaigning for local bond issues, working in social-service agencies, counseling in playgrounds and camps — in short, for almost any form of productive service, whether or not it was performed for pay.

Through the core courses, all students who receive the A.A. degree at the community college attain similar learning objectives (and receive equivalent credits) although the time spent in study may vary greatly among individuals. Some students study at the college for only a few months before receiving their degrees; others spend several years in repeating various units. The average student completes the four core courses in two years and seven months. However, in all cases, the degree is evidence of the attainment of a common core of learning.

In addition to providing a common core of learning for all students who receive A.A. degrees, this arrangement has effectually eliminated what was once called "remedial" or "less-than-college-level" instruction at one extreme and "honors" programs at the other. The single core-course system allows the staff to add units "up" or "down" as the abilities exhibited by entering students change. There is no need for "remedial" sections. And by being allowed to proceed at their own speed and to "test out" of units, the more capable students are freed to take specialty courses, organized in the community under college auspices, or to stay at the college and study on their own. However, most students who exempt or complete the core courses satisfactorily accept their degrees and move on to other institutions for further study. Universities generally accept the Associate in Arts degree as meeting the general education requirements of their lower division and allow students with the A.A. to enroll as juniors in almost any program offered.

A transcript for each student is printed out at the end of each quarter or more often if it is requested. It includes an accounting of the units he has completed; units have an average value of .3 credits. Thus, a student who completes a year of study in one core course (approximately twenty units at two weeks per unit) receives six credits. Specialty courses may carry one credit or one-half of a credit depending on the complexity of the objectives.

At the time of his initial enrollment, each student is issued a permanent plastic card similar to a credit card with his name and Social Security number embossed thereon. He presents the card along with his most recent transcript to the instructor each time he enrolls in a unit. The instructor checks the transcript to be sure that the student has met the prerequisites for that unit. He then imprints a roll sheet with the student's card (much as a credit-card purchase is recorded) and admits the students to his section. When the student successfully completes the unit, his instructor sends a punch card to the computer facility where appropriate entries are made in the central storage file. A similar procedure is employed when a student "tests out" of a unit.

All the branch centers feed data into the one data bank. Credits and units are freely interchangeable among the centers. Of course, there is no penalty assigned to a student who enrolls in a unit but fails to achieve its

Student Name _____ Number _____ Date _____

Core Courses   Units Completed

	1 2 3 4 5 6 7 8 9 10 11 12 13 14 15 16 17 18 19 20 21 22 23 24 25 26 27 28 29 30 31 32 33 34 35 36 37 38 39 40	TOTALS
Communications		
Science		
Social Science		
Humanities		

Total Core Credits @ .3 per unit _____

Special Purpose Courses   Units Completed

Data Processing		
Vocation 1		
Vocation 2		
Foreign Language		
Community Service Activity		

A complete set of objectives achieved by
this student to date is available on request.

Total Special Purpose Credits _____
GRAND TOTAL CREDITS _____

objectives—the instructor simply does not send in the card that indicates the student has "passed" the unit.

Schedules are posted quarterly that list all courses, units, and sections—much like a menu in a restaurant window. The schedules include the current objectives and prerequisites for each unit so that a student can tell at a glance whether he is qualified to enroll in a unit. Copies of the unit objectives are kept on file so that, at any time, a student's achievements can be obtained by transfer institutions, employers, or other interested groups. The transcript includes a notation of this fact.

RESEARCH AND CURRICULUM

The research conducted by the college is directed primarily at keeping the curriculum up to date and maintaining effective instructional procedures. A continuing study of students is made for the purpose of modifying learning objectives and media as required. This research is geared to concrete measures of the effect that education has had on the students' attitudes and achievements. The college sets criteria like the following:

> Within six months of completing the *Social Science* course, 90 per cent of the students who are eligible will have registered to vote.
>
> Fifty per cent of the students who are enrolled in the *Humanities* course will voluntarily attend at least one stage production.
>
> Of the students who obtain employment in data processing after completing the course, 85 per cent will be rated superior to new workers who come from other sources.

The college research office assesses the attainment of these objectives by a variety of follow-up procedures. Students completing the core curriculum are systematically sampled and interviews are conducted periodically. Four-year institutions feed back information regarding the progress of transfer students in the first university courses. In addition, interviews are conducted with students who have failed to complete programs at the college. All students who enroll for even one specialty course are viewed as members of the population from which experimental samples are drawn. Young people of the community who are not enrolled are utilized as members of control groups. Various types of questionnaire follow-ups are also employed, but the personal interview technique typically yields more fruitful data on which curriculum modifications may be based.

The curriculum is reviewed on a regular basis by standing committees—one for each core course. The committees include faculty and student representatives, a delegate from the college's "objectives" specialty team (see Chapter Five), a professor from a university, and several lay citizens from the local community. The chief responsibility of these committees is to assess the core curriculum in the light of research findings and the changing character of the community which the college serves. Each group meets during the two-week Interim Period at the end of each quarter to review data on student achievement in the course units just completed and to examine the results of student follow-ups conducted by the research office. It recommends changes in objectives when appropriate, and considers the value of various instructional media. Changes in learning objectives may be proposed to the committee by the faculty or students at any college center.

The curriculum committee recommends objectives and media for the entire college, but it often approves modifications for only one of the centers. If an objective is to be used in a unit at only one center, or if a unit content is to be modified, the committee allows the change only if the level of complexity of the unit's objectives approximates that of the equivalent units at other centers. Thus, if one center wishes to emphasize American Negro literature rather than American literature as a whole, approval is granted only if the unit objectives at both centers require the same level of thinking to complete the unit satisfactorily. Thus, flexibility and some local control is maintained. However, although students may work toward alternative objectives and learn different topics through the use of varied media, if a unit calls for "analytic" thinking at one center, it cannot conclude with simple "recall" objectives at another. (Bloom, 1956.) Factual content is transient; what is important for one student may be of little interest to another. The true end of instruction is to help all students learn how to think.

The broad representation on curriculum committees helps keep unit objectives relevant to community life and prevents their trivialization. For example, the *Communications* course committee includes not only a university English professor but also the editor of the city newspaper, a television station manager, and two other local citizens. Other checks on curricular objectives include their being reviewed by other institutions in the consortium to which the college belongs and by curriculum committees at the university. Constant reactions from these diverse quarters as well as scrutiny by lay and professional organizations in the community help maintain a balanced curriculum.

The college as a whole engages in research based on, and designed to support, the teaching–learning paradigm but the college is also participates cooperatively in other types of research projects. Universities employ students as subjects for more specialized experiments and industrial concerns often view the college as a laboratory. The college does not initiate studies of enrollment trends, site surveys, or projections of financial resources because those types of specialized studies may more economically and efficiently be made by such groups as private or governmental research agencies. Some other studies are potentially of interest — certain psychological assessments of students and faculty, for example — but for these too the college seeks and receives outside aid. Research initiated and entirely conducted by the college focuses on student learning, curricular offerings, and institutional forms.

Through its continual redefining of objectives, the college is involved indirectly in another form of study revolving around such questions as "What makes a good community? How should people act when issues of particular social import arise?" By studying such problems in their relevance to curriculum development, the college takes positions and leads students to form careful opinions about community life, and also it helps the community to redefine its own values. To the extent that it leads to deliberate goal-setting, this form of study is basic to the life of the community. And because students sit on the curriculum committee as equal members, they are brought directly into the process of determining directions for their college and city.

ADMINISTRATION

The difference between roles of the faculty and the administration is much smaller than it was ten years ago. The administrators at the college are concerned with coordinating services, allocating resources, effecting liaison with the community, and insuring that both internal and external communication links are kept free. They serve as coordinators of certain projects, especially those that are peripheral to the college's main task. An example of this type of project is a community research study in which expertise housed at the college is employed on a contract basis to study community problems.

The management of the computer facility and the physical plant is also assigned to the administration. The staff includes a Director of Public Relations who also obtains scholarships and community-work positions for the students. Another administrator is solely responsible for seeking money from government agencies and private foundations to be used for such purposes as the purchase of special equipment that is necessary to produce films and other media.

The administrator most closely associated with the college's main function is the Director of Faculty Personnel; he establishes leave policies and arranges assignment schedules. Although he also helps in recruiting and selecting instructors, the final decision is left to the faculty after the prospective instructor's period of training and apprenticeship is over and has been reviewed. This method of selection is essential because the faculty's responsibilities for producing media, constructing test items, etc., are vital duties. Faculty members would find their work load increased if they had to "carry" an incompetent member; they must have the final say on the hiring of their fellow instructors.

More than any other single factor, the assignment of specific faculty tasks has allowed the faculty and administration a degree of self-policing that was not possible in the 1960's when their roles were vaguely defined. The administrators represent the college to the community. They must often say "no" to individuals and groups within the community who want the college to assume responsibilities that do not fit into its main function. Generally, the administrator's control over the faculty member is much less marked than it was ten years ago. The administration's position to-day resembles that of a hospital administrator who keeps the institution running so that the doctors are better able to cure patients.

The administrative staff must carry on an unending job of public relations in convincing accrediting agencies that the college's programs fit the purposes outlined in the institution's charter. The members of accreditation teams still employ archaic standards. They confuse means with ends; they seek evidence in the form of buildings, volumes in the library, and other quantifiable artifacts that the college recognizes as media, not as ends in themselves. For example, one team was aghast at the fact that the college was not sorting students into tracks but was accepting responsibility for the learning of all students. The team simply was not used to examining the concrete evidence of a student's performance. The re-education of accreditation teams is a continuing problem.

Academic advising is done by the faculty. Counseling is no longer a distinct function in the college. Much of the outmoded need for counseling derived from the days of *in loco parentis*, a concept that never really suited the community college, and from the attempt to fit students into irrelevant curricula and instructional forms. Counseling was necessary because the forms could not be changed quickly enough to meet the changing needs of the broadening base from which the community college drew its enrollees. Given the varied modes of instruction and the flexibility of the curriculum, students now seldom need to be "adjusted" to the curriculum. The curriculum is dynamic; instructional forms are varied. Students can find their places quickly within the variegated and clearly defined structure of the college.

THE COSTS OF EDUCATION

The community college of 1979 costs no more to operate than it did in 1969 or even in 1959. In relation to the number of students enrolled, the budget is about the same that it has been for many years; a major difference is that the college's focus on concrete objectives enables it to guarantee student learning. Previously, the budget only assured that students would be allowed to attend school; there were few attempts to relate the amount of learning to the money spent. Now, financial arrangements with the supporting district specify, in effect, "This much learning for that much money." Accordingly, the college receives financial credit on a percentage basis for students who "test out" of units in the core courses as well as for those who progress through instructional sections. (The tendency for the college to maximize its funds by making it easy for students to achieve unit objectives without repeating is checked by its responsibilities to outside administrative agencies.) The amount of state aid the college receives is calculated on the basis of student achievement rather than on average daily attendance. The daily-attendance principle, stemming as it did from the "Carnegie unit," had long outlived its usefulness by the time the community junior college began to flourish. Once the real purpose of the college was made clear, it became relatively easy to change the modes of financial accounting.

Several new ways of cutting expenses have recently been put into effect. The instructors' salaries are more than double what they were ten years ago; the increase has been made feasible by the widespread use of technological aids and nonprofessional assistance for many tasks once assigned to instructors. For example, qualified students can stimulate personal interaction in the tutorial sections without draining the more costly time of the faculty. Ten years ago, faculty members spent half their time marking quick-score tests, checking materials in and out of storage facilities, and performing a variety of general maintenance functions. A nonprofessional staff has taken over almost all of these tasks at half the cost.

Other savings have been effected in management functions. Fully automated scheduling, record-keeping, and data-processing has enabled students to come and go at will, eliminating the cost of laboriously registering them as they enroll and drop out. Admissions and enrollments are no longer costly, because the practices of advance enrollments and the probation and suspension of students have been abandoned.

Along with his corps of aides, the instructor has taken over many formerly expensive administrative tasks. Community and student services outside the scope of the teaching–learning paradigm have been dropped. The proliferation of course offerings, another wasteful luxury, has been discontinued. Formerly, it was not unusual to find almost half as many courses offered at an institution as there were students enrolled, but the core courses eliminated that. By deliberately blocking out a set of functions that it alone can best perform, the college has dropped many of the extraneous, expensive endeavors that formerly drained its budget.

The construction and maintenance of elaborate buildings was a major expense of the old college. Most of the modern college is scattered among structures that were not even built to house schools, where land is cheap and rents are low. The multimillion-dollar campus, constructed to last a thousand years, is no longer an expense.

Chapter Five

Students and Staff

STUDENTS

Community college students reflect a broad spectrum of community feelings and mores. The population base from which community college students are drawn has become even larger than it was in the 1960's. Studying the students as a group in 1979 is tantamount to examining almost the entire population of the community in which the college is located. Although most city residents attend the college at some time or another, young people between the ages of 17 and 20 still comprise the majority of the student body. These students are drawn from all segments of the population, but they have in common their age and the fact that they are in the process of formulating approaches to life. This has not changed.

The community college student of 1979 is still searching for meaning, still questioning his identity, still and increasingly reflecting community mores even while he disputes them. If, in the Eisenhower Era, students were "gloriously contented," it was probably because their elders were contented, too. If, in the 1960's students were critical of society, so were many non-students. More than ever before, the community two-year college student is a part of his city. He is distinct from his counterpart who resides at a four-year campus and who, in his quest, removes himself from his home community physically and, frequently, spiritually.

Most students at the college of '79 are not social critics. Few of them have played the activist role so often displayed at the university. One reason may be the fact that they are residents of a city, not of a college community. Also they spend less time at the college, both on a day-to-day basis and in terms of years. Those who are inclined to question vociferously are likely to do so away from the campus. A few community college students have followed the lead of their university counterparts by engaging in social and political protests both on and off the campus; even for many of this group, however, protest has been a case of faddism — following the trend toward "activism" just as students have followed it in fraternities, sports, and other areas of "college life."

The junior college student seldom has participated in revolutionary or reformist movements. Although he questions the value of his institution less than does his counterpart at senior colleges, he expects less from his school. Because he lives with his parents and often works thirty or more hours per week, entering the college has not separated him from his earlier environment. He does not seek psychic or social restructuring as a goal to be attained through the college curriculum. The few students who seek this type of curricular "relevance" drop out without attempting to change the structure. The constraints which led young people in earlier generations to seek self-awareness mainly through introspection and informal contacts with their fellows are, to a large extent, felt by today's community college student.

Personal maturation is a matter related to, and formerly confused with, more general considerations. Even now, in 1979, after more than a decade of widespread reforms in the curriculum and modes of instruction, some students deplore "curricular irrelevance" and the "depersonalization" of instruction. They seek a place to "be," to "find themselves." They want to gain "meaning" and self-illumination, and they question the college's apparent inability to give it to them. In the student-organized experimental colleges of the 1960's — through sensitivity groups, dialogue sessions, and similar activities — young people attempted to create settings in which "self-hood" might be found and exercised. These movements succeeded, not because they provided self-knowledge, but because they induced curricular and instructional changes in many formerly tradition-bound colleges. Curricular reforms have brought the college of '79 directly into line with social needs, and maintain a dynamic potential, but students' striving for personality development remains a private matter.

FACULTY

The college attracts many types of instructors from many sources, especially from work situations in the community at large. Many of the best faculty members have been out of graduate school for a period of time; they worked at other jobs and then decided to seek positions in the college. The Master's degree is the minimum requirement for the beginning instructor at the college, because of the recommendations of the accrediting agencies and because the possession of this degree suggests a certain level of commitment and self-direction. The certification of teachers by the state was abandoned a few years ago; it is not missed because it did not guarantee competence in *teaching*, only in a particular academic discipline.

Instructors are selected by the faculty at each center. Few applicants have been specifically prepared to teach in community colleges, even fewer have been prepared in programs built upon a definitive teaching–learning paradigm. The idea that an instructor is worth only as much as he contributes to the purposes of the institution is not one that has been accepted by most applicants, if indeed they have ever considered it. Applicants are informed of the objectives toward which they will strive, and the role that they will assume within the institution is delineated. The centers try to recruit people with sufficient flexibility to accept new roles easily.

The selection procedures are less relevant to the instructors' academic practices than is the college's own teacher-preparation program. In addition to acting in some capacity as a learning manager for students, each instructor must work with a team in an instructional specialty. The college itself prepares its instructors to perform effectively on these teams. Short courses in each of the areas of instructional specialization are offered to the applicants; they cover construction of objectives, preparation of test items, diagnosis and plotting of learning paths, production of media, and long-range curriculum planning (which includes the use of follow-up data). Of course, each one includes its own pre- and post-training assessment devices and sets of replicable media. Upon completion of the courses, the neophyte instructor is assigned as an apprentice to the team in his chosen specialty if he has demonstrated competency. He is paid at the full rate as a beginning instructor during the time that he works with the team in a particular area.

The members of the college-wide specialty teams are assigned to the different centers. Each center has its own test specialists to help other instructors prepare new items, its own media specialists to help with film and tape production, and so on. At least once each week, each team of specialists meets with its apprentices and aides to consider and solve problems. Members of the teams serve, in effect, as consultants to their colleagues who specialize in other instructional tasks.

Paraprofessional help is allotted to the college centers as required. Aides, proctors, and tutors are drawn for the most part from the college's enrollees. The college employs an adequate staff of clerks and typists, because it long ago realized the false economy of asking instructors to type, mark examination papers, and perform similar maintenance functions.

Faculty job specifications are written annually to allot the specific tasks which must be fulfilled. The instructor's teaching objectives and his duties as a member of the team of specialists in his field are delineated and included in his contract. Under this system, instructors rarely are dismissed. If it seems desirable, they may be reassigned to different tasks. Those who choose to stay within the institution usually find a place doing work in which they prove competent.

Once he realizes that the institution's team approach to particular problems and work areas is "the way it is done here," it is usually easy for a new instructor to overcome the tendency toward operating as an independent practitioner. After a short apprenticeship, some instructors leave the college because they do not find what they were seeking when they decided to enter the teaching profession. Almost invariably, however, those who stay become valuable contributors to the purposes of the institution as well as competent specialists in particular areas.

Instructors at the college have gained the clear identity and status which their predecessors had long sought. They are recognized as setters of the objectives which in a sense define and recommend modes of behavior for all citizens in the community. This function alone is far different from that of teachers long ago who were commonly tolerated for their gentility, but considered ineffectual in shaping the lives of the young. The instructors still identify with and assume a role not very different from that assumed by their fellows in other institutions. However, a significant difference is that they understand and accept a specific set of functions. Many of the college's most influential instructors rarely meet students, and thus rarely play "teacher" in the archaic sense of the word. Their influence is reflected in their curriculum-planning, test construction, and objective setting.

Thus, in the college of 1979, students know what to expect because specific objectives are stated; faculty members possess specialized capabilities and are recognized as professionals in student learning. The long-held dream of educators — students and teachers working together as partners in the quest for human knowledge — is being realized.

Part Two

Means, Ends, and Anomalies

What is *today's* community junior college trying to do in the total scheme of American education? Cut through the public relations rhetoric and the jargon that emanates incessantly from the colleges and their professional associations and what is left? A group of functions? A set of vague goals? A picture of a structure in which people labor with little awareness of what may result?

Any educational institution is a medium that has an impact on its environment and on the people within it. The effects of the institution's influence may be predictable or serendipitous, deliberate or haphazard—but they exist. A peculiarity of institutions of higher education is that the people who work within them—they who are themselves part of the system as medium — also have the opportunity, and hopefully a desire to shape the ultimate purpose of their labors. To the extent that they accept their function, they can define the results that their efforts produce. And the junior college, similarly, helps to determine the goals of the community that it serves.

As an institution becomes large and complex, more and more time is allotted to its maintenance and less time is devoted to the definition and redefinition of its purposes in the light of changed environmental conditions. Community junior colleges collectively comprise a large and complex institution, busily adding seventy-five colleges a year to its corpus. Each college continually grows (10,000 students is no longer unusual nor even particularly noteworthy), and the number of multi-campus districts is increasing correspondingly. Thus, the general system becomes more complex. Accordingly, more and more junior college educators spend less and less time in considering basic goals. Instead, they are occupied in adjusting procedures so that their institutions can operate smoothly. In their eyes, the college to a large extent has become its *own* end, and each institution is evaluated in terms of the way in which it enhances or detracts from the educational system. Effects on the lives of individual students or on the varied communities in which the colleges are located (and which they were designed originally to serve) recede to distinctly peripheral places in the planner's thinking. Instead of the college as a medium, the college and its perpetuation have become the ends.

The following section pertains particularly to today's publicly supported community junior colleges — institutions that are organized as separate entities by individual districts, within or outside a state-supported educational system. University branches and extension centers will not be discussed specifically within this rubric; the private junior college, with specialized aims, is excluded from this text because it is not often an integral part of its community. The title under which the institutions operate vary greatly; some use the term "college," others "junior college," some "city college" or "community college," but in all cases the institutions considered here are publicly supported colleges that offer Associate in Arts degrees and various "less-than-degree-level" programs.

The community junior college is emphasized here because it represents a most important segment of the American higher-education complex. The proportion of public to private junior colleges changes continuously. In 1933, 42 per cent of the junior colleges were public, 58 per cent were private. By 1946, the number of public and private institutions was almost equal; and by 1956, the 1933 figures had been reversed. Enrollment changes are even more striking — more than 90 per cent of all junior college students are now in publicly supported institutions. The trend continues; now, when one speaks of a "junior college education," it is likely that he refers to the public community college.

It is not the purpose of this section to delineate or characterize the junior college's position in the total scheme of American higher education. Several textbooks and many publications produced and distributed by the American Association of Junior Colleges do this quite well. However, certain organizational anomalies and curricular and instructional practices of questionable value will be examined.

Just as the junior college postulated for 1979 does not represent the only form an educational institution might take, the comments in this section about the current status of the curriculum and instruction are not universally applicable. But they do indicate some general guidelines that might be applied to junior colleges as a means of assessing the strengths and weaknesses more clearly. Most of these comments pertain to the "academic" portion of the colleges' curricula—their "college level" or "general education" offerings. As applied to some institutions, certain criticisms may appear overdrawn; however, as applied to others, they may not seem to go far enough.

It may seem somewhat untoward to challenge the junior college, because in its short history it has become a familiar and—among people committed to democratic education—a beloved institution. To question it is to call forth from its apologists the defenses erected over the decades when they were struggling to gain initial support. Yet the junior college must be examined critically so that it can loose itself from the tired premises it has inherited from secondary and higher schools and thus be free to move into a new phase of development. Change is needed, and as Warren Martin (1968, p. 22) has put it:

> The best hope . . . for encouraging an interest in change is in showing the inherent conflicts in the dominant educational model and, at the same time, probing for alternative ideas and forms that might resolve these conflicts and provide better responses to the challenges emerging now.

Chapter Six

A Question of Identity

The philosophy that each individual, regardless of economic or social status, should be provided the opportunity to develop to his and society's ultimate benefit, found its way into the mainstream of American thought with the advent of the land-grant college. The community junior college is today in the forefront of the thrust toward democratized higher education that derives from that era. Post-secondary schooling is regarded increasingly as a necessity for an ever-growing portion of the population, and the junior colleges are bearing much of the added responsibility.

Junior colleges have absorbed increasingly larger segments of higher-education enrollments. In 1920, they enrolled 1.4 per cent of all college students. The proportion increased to 10 per cent in 1940; 12.1 per cent in 1960; 15.2 per cent in 1965; and will reach an estimated 16.9 per cent in 1975. By 1980, junior colleges will enroll 22 per cent of all college students. (Tickton, 1968, p. 18.) The rate of increase is even higher when junior college enrollments are related to *undergraduate* higher education only. By this mode of accounting, junior colleges in 1965 accounted for 17 per cent of the population. And considering lower division enrollments only, junior colleges have more than 30 per cent of that group within their doors already. (National Science Foundation, 1967, p. 5.)

Why is the community college movement of such magnitude? One answer is suggested by viewing the general situation of American society in the first half of the twentieth century. Several broad social and ideological trends can be related to the rise of the community college. First, as one of the results of the democratic revolution which began in the eighteenth century, Americans' absolute respect for authority has steadily broken down. The idea that one's elders were to be obeyed indiscriminately gave way in the twentieth century as the belief in the divine right of kings to rule had collapsed at the onset of the worldwide trend toward democracy. And in both situations, class differentiation changed and became less distinct. Whereas, in an earlier age, social classes had been distinguished largely on the basis of ancestry and material possessions, a new class division has emerged on the basis of knowledge, training, and education. It is more accurate now to identify a person's class by the way he employs his time and efforts. This, of course, has made education a crucial factor in class mobility.

Another force that has stimulated change in American society is automation. The history of automation, the way it has changed job patterns, has been traced many times. For the purpose of understanding the organization and operations of the community colleges, it is sufficient to note here that by the mid-twentieth century there was little need for an unskilled work force, and there were practically no jobs available for male high-school graduates with no other training. Similarly, there were few jobs for female secondary-school graduates who had not been prepared to handle relatively sophisticated equipment. The lack of jobs for the unskilled—and the correlative availability of jobs only for the trained— has led to a situation in which young people, not needed in the work force, tend to go to school for longer periods of time. The technology which led to automation is forcing the unskilled millions into school.

Although it has been traced and well understood, this phenomenon means more than that the schools must prepare people for employment. There are currently few socially acceptable places for a young person to *be* other than in school; this fact is an outgrowth of the technological revolution that has not yet been fully realized. Under the impact of having nowhere else to go, some youths have turned to drugs or petty crime. However, most of them have found their way onto campuses where they seek, if not further training, association with their fellows in an approved environment.

Another twentieth-century phenomenon is a change in types of learning stimuli. Non-institutional opportunities for learning are all around us, not merely in the apprenticeship or direct-learning experiences of past generations but in a new realm of abstractions-given-form. Television brings a world of ideas and images into every home; radio brings it into every automobile. The senses are assailed by the information input. It is almost impossible for a conscious person to ignore such data, coming in a variety of forms from an infinity of sources. Not yet known are the effects of the electronic revolution on the community's store of knowledge and pattern of behavior. Surely, changed approaches to education and learning are among the implied consequences.

Another force that acts on the community junior college is economic competition. In the broad sense, learning has become big business. "Research and development" operations comprise a major area in America's industrial growth. Concomitantly, industrial encroachment upon what has been for centuries the preserve of academicians is increasing. Industrial concerns have always conducted training programs for their employees, but now they have moved into education in a much more concerted way. Education offers considerable profit potential, and where business moves, the marketplace intrudes. Academicians, long accused of attempting to escape entrepreneurship by hiding behind walls of ivy, must now compete with industry for influence over the form and context of education.

With it all, the community college is being asked to accept a general-welfare function. (McGrath, 1966, p. xi.) Just as mobility across socio-economic lines is now, more than ever before, furthered by education, social integration is being pursued ever-increasingly in the schools. Havighurst (1967) maintains that "Public community colleges are the main instruments of educational opportunity for Negro youth." Education's policy makers at the highest level insist on seeing the schools as agents for community change. The Supreme Court's integration decisions and federal legislation that has authorized millions of dollars for certain school programs reflect similar thinking.

The rubric of education for all; a burgeoning need for vocational training; young peoples' need for an institutional locus; the call for schools to be direct agents of social change; and the growing competition from industry and the communications media in mass education — this is the milieu in which the community junior college now exists. How can a single institution, no matter how comprehensive it purports to be, confront all these pressures?

Even the functions that are now accepted as part of the junior college pattern—transfer education, guidance, general education, technical and crafts training, adult education, among others—constitute a comprehensive and tremendously complex program for any single institution. In an age of specialization, comprehensiveness seems somewhat anachronistic, if not unfeasible. It is unlikely that a single institution—especially one modeled on archaic education forms—could perform all these tasks well.

One problem is that the heterogeneity of purposes, of students, of programs, and of personnel is not reflected by the institutions themselves. There are large-city junior colleges within school systems, autonomous institutions in small urban areas, multi-campus independent districts, non-urban colleges attached to local high schools, two-year branches of universities, colleges organized as parts of state systems, and so forth. But this diversity in affiliations does not necessarily indicate a similar diversity in approaches to curriculum, instruction, and student–personnel policies. Instructional forms may be very similar in a large urban branch of a multi-campus district and in a small, rural, independent junior college. The curriculum that was developed originally in (and for) universities may be the pattern for courses and programs in any of the types of junior college listed. In most junior colleges, courses are apportioned among divisions or departments that follow the rigid prescriptions of the research-oriented universities. Even the apparent diversity among junior colleges is not borne out by certain types of research. A study of thirty-two junior colleges, forty liberal arts colleges, and twenty-seven universities assessed student perceptions of the campus environment with Pace's College and University Environment Scales. Findings indicated that junior colleges spread over only half of the total possible range of diversity in all areas of measurement. For example, they were in the bottom half of the "Awareness" scale. (Pace, 1966.) Should institutions rightfully be classified as different from each other solely on the dimension of the type of government or control? Other parameters might well be employed so that a more useful picture can emerge.

Change has been the hallmark—indeed, one of the few certainties—of this century. The farther into the century we progress, the more rapid becomes the pace of change. And with twentieth-century changes have come demands for post-secondary education in a variety of forms for an ever more diverse student population. The community college, a response to new social needs which was expanded into areas of learning not being dealt with by other institutions, is in itself a significant change in higher education. But it may be that, in a sense, junior colleges have not accepted their pioneering role, and have failed to consider all of their options—even to identify their problems clearly. There is much questioning about whether the manner in which the institutions are organized, the way they operate, and the personnel with which they are staffed are appropriate to their vital tasks. Society, not infrequently, has to remind educational institutions of their inadequacies. (Legters, 1968.) Must the junior college wait for other elements in the community to force it to redefine itself?

According to a common view, junior colleges are designed to fulfill several roles. They offer vocational training for students who cannot receive it in other educational institutions, provide for other young people "general" and "transfer" education, and so on. The usual thinking then proceeds to the assumption that a junior college with a working group of counselors must be fulfilling the guidance function; a college that offers a variety of courses and programs must be meeting the diverse instructional needs of students; a faculty composed of instructors with Master's degrees who do not publish articles makes its school a "teaching institution"; a system with an open-door policy "provides opportunity for all to achieve to the limit of their ability." The existence of facilities and processes aimed at certain ends is accepted as adequate indication that these ends are actually being served.

There are, however, other ways of viewing educational structures. One alternative is presented by this book — that of looking upon the colleges as *media* for designing and achieving specific ends. From this viewpoint, the counselors may do more to discourage than to guide; the various courses may not be relevant to students' needs and desires; the premise that a faculty which does not do research must perforce "teach" is viewed for what it is — a fallacy in logic; and the open door that allows all to achieve can be seen as a door to frustration and failure for many.

The use of precise goals as the chief criteria of success requires a picture of the way the junior college changes the lives of its students and transforms its community — how much learning it causes to occur. The ends, not the means, become the focus of attention. The junior college should not be dedicated to furthering itself through program aggrandizement, expanded financial support, and public relations work; instead, it should become a medium valued only insofar as it produces predictable, demonstrable effects. It is, then, on its *effects* rather than on its processes that it should be adjudged more or less successful.

This alternative way of viewing the institution can lead to more realistic planning for what can eventually become a new phase of community service. It can help junior colleges find the identity they seek and it can lead them to understand several contemporary crises which they only dimly recognize as yet. Planning cannot end when a junior college achieves modes of support, a campus, a staff, and procedures. Identity comes not only from marking out "an area which was not being covered by other institutions" (Gleazer, 1968b), but by *effecting learning* within that area.

It is by no means certain that the time is yet ripe for such alternate views. Junior college educators are not easily convinced of that necessity. Small wonder, for the focus on function and process have thus far served the junior colleges well. Most are still riding the crest of a wave of support for their efforts. In many states, community colleges represent still-new visions of opportunity for the young. Communities in which the colleges are symbols of achievement still pass bond issues and tax overrides. College systems are growing rapidly. If hundreds of students drop out after a few weeks of attendance, it matters little, because at the beginning of the next semester, thousands more will be there to take their places. Administrators, by their own standards, are successful if they can keep up with the burgeoning enrollment. If students who transfer to the university earn grade marks nearly equivalent to those they earned at the junior college, the college is seen as having "taught" as well as the four-year institution. And if a few students are redirected into programs "more consonant with their abilities," the college has fulfilled its guidance function.

Perhaps not until the momentum of increased support and student enrollments comes to a halt will the institutions realize that even now most of their practices offer less flexibility than they seem to offer. It is very heady being asked to take on all the jobs that other elements in the society had not been able to manage — keeping the young out of the labor force, training them for jobs, inculcating them with a set of moral values, helping them gain a feeling for their place in society, providing an overflow receptacle for those whom the universities are unable or unwilling to serve. And for each of these tasks, money has been made available. There are funds for buildings and for staffs and promotions for those educators who "understand the problems of the community college." So far so good.

But rigidity can creep up on any institution and the most insidious form of rigidity is that which affects vision. The community college has grown strong in the mid-twentieth century because it did retain a great deal of youthful flexibility. But a system cannot be considered flexible merely because it can expand its size seemingly indefinitely. It must demonstrate its responsiveness to the changing needs of the communities which support it, or it remains in perpetual danger of losing that support. Flexibility is more than infinite capacity for expansion and overly publicized innovations in methodology. Flexibility requires a capacity for taking new directions.

Inside and outside the community colleges, doubts persist. The problem of identity has long been an issue. After more than a half century, instructors are still asking, "Exactly what is this college set up to do . . .?" (Garrison, 1967, pp. 77-78.) As if to prove his college's manhood, a president states proudly that the high state of student attrition "indicates we're not soft . . . . About one-third flunk or quit the first year." (O'Connell, 1968, p. 5.) (No doubt his college would be twice as good if *two*-thirds flunked or quit!) And repeated cries for innovation cannot be ascribed simply to change for its own sake or for the sake of economy in operation. (Johnson, 1966.)

Students, too, raise questions. For the most part, junior college enrollees are not inclined to speak out, but might not this comment by an Antioch College student be considered representative of the feelings of at least some of them?

> Our education is becoming increasingly less related to the concerns of society. By refusing feedback from non-academic sources, academia has become a closed loop system whose existence seems to lie in perpetuating itself. Reacting defensively to increasing charges from the outside that much of what we are forced to learn is useless, it continues to justify itself by assigning values to the little awards, grades, credits, and degrees it so graciously gives out. (Dixon, 1967.)

Educators often question the junior college. Some go as far as to say that students in community colleges receive, "despite fancy jargon used to obscure the fact, custodial care." The Associate in Arts degrees obtained by a few represent a "consolation prize," but "no knowledgeable person" is fooled "as to the quality or utility of the education they received." (Kauffman *et al.*, 1968, p. 29.) These are severe criticisms.

Are their statements being echoed by citizens who refuse any longer to support community colleges without question? Despite its long established tradition of free public education, California has recently cut back support. Community colleges in that state had enjoyed a generation of ever-increasing favor, but in the past few years, tax overrides and bond issues have begun to fail in alarming numbers — exactly half of all school bond issues were turned down at the polls in 1965–66. (Nationwide, 25 per cent of the bonds offered were rejected as compared to only 11 per cent in 1960). (*Time*, 1967, p. 44.) It is just possible that there is causal relationship between financial cutbacks and criticisms such as those raised by many educators.

Who can blame teachers and administrators who work within the system? They are kept busy with maintenance functions and have little time for broad reflection. Educational forms reflect their own environments, and in most areas of American life, "how?" has superseded "why?" The perpetuation of the colleges in their current form reflects a belief that their growth derives from their usefulness. As a place for young people in a rapidly expanding population, for those who are no longer needed in the work force, the junior colleges may indeed be doing an adequate job. But that seems a limited use of the tool that has been created and even the most complacent administrators complain about the lack of respect accorded them by the broader educational community.

The institutions drop the word "Junior," from their titles, break away from local school districts and form state boards of their own. Yet all the calls for status and recognition are useless unless the colleges define themselves more clearly — decide what they want to do and can manage well, and what they must leave to others. Community colleges cannot achieve the identity they seek by serving "almost in bondage the demands of the multiversities. Asking these institutions to take the lead in experimentation is demanding a great deal, proposing a revolution in fact," but it is essential, if not for survival, at least for status. (Kauffman *et al.*, 1968, p. 59.) For the junior college to achieve identity it must break away from its rigid yet vaguely defined mold and take the lead in providing "new forms of education both for those who find no place in college and for graduates who missed crucial stages of personal development." (Sanford, 1967, p. 189.)

Whence will identity be derived? Even if the junior college views itself as being largely custodial and only partly educational, it is spending too much money for custodial care and not enough for instruction. It would be much cheaper for the community to provide other places for the young to be while they await maturity. On the contrary it might not be more expensive to provide a highly efficient learning and training system if that were to become the college's acknowledged and determined purpose.

Reaching a sense of identity is a long, perhaps continual, process. In order to begin such a process, direction achieved from *within* individual community colleges may be necessary — direction derived from a focus on defined learning. Many current institutional crises, including that of identity, may be related to the fact that the community college, dedicated from its inception to community upgrading, *has yet to demonstrate its effects.* Goals, ideals, dedication, and good intentions alone may never be enough. There must be a bridge between these concepts and the measured effects of their being applied.

Chapter Seven

Images: Campuses
and Marks

An organization's effects on its client population may be either enhanced or adversely affected by each individual's perceptions of the system
itself. A system projects images, communicates messages to the onlooker
and participant. In many cases, the messages are subtle, perceived more
by some than by others, but they are nevertheless influential. Examples
of this phenomenon may be obtained by viewing two seemingly disparate
features of today's junior colleges—their campuses and their grade-
marking practices—as they contribute to the images projected by the
institution.

CAMPUSES

The community college is distinctly American. Most of its forms
have evolved from liberal arts colleges. The early American college was

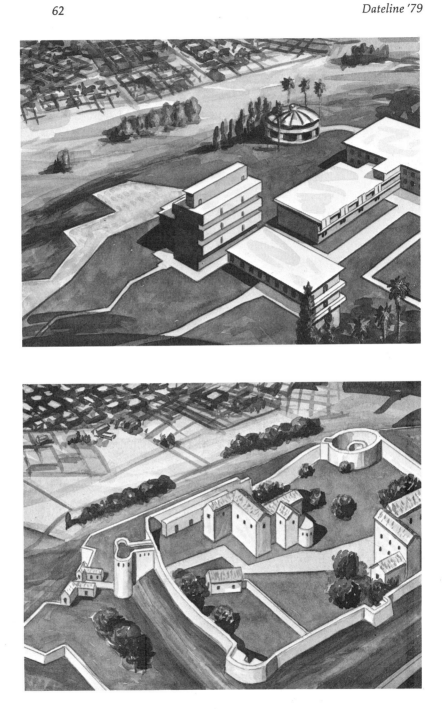

One of these is a "community" junior college.

rural; although its organizers could have found precedent for urban locales in the great medieval universities of Europe, they chose to build in the countryside, as far as practical from the cities. For example, the 1789 charter for the University of North Carolina stipulated that the university could not be located within five miles of any seat of government. In 1801, Georgia selected a hilltop for its university and called it "Athens." (Rudolph, 1965, p. 92.) And to this day, many college catalogs carry notations relating the institution's potential benefits to its pastoral qualities.

Early colleges developed a pattern of life known as "the collegiate way," a form dependent as much on students' residence as on library, faculty, or curriculum structures. An environment away from the temptations of the city was regarded as essential to maximum learning. Presumably, a youth could be removed from his home milieu, placed behind walls for a period of time, and after appropriate indoctrination, returned to his community as a changed person. The collegiate atmosphere included a regulation of conduct which suggested not the free spirit of scholarly inquiry but the atmosphere of an English boarding school.

By the time the community junior college arose, a style of architecture distinctly identifiable as "College Gothic" had developed as housing for the paternalistic liberal arts college. Thick walls, vaults, high ceilings, and massive facades gave this college the appearance of a medieval church or fortress, which perhaps betrayed its spiritual and intellectual roots. Understandably but incongruously then, in their early years community colleges also sought isolated settings and erected "Gothic" buildings. It was not always possible to duplicate a rural locale, but the idea of "campus" and the architecture was followed — often complete in detail to the surrounding brick wall.

Thus, crenelated structures arose in the midst of cities. If a college could not practically be built on the brow of a hill outside the town, an expansive lawn and an iron fence could yet make it look "collegiate," hence genuine. For how can true learning occur except in an isolated, preferably bucolic, setting? And more important, if the structure *looks* like a college, is it not more likely to be *identified* as one?

The matter would be one of mere historical and architectural curiosity were it not for the image projected by the physical form of any institution. In the case of the community college housed in massive structures on a "campus," the problem is in the incongruity of the image. The twentieth-century community college has dedicated itself to providing educational opportunity for all people of its community and to a curriculum relevant to the locale from which it draws its students and support. What can be more anomalous than a community college dedicated to these principles housed in a structure that looks as though it had been designed to repel attacks by barbarians? Its walls defy entrance except by the hardiest members of the towns. Although full-blown "College Gothic." architecture has been abandoned, columns, walls, arches, and expanses of lawn betray the heritage. "College is for the elite who can afford to send their children away for extended periods of time," the walls seem to say to potential enrollees. "Who are you to seek entrance?" And to those who work in the institution, "Your curriculum and instructional forms must be 'collegiate' in these hallowed halls."

Form may follow function up to a point; then form begins to follow form. Eventually, form *evokes* function. To illustrate this point, consider the extent to which the classroom, a rectangular box with forty chairs facing forward and a podium facing aft, mandates to students, "Thou shalt sit and be still," and to instructors, "Thou shalt stand and speak."

Planners sometimes consider the broad views of junior colleges as parts of their communities. Because architects are sensitive to the relationships among functions, forms, and images, they often attempt to plot college environments that will serve particular purposes and they frequently design urban campuses that blend into the cities in which they are located. But with rare exception, whether colleges are built in large or small cities, in urban or rural districts, in high or low socioeconomic areas, they follow the model of the monastery–fortress. There are those who consider the college an instrument of urban renewal. (Caudill, 1965.) But of what use is urban renewal if acres of decaying buildings are torn down only to make room for a group of massive structures, architecturally unlike the surrounding ones — buildings that turn their stern backs to the people they are supposed to serve?

The very idea of "campus" is archaic within the context of a complex modern city. In his enlightened treatment of this issue as it relates to the urban university, Birenbaum states:

> The wide open spaces, the monumental and inflexible architecture, and the insulation combine into an anti-urban phenomenon. The campus is more than a place; it is a system. It assumes turning the flow of human relationships inward. Its success depends upon imposing an isolated, contrived community upon the lives of its inhabitants . . . . The result is . . . a phony world . . . . (Birenbaum, 1968, p. 58.)

The modern community college cannot really afford to have a campus — physical *or* spiritual! The image of the junior college as a fortress is incompatible with its charge to educate all and to upgrade its community. As a medium of transformation in community life, the institution is not enhanced by structures that symbolize strength and defiance. It is not only unnecessary for the college to separate itself architecturally from its city, it is another way of lessening its effect. How much more could a junior college do for its community if it were less isolated?

One of these is a "community" junior college.

THE MARKING SYSTEM

The marking system — another heritage ungraciously offered by the university and accepted by the junior college — persists and projects images. It suggests to students that instead of being taught they will be judged, sorted, screened, and weeded out and that society will be protected from them. This system puts students in competition with one another and encourages them to perpetuate a kind of pseudo-learning behavior that makes them extremely effective in "psyching out" a curriculum without ever learning that which was supposed to have been taught.

Except for occasional programs, it is a rare junior college course in which advance commitment is made that a specified percentage of students will achieve predefined skills. Bloom (1968) explained:

> Each teacher begins a new term (or course) with the expectation that about a third of his students will adequately learn what he has to teach . . . . This set of expectations, supported by school policies and practices in grading, becomes transmitted to the students through the grading procedures and through the methods and materials of instruction. The system creates a self-fulfilling prophecy such that the final sorting of students through the grading process becomes approximately equivalent to the original expectations.

The operation of the grading system is often relatively unsubtle. Course outlines in use in junior colleges sometimes carry the statement, "No curve is applied, however, experience has shown the pattern of grade marks in this course to be: A's, 10 per cent; B's, 20 per cent; C's, 40 per cent; D's, 20 per cent; F's, 10 per cent." Is it not likely that by changing examination questions as the course progresses and by other similar practices, the instructor will unintentionally make the pattern come out the way it is "supposed to"? Such is usually the case, regardless of the changing populations of students and the students know it. The marking system, itself, then becomes an instructional form to the extent that it communicates images to the student and serves as a barrier between him and content of the course.

Practices of this sort are so ingrained that we tend to ignore their effects. The junior college persists in studying grade-point differentials (the difference in grades earned by junior college students and those earned by the same students when they transfer to a four-year institution) intensively. More research on the "effects of instruction" in the junior college is conducted on the grade-point differential than all other forms of instructional research combined. Yet the insistence on the use of marks and the constant study of the grade-point differential can only indicate the junior colleges' acceptance of a role as a *sorting* institution. The fact that sorting students is *not* the same as *instructing* them is unfortunately overlooked.

It is a pernicious system. College grades bear little or no relationship to any measures of adult accomplishment. Marks are very useful in predicting other marks, but little more. Yet "with the exception of the negative assessment assigned a student who violates moral, ethical or legal standards," (Hoyt, 1965) the grade-point average is often the only assessment of educational progress attempted.

Why does the use of the "normal curve" persist? This practice communicates to the student that he is to be judged rather than taught; it tells him to compete rather than to cooperate with his fellows. Is the method of assigning marks an escape — a rationalization in the psychological sense of the term? (W. Trow, 1963.) The practice tends to project the failures of the instructional system onto the students, giving low marks to those who have not been adequately taught and high marks to those who do well — some of whom may not even have needed the instruction. Any value inherent in the grading system must be minimal. Assuredly it does not offset the negative image projected by the system.

Other superficially innocent practices that in fact limit the college's teaching potential can be cited. For example: To what extent are college doors closed to students who find it difficult to complete applications, pay fees by check, take entrance tests on certain dates, and make similar advance commitments associated with enrollment? (Knoell, 1968.) But the pervasive concepts of campus and marking seem most obviously debilitating. Many educators are concerned with the impact of anomalies in instructional form, and they seek corrective measures. The physical facilities are sometimes planned to be extensions of city streets — the buildings look much like those in the surrounding neighborhood (though they are still "campuses"). In addition the "Pass/Fail" or "Credit/No Credit" method has replaced the five-tier sorting system in some courses. Still, most junior colleges proceed in a fashion that suggests their inability to confront the incongruities and failures of the conventional system.

Chapter Eight

The Pragmatic Student

A dominant characteristic of students in the current generation is that they are *gloriously contented* both in regard to their present day-to-day activity and their outlook for the future. Few of them are worried—about their health, their prospective careers, their family relations, the state of national or international society or the likelihood of their enjoying secure and happy lives. They are supremely confident that their destinies lie within their own control rather than in the grip of external circumstances.   —PHILIP E. JACOB (1957, p. 1.)

The majority of American college students are being had .... There is a growing conflict of interest between students and faculty regarding basic educational philosophies and the curriculum which reflects their philosophy. Students are increasingly interested in an education which will help them deal with social, national and international — and personal — problems. The traditional curriculum, behind which the faculty stands, provides numerous roadblocks to the student seriously interested in these problems . . . Only recently has an identity crisis in the college years become the most important aspect of a student's education.   — PHILIP WERDELL (1967.)

The difference between these two characterizations of student outlook is profound. Did the intervening decade bring such a change in percepts and expectations; or do the reports simply represent different ways of viewing the same complex phenomenon?

The identification of a typical student approach to junior college is difficult for several reasons. There is a paucity of research on the personality characteristics of students, on the college's effects on students, and on what students expect to gain from the college experience. A consistent methodology is lacking. Published studies are either so narrowly based that generalization cannot be drawn or so broad that the meaning is lost. Furthermore, the investigator's percepts and biases are reflected in the findings. Which questions does one ask of students, and why? Matters deemed important in one study are ignored in others.

On certain dimensions of personality, 10,000 students enrolled in an urban college may be less unlike each other than are a "select" group of a few hundred students who attend a small liberal arts college. It is not safe to assume that heterogeneity of outlook follows demographic heterogeneity. Here it is most apparent that "many more studies of student characteristics [are] . . . needed to complete the qualitative description of the clientele of the community junior colleges." (Thornton, 1966, p. 158.) As Sanford (1967, p. 52) says, "The great majority of entering college students bring with them the after-effects of earlier struggles with overwhelming tension, and it is probably safe to assume that none is absolutely free of unconscious motives and mechanisms of defense." But what are the correlations between students' anxieties and their "practicality" or the way they accept or reject college offerings?

Some "questionnaire" research indicates that junior college students are pragmatic — less inclined to graduate training or to studies of the humanities for their own sake; more likely to attend college because it will lead them to higher status employment. (Richards and Holland, 1966.) Most studies of students focus on such population variables as age, sex, and economic status or on broad "achievement-related" measurements: previous academic success, preference for a major field of study, transfer aspirations, and the like. (*Junior College Research Review*, 1967.) Numbering in the hundreds, these investigations tend to indicate great heterogeneity in student populations along varied dimensions. However, in spite of inconsistencies in the data, the typical junior college student is commonly acknowledged to be "a product of a lower socio-economic stratum, . . . less able (in the academic sense) and less mobile (in the geographic sense). He is, on balance, not strongly attracted to the junior college." (National Science Foundation, 1967, p. 88.) Rather, he is there because, to him, the college is one of the few available — if not the only — options for education beyond the secondary school.

Junior college students are typically divided by researchers into "adult" and "college age" subgroups because, in many states, financial aid to an institution is differentiated according to the number of students in each category. Few writers lament the pragmatic orientation of adult students; they accept without question the fact that most attend college "in order to obtain a better job." (Blocker *et al.*, *1965*, p. 125.) But many of them do deplore the apparent similarity between the adults' outlooks and those of the "college age" group. (Sanford, 1967, p. 33.) It is frequently alleged that the younger students should use their years in lower-division college work to explore ideas, to develop their own personalities, and to question their places in society. Instead, these students apparently come to the college for a set of experiences and a slip of paper that will qualify them to enter the world of work. The "conscious search for meaning," is evidently rare among the junior college students. Rather, "two-year colleges attract pragmatic students seeking vocational training; they are less attractive to talented students who are intellectually and academically oriented, who plan a degree in one of the traditional subject areas, and who expect to take part in a wide variety of activities in college." (Richards and Braskamp, 1967, p. 13.)

Assuming these generalizations to be accurate, the "pragmatic" student should not be blamed for seeking a set of experiences relevant to his life while he is enrolled in college. Although this student is less inclined than his university counterpart to use the written or spoken word to express his feelings, his behavior does imply dissatisfaction. What proportion of the high dropout rate in the community college can be ascribed to disillusionment with the curriculum, instructional forms, and general patterns of organization? Even in two-year institutions, student activism is a force (Lombardi, 1969); the fact that both educators and lay citizens tend to overreact greatly to the "revolt" should not obscure the students' intent to bring more meaning into what is often at best a situation divorced from "real life." Today's junior college students organize tutorial projects, election campaigns, and civil-rights activities on and off campus. No less than the university students—perhaps even more so because of their close association with their communities—they want to "hear it the way it is." If college is not relevant, they will seek relevance elsewhere or in their own activities.

What *is* relevant in college? Probably few of the experiences commonly organized and administered ostensibly for students would qualify. For example, guidance is acknowledged as a major function of the community junior college, primarily because students display a "lack of realism" in their choice of occupation and in their selection of a curriculum "appropriate to their abilities." (Blocker *et al.*, 1965, p. 117.) One point of view is that "it is unethical to admit students without regard for their chances of succeeding." (Wrenn, 1951, p. 420.) Guidance counselors, whose role is implicitly assumed to help students must "redirect" students and otherwise lead them to accept "more realistic" goals.

However, while institutions often point with pride to counselors' successes, many students react with the accusation that premature, forced choices are unfair. They should not be penalized, they say, for their "lack of realism." Instead, the college should be receptive to their vagaries and tolerant of their changing goals, of their desires to try out different curricula. And although the counseling staff may display "tolerance," this virtue is less frequently found in the faculty which often insists on the screening of students so that their courses can maintain good "content coverage." For whom is guidance relevant?—for the student who wants time and a place to explore avenues of potential interest, or for the institution which uses guidance to protect the university, society, and its own faculty from the "incompetent"?

The pragmatic junior college student has never accepted extra-curricular activities; his "lack of school spirit" is often lamented. Administrators often excuse the student by saying that his outside employment or home life leaves him no time for fun and games. For the student, however, reality is more influential than precedent—quite the opposite of his elders who are comfortable within their traditions. Perhaps he views extracurricular activities as an attempt to buy him off with false coin, to divert his energies from involvement in social issues, or to prolong his adolescence. Perhaps the student does not often seek outlets for his energies within the forms encountered at the junior college because few opportunities for realistic involvement with his community are available within the traditional program. Pragmatism is a many-faceted trait.

Research studies have verified that more junior college students come from lower socioeconomic groups than equivalent percentages of four-year college students do. Consequently, they are less inclined to wait for educational "pay-off." For many of them, the job must be clearly available at the end of the program or curricular sequence. Conversely, because of his socioeconomic background, the liberal arts college student is usually in a better position to postpone employment until he has spent more time in school. Except for a tiny minority, a Bachelor's degree or graduate education does not loom as a significant possibility for junior college students—hence, their "pragmatism."

But broad categorizations do little for educators who must fend off community accusations of "coddling" malcontents while they try to plan programs and curricular sequences for all. Many students attend the junior college for reasons that are neither "pragmatic" nor "unrealistic." Some of the relatively affluent but academically inept (Jencks and Riesman, 1968) attend because "it is what one does when one completes high school." (M. Martin, 1968.) September arrives and, as they have for the past twelve years, they present themselves for enrollment in a public school. They are unsure of themselves in a changing society. Barred from all but low-status employment unless they receive further "education" and inclined to experiment in personal and/or social involvement—still, they are "in school." How to serve this group—a twentieth-century American fellaheen that represents an ever-increasing proportion of the junior college student population?

If such a student reacts negatively to college it may be because he *is* realistic. He may have been led to believe he *could* explore, choose, take time to "be" while in attendance. Instead he is faced with an "impersonal, and to him, implacable set of curriculum demands for verbal abstraction and memorization of technical terminology to which no real personal meaning can be attached for the simple reason that the demands are irrelevant to his past, present, and anticipated future." (Pace, 1967.) He may have been told to set his own goals but then forced to choose a specific program of study. What of the student whose goal is *not* to choose a vocation, a transfer institution, or even a curriculum? Is he being "unrealistic"? Is he less "pragmatic"?

The junior college publicizes free choice and a curriculum to "meet the needs" of all. However, that ideal is far from being realized—less for the reason that students cannot be sorted, screened, and redirected into programs "consonant with their abilities," than because they *are* so sorted, screened, and redirected. Only rarely is a student allowed to choose not to choose. And when he *is* "placed" (how our words betray our attitudes!) in a program "at his level," he is faced with probation, suspension, or failure if he is not quick enough to select and read clues from his environment—clues which allow him to "succeed" in the competition with his fellows. True, he may select his own path, but only within the constraints of narrow curricular and instructional sequences. For despite the plethora of courses and programs, variety in instruction is more apparent than real.

Many of the junior college's institutional problems arise from the attempt to differentiate among people who exhibit an infinite variety of characteristics. "Low-ability students?" "Poorly motivated enrollees?" What do the terms mean? The junior college enrolls all applicants and, in its redirection activities, pretends it can make accurate discriminations; it acts as though the terms — constructs at best — have a fixed meaning. Which test used in the junior college's counseling picks out "motivation"? What is the validity of "ability" tests which are by all accounts of dubious value in predicting the "success" of "low-ability" students. (Schenz, 1964.) Test-makers acknowledge that vocational choices can be predicted most accurately simply by asking the students about their preferences. (Holland and Lutz, 1967.) Perhaps junior colleges have gone too far in their efforts to find inventories that assess the needs and abilities of students. In spite of the fact that the criteria for "success" are notoriously nebulous in most courses, the zealous sorting of students continues, resting heavily on the use of grade marks and guidance-testing.

In its support of community junior colleges, society has determined that public education is not a privilege but a right. No one in the community can be denied this right. Barring students from college because of their "low ability" or "lack of interest" is becoming as unacceptable as barring them because of their poverty. To say that a student cannot profit from the college experience in some manner is passé. But practices belie the philosophy. Failing students in courses and putting them on suspension *on the basis of undefined criteria* is accepted practice in the junior college — and in other fields of American education — even though it is socially undesirable, pedagogically unnecessary, and philosophically immoral. To the pragmatic student, college means money to be gained in higher-status employment. In any other field of human endeavor, an institution that excludes an individual without spelling out the criteria on which this rejection is based ("You're just not college material") might be sued! How "unrealistic" is the student when he rejects the college on these bases?

Chapter Nine

Curricular Myths

The ghost of a silly seventeenth-century squabble still haunts our classrooms, infecting teachers and pupils with the lunatic idea that studies must be either "classical" or "modern."
— R. G. COLLINGWOOD (1939, p. 6.)

We are the inheritors of an educational ideal intended for the training of elites. The notion of a well-rounded education assumes that the study of humane letters prepares those who are to rule or administer (somehow) for their intended tasks. This ideological relic — it has no relation to any reality I know — allows us the comfortable pretense that the functionaries we train receive an education which makes them whole, humane and enlightened. — LOUIS KAMPF (1968, p. 55.)

"Curriculum" can be defined as a total set of experiences designed for students—experiences which are supposed to take their minds from one place to another. The word "curriculum" comes from the Latin word "currere" that means "to run." Its closest associated words are "course" and "courier." However, "curriculum" is most often used to mean the whole body of courses offered in an educational institution or by a department thereof. The experiences planned for students outside the course framework are "extra-" or "co-curricular." Curricular research, then, "studies the relation between subject matter taught a student and his behaviors subsequent to having been taught it and which are considered relevant to it." (Henderson, 1963, p. 1008.)

Depending partly on the meaning, curriculum can be viewed in many ways. One problem with the definition of "curriculum" as a sequence of courses alone arises when one attempts to plot the behavior exhibited by a student before and after he attends college. Which portions of his experience stem from, or were affected by, the formally organized courses? Which by formally organized extra-curriculars? And which by informal experiences and contacts not under the direction of the institution? Another problem with this definition arises from the overlap between designed experiences and serendipitous experiences. For example, a student goes on a field trip that is a part of a particular course. On his way to the site, he sees something that has a profound effect upon his thinking—either in this course or in another one. Has the formal course affected his view?

Most junior colleges separate their course offerings into categories labeled "transfer curriculum" and "terminal curriculum"; the latter category is often subdivided into "remedial curriculum" and "vocational-technical curriculum." Community-service courses or courses for part-time "non-credit" students are sometimes also viewed as separate elements in the curriculum. Frequently an evening division has a curriculum of its own—one which combines elements of all the others. Each curriculum is usually assigned specific types of courses and areas of subject matter.

INFLUENCES ON CURRICULUM

What happens to the students as a result of attending an educational institution? Clear answers must be obtained if curriculum is to be realistically designed, assessed, and revised. The distinctions among curricula (transfer, terminal, vocational) cannot be defended validly except in relationship to this question. But curricular goals are nebulous; and concrete change in students is seldom considered or measured.

The current structure and amorphous goals of the junior college curriculum are part of its heritage from the public school system. For more than a century, the schools have been gaining a monopoly on instruction that is designed to produce the status and garb typically associated with the middle and upper classes. Simultaneously, the family and the church as media of learning have dropped in status and significance. The public schools' monopoly has protected them in their failure to plot deliberate goals. Goal-structuring, perceived as an undesirable constraint by many academicians, is often thought unsuitable to the traditional concept of the flexible curriculum. The researcher who notes that "many transfer students conclude their college training in junior college, whereas some terminal students continue" (Matteson, 1966), is saying something that college leaders have today long known. Yet the *functional* distinctions persist.

Curriculum today is constructed and revised in a context that can be explained from the viewpoint of any of the social sciences. From a philosophical point of view, the curriculum should be designed to fulfill the democratic ideal of public education for all to the limits of their ability to learn. The sociologist would say that changes in the population of college students have broadened the base of skills and attitudes they bring to the institution and that academic heterogeneity requires varied curricula. Psychology supplies various hypotheses about instruction and learning, together with constructs of motivation, frustration, anxiety, and analogous factors presumed to affect human behavior. The political scientist views curriculum construction as it relates to support from, and interactions with, various groups within the community from which the college draws its finances and from the larger polity which passes legislation. These are broad ways of viewing the factors that determine a given college's curriculum.

A more detailed look reveals different degrees of influence acting on the curriculum from myriad directions. The institutions to which junior college students transfer exercise much pressure—some direct, many more indirect—on the "college parallel" programs. Direct influences come through the emulation of the university's organization and course offerings and through the four-year institution's giving or withholding credit for certain courses. Indirect influence in many forms is typified by the practice of training junior college faculty in the universities; as products of the system, they tend to offer in the junior college courses similar to those which they experienced at the university. "Technical" programs are influenced particularly by the need to prepare students for certain jobs and by career advisory committees. Textbook publishers serve also as agents of curriculum change, directly through sales-promotion and indirectly by making only certain types of instructional materials available.

Other influences on curriculum include accrediting agencies, boards of trustees, state laws that directly demand certain offerings, and the availability of extramural funding. On the latter point, it is difficult to conceive of a program which a junior college would not offer if an outside agency made financial support available. And, not least, most community colleges will offer any course for which students can be found on the grounds that is an "educational service." (O'Connell, 1968, p. 51.)

Within the institution, curriculum committees, composed of faculty members and administrators, wrestle with the nuts and bolts of curriculum construction. (One sometimes wonders why students are not more frequently found sitting on curriculum committees.) The constraints within which committees operate include most notably the backgrounds and orientations of the members. It is difficult for many academic subject matter specialists to view curricular effects except from a one-dimensional perspective. Divisional and departmental loyalties—the slicing of knowledge into component parts—are often served despite the fact that departments have long been obsolete in the undergraduate setting. Departmentalization in the junior college (another legacy of the university) is a pervasive force which hinders the introduction of interdisciplinary or subdisciplinary courses and programs. It has been described as a form of institutional inefficiency which leads to an unnecessarily large number of courses in four-year institutions (Anderson, 1960, p. 258); there is certainly no reason to think it is less of a liability in the junior college.

MYTHS ABOUT CURRICULUM

Even if junior colleges were to be recognized along divisional rather than departmental lines and if all influences on curriculum were to be examined rationally, several limitations in vision would still narrow the range of choice in changing curricular structure. These limitations may be called myths, each of which is widely accepted (and insulated) as "fact."

The first myth is the conception that only courses for which transfer students are allowed university credit are "college level." This attitude disregards the history of American higher education which indicates that subject matter and patterns of thought and behavior taught in college are subject to constant change and redefinition. What is "college level" at one stage in history disappears from view at another. The fate of the classical languages—Latin and Greek—is a prime example of this phenomenon. A century and one-half ago the student who did not study the classics in the original language while he was enrolled in college could not receive a degree; he was not an "educated" man. Conversely, when engineering was introduced to universities in the mid-nineteenth century, it was a "trade." Architecture, first taught in the university of the 1860's, journalism at the turn of the century, and business management a little later were similarly viewed. Even among the "academic" fields, reshuffling occurs constantly. The Seven Liberal Arts have been supplemented by a variety of disciplines—any one of which might not be considered by the purist as being "college level." Sociology, psychology, and linguistics are examples; many others could be mentioned. Courses in these "subject areas" are certainly "college level" now, and they enjoy respectability and acceptance.

Each new form of educational institution has in its own turn reshaped the meaning of "college level." The universities, beginning in the nineteenth century, brought medicine, law, and modern languages to a level of academic respectability. The land-grant colleges furthered the trend with their broadening of "college level" work to include vocations (agriculture, business, journalism) which are even now somewhat less than "professions." In its turn, the junior college will revise the meaning of "college level," but not until it takes its own lead in defining the areas worthy of its attention.

A second myth holds that some absolute standard of "college level" course content exists, which can be determined by the nature of the subject taught. This way of thinking ignores the fact that subject specialties themselves have no absolute standards. Rather, there is a spiral effect in thinking about a problem through the filter of any academic discipline. One can apply the thought processes of a sociologist or political scientist to a phenomenon without having been thoroughly trained in that discipline. One "college level" sociology course may require that students recall data which would be used as input by a researcher, while for a supposedly similar course, students are asked to concentrate on using sociological concepts to organize data which they need not commit to memory.

In many elementary schools, children are now being taught to apply scientific methodology to problems. In a sense, their experiences may more logically be considered "college level" than a university course in which students memorize formulae and tables of information in the sciences. At what point does a course in a science become "less than college level"? It might be argued that no absolutes exist because there are no curricula which can be *prima facie* considered inferior to others. If the many attempts to classify educational objectives according to hierarchies of complexity were applied to courses in particular subject areas, some university courses which demand only recall of data would have to be considered less "college level" than the elementary school class that requires pupils to make inferences and test hypotheses.

The widely held belief that education for immediate employment is less "collegiate" than education for work which will not be performed until further training has taken place is myth number three. In a broad sense, practically all graduate training is directly employment-related. Most doctoral programs prepare people for professions. A two-year junior college "occupational" program differs in the length of time the students have already spent in school, but not in its relation to a world of gainful employment. The persistence of the illogical disdain for post-secondary occupational training can be ascribed mainly to tradition and to the artificial distinctions made by the academic pecking-order.

A fourth myth is that everything must be formally taught to be learned. (Commager, 1960, p. 14.) The role of the teacher is typically studied apart from the learning responses of students. One can postulate the extreme example of an institution organized exclusively around "teaching." In this college, rooms would be occupied by "teachers" lecturing to empty chairs. The fact that in school some people are *attempting* to teach other people is, although not entirely irrelevant, surely overemphasized in its contribution to the learning process. The best that any instructor or instructional program can hope to provide is "stimuli" or "inputs" to learning. Teaching is the process of helping to bring about change in students along predictable dimensions. But learning in the modern society occurs in many places under many circumstances; deliberate teaching is more often than not unrelated to the learning that actually occurs in the lives of most people.

A corollary to the idea that everything must be taught is a fifth important misconception: Because all knowledge is the province of the scholar, a college, it is thought, should take all knowledge as its province. Even if the junior college were the home of a community of scholars (which it is not) and even if those scholars were in possession of the total store, or even a significant portion, of all knowledge (which they are not), other agencies in the community could still well perform many necessary teaching functions. To say that all knowledge should be considered in the college is to deny the role of other agencies that may be better equipped for particular types of educational endeavors. It must be re-emphasized, moreover, that it is ways of thinking—not facts—that should be central to the planning of course content.

The current misguided emphasis is no more apparent than in a demand that all courses in American history, for example, "cover" the same points. Everyone "studies" the Civil War, the Progressive Era, the Great Depression, and so on. Arguments in departmental and administrative curriculum committees often range around whether to use a text which emphasizes this or that approach to the Return to Normalcy; whether or not to spend an extra week on Populism or Progressivism at the expense of the Reconstruction Period and Grant's administration, etc. A curricular innovation, debated for months and hailed as being indicative of "individualized course content" and "meeting the diverse needs" of various students, often turns out to be some emphasis on Black Studies which tosses a few Negro heroes into the pool of those "treated" in the course.

In the design of curriculum, the level of conceptual complexity required of the students should supersede the data presented. Memorizeable content is the most quickly forgotten portion of the curriculum. If a student who takes *American History 7A* from Mr. Jones succeeds when he can recall pertinent facts, while Mr. Smith's students must learn instead to assess the significance of such information, what matter that both teachers "cover the same topics"? There is greater difference between these two courses than if one dwelled upon the administration of Rutherford B. Hayes and the other presented Franklin Roosevelt's foreign policy.

How should the courses be taught? What method should be employed? A sixth myth holds that the method of instruction is all-important. Lectures, audio-tutorials, large-group and small-group discussions, live versus replicable media — all are defended as though the existence of the institution and its image in the eyes of accrediting agencies and universities depended on the selection of media. But a lecture is often the same whether it is given to five students at a time or to five hundred. Is it received differently by any one student if he hears it along with four instead of with 499 others?

Teaching methods must be considered in terms of their effects on individual students. To what is the *student* attending? Students probably pick up relevant cues from examinations and other assessment devices more than from subtleties of instructional methods. He who would significantly influence curriculum must attend to the tests, which, by stressing rote learning, may obliterate an instructor's attempts to teach concepts instead of facts.

A standardized format of instruction must of necessity mean that instruction methods will be inappropriate to the content of at least some courses. Junior college instruction in psychology, for example, rarely deals with live people; sociology courses often study community social problems only in the abstract; courses in English usage often afford little practice in writing. Students are rarely encouraged to study society in field situations; it is hard to find an instance in which students are given "credit" in political science for campaigning for political candidates, for example. Workbooks, in which students underline or circle correct forms, and "grammar" courses, in which they are supposed to learn how to write by studying the structure of language, are the norm, not the exception. No instruction method can be valid unless it suits both the kind of information being taught and the students who are supposed to do the learning.

One more myth holds that where value-free instruction exists, students will somehow learn on their own to apply critical thinking to social, political, and personal issues. There is prevalent in the community college a belief in a dichotomy between fact and value, yet the selection of topics to be "covered," is shot through with value judgments. Could a school *offer* a course in American literature without deciding which authors merit attention and which can be ignored? And by what standard is American literature taught in preference to English literature?

Values abound in every image the community college presents to its students. The very words employed in the institution carry meaning. Might a student not think himself a burden to his instructor when he is counted as part of the teacher's "load"? The "tracking" system which groups students into "remedial" sections where they have a better chance to "succeed" suggests pre-judgment. "Value-free" instruction is itself a myth. The grade-marking system that says, "We are here to *sort* you rather than to *teach* you" may do more to effect cynicism than any course in "Great Philosophers" can overturn. Can an institution which tends not to examine its own processes critically hope to encourage students to apply critical thinking to the problems of the larger community?

Probably the most pervasive myth surrounding the curriculum is that the junior college is an open system that channels the needs of the community into curricular design. It is true that changes may occur in response to changed student populations and community pressures, but these changes tend to be made only within the constraint of what is essentially a *closed* system of marks, methods, prerequisites, transfer requirements, and the campus itself. Tradition and departmentalization exert as much influence within the community college as they do in the most traditionalist liberal arts college.

The closed system accepts information only from within itself. A leading example of this is found in the fact that the differential in grades earned at the community college and those earned at the university to which students transfer is universally accepted as evidence of the extent to which the college has "taught." One of the most convincing arguments for curricular change is "We can get money for doing it!" Running a close second to this justification is "They are doing it that way in several other colleges." Neither argument suggests an institution operating as a system open to its home community. (Keuscher, 1968.)

But the cruelest myth of all is the one which perpetuates the fiction that junior colleges offer a liberal general education to their students. General education — the learning of those values and behaviors through which a student may conduct a personally satisfying life and fulfill his responsibilities as a citizen — has a long history in the American college. Dating back to the colonial colleges in which all students studied together (the idea of "major" or specialized field was largely unknown) the concept was revitalized early in this century as a reaction against the course proliferation that had become a serious problem in the many universities in which a free-elective system was in vogue. There, students might enroll together as freshmen and, never having taken courses in common, graduate four years later with what was ostensibly the same degree. By 1920, many universities began to institute integrative patterns of general education — programs which all students were to follow. Columbia University and later the Universities of Minnesota and Chicago were leaders in the movement to teach the interrelationships among fields of knowledge.

The period shortly after the Second World War was the high-water mark of general education in the American university. It was at that time that the Harvard book *General Education in a Free Society* (1945) stated a rationale for university programs, and that Johnson's *General Education in Action* (1952) catalogued the junior college efforts to provide integrated learning experiences for their students. By the late 1950's, however, the concept had once again moved out of favor, largely because of a newly perceived need for early specialization; there was a public demand for professionally trained experts to advance technology.

For the most part, community colleges have followed university trends in this respect; integrated courses arise, become specialized as they are brought in line with the university's offerings, and then split into separate departments, eventually to be replaced by other interdisciplinary courses. Educators have called for general education in the junior college because it would provide an excellent scheme for rounding out elementary and secondary school programs and would complement the more specialized technical programs. (Hutchins [1966] has called the junior college "the last hope" for "basic liberal education.") But junior college curriculum planners cling to a belief that universities will not accept students who transfer with "unorthodox" courses on their records. This concern is largely unwarranted, however, because in most instances when junior colleges have taken the lead in attempting general education and in diligently arguing the idea with transfer institutions, the difficulty has been overcome (Johnson, 1952, pp. 386–395) — as, for example, in Florida. (Reynolds, 1966, p. 115.) Unhappily, too few junior colleges have taken such leadership in breaking down the university's dictates through direct assault.

A program must be valid for its own purposes and not designed to fit upper-level specialties. A general education curriculum which demonstrably leads students to read and interpret scientific information in the popular press, for example, has more validity in the community college than a sequence of science courses which meet the specific needs of pre-medical students. This is not to imply that general education biological science has no value for premedical students but to simply suggest that the tiny number of community college students who *do* become medical students are currently the tail which wags the dog of many science curricula. Similarly, communications courses should not be justified by the extent to which they train students for university-type report-writing; they should serve the communications needs of the majority of students. In brief, a general education program should be so constructed that students will have received a defensible education if they never take another formal course. (Mayhew, 1960.) And for many young people, the junior college is indeed their last exposure to school.

The current distribution requirements, prerequisites for transfer, and university-type specialized offerings simply do not lead to an integrated, interdisciplinary general education of a type that suits the broad purposes of the American community college. A student who "has to take any one science course, any one humanities course, and any one social science course, with little regard for logic, coherence, intellectual relevance, or any other criterion except the three different labels" (D. Bell, 1968, pp. 401–406) has not received a general education.

"College level," "standards," "vocational," "content," "academic" —these are some of the many terms that are used unstintingly even though their meanings vary greatly. The most cursory examination can show how unrelated they are to the real purposes of the junior colleges, yet they are the stuff myths are made of and, as such, they exercise an insidious influence on curriculum. Is anyone learning anything as a result of his passing through the curriculum? What effect are the courses having on his life? These are the types of questions that must be asked of all programs. To the extent they divert attention from the pertinent issues of education, curricular myths weaken the college's impact.

Chapter Ten

Instructional Archaisms

Any theory of instruction must be "principally concerned with how to arrange environments to optimize learning according to various criteria." (Bruner, 1966, p. 37.) Stated another way, a theory of instruction must explain the ways in which what one wishes to teach can best be learned. It must specify an environment or set of experiences which implants a predisposition to learn, the way a body of knowledge can best be structured for presentation, the most effective mode of presentation, and the pacing of rewards and punishments—all to the end that optimal learning occurs. Unhappily, there are as yet no consistent theories of instruction. It is difficult to point to even a few "empirically validated principles of instruction that could form the primitives of a theory of teaching." (Oettinger, 1968.) Most of what passes for instructional theory is actually *learning* theory rooted in stimulus–response or cognitive grounds.

If there are no theories of instruction to which the critic may repair, on what bases may junior college teaching be examined? There are many ways of viewing the question. One approach is to consider the early universities and public schools which the junior college tends to emulate. Because instructional patterns are not founded on theory, they are curious combinations of the information-transmission modes developed in early colleges and the organizational characteristics of the lower schools.

The dominant forms of instruction in Western colleges and universities stem from the teaching performed by the church and by itinerant scholars of the Middle Ages. At that time, few books or other tangible teaching devices were in use. An "instructor" was often chosen because he owned the books or, in some cases, because he alone could read. The lecture—the reading of books to a group who had none—was a prime form of deliberate information-transmission. Although instructional processes in higher education appear to be different now, they are not far from those of the medieval and Colonial American college. Despite the widespread introduction of overly publicized "innovations," lecture and discussion still form the major thrust of teaching in the American college. Although books are available to everyone, the lecture is still widely employed as a verbal text.

Despite protestations to the contrary, the public schools are built on a cultural model which suggests that all *cannot* profit from instruction. The standard by which progress through its educational system is measured is set up by the system itself; the system's word is taken about the qualifications for entrance, curriculum, and graduation. The public-school system in America has been organized, staffed, and maintained by a dominant majority that insists on using it as a device to screen "capable" from "incompetent" youngsters. It assumes from the start that all will not succeed. The "capable" are those who can fit into the school without perceptible shock because their homes "set" them for the patterns of activity they find in the classroom. The incompetent are often those who have not been pre-fitted to the system. In short, instruction is most efficacious when it is least needed; it "succeeds" when it is almost superfluous. Rather than instruction, the schools offer primarily a form of custodial care, holding the young until natural maturity catches up with them. Teaching and learning are in a distinctly secondary position.

Instruction in the junior college is based neither on instructional theory nor on theories of learning, but on practices stemming from higher education's roots in the monasteries and from the public schools' attempt to cope with a sizable influx of students. Curiously, the junior college accepted the organizational forms of the lower schools along with the lecture-discussion mode of information transmission from higher education. The instructor's role as classroom despot, the compulsory-attendance requirements and roll-taking, the prescription of a single instructional mode which must be shared by all students, and its custodial function — these are the junior college's inheritance from the lower schools. The lecture and the discussion as prime instructional models, the design of courses that serve primarily as prerequisites for other courses, the consideration of laboratories as mere adjuncts to classrooms, the use of entrance tests as placement screens, and the status of the instructor as an independent practitioner with sole autonomy over his courses — all stem from higher education. The junior college cannot yet point to one instructional form which it alone evolved.

In the junior college, group instruction — from thirty to forty students — is the core medium of teaching. Other instructional media — language laboratories, remedial learning laboratories, and hardware used in a variety of ways — are viewed typically as supplements to group instruction. All are adjuncts to "teaching," which itself takes place in the classroom — the eminent domain of the instructor. Separate sections of what are purported to be the same courses are more often than not actually different courses; perhaps they utilize the same reading lists, but they almost always employ different objectives and test items. Departmental exams are often found but, in many instances, they are subverted in a variety of ways by faculty members who demand autonomy under the guise of academic freedom.

One more example of archaism relates to the element of time. College courses generally are structured according to the span of time it takes for the "one who knows" to articulate the subject matter for the benefit of his audiences. Although the spoken word is the slowest form of communication among the many currently available (reading, viewing images, etc.), it is still thought of as being the quintessence of "teaching." Time blocks are organized to fit the time needed to engage in discourse, and the clock-hour unit is used as though it had a relationship to the sum of a student's knowledge. Those who listen to the master "receive" as much information as he can dispense in the allotted time. If they spend less time in his presence, it is assumed they have learned less. College transcripts indicate hours; degrees are based on hours; the financial support of the institution, the time spent by the faculty members on campus, the work load of any staff member, and many other elements related to the instructional process — all are apportioned by the clock. All these procedures stem from the Medieval period when the amount of information available to a person correlated almost exactly with the time he was exposed to verbiage — books being extremely rare. The core of instruction is typically fashioned as though other forms of information-transmission had never been discovered.

Although the junior college is not alone in its reliance on archaic instructional forms, it does suffer several unique anomalies. The description of a junior college as an institution where greater attention is paid to individual students is still used — currently with questionable validity. The claim was first made by early private junior colleges of limited enrollment. Today, when public community colleges often enroll more than 10,000 students, it is justified by comparing junior college instructors' "student-contact" hours with the hours spent in the classroom by university professors; this argument has merit to the extent that one considers teaching assistants less than competent.

The junior college might well question the implicit assumption that the ideal educational situation is one in which every student has personal attention from his instructors. The real goal should be that each student be educated to the extent of his capacities. Personal attention is a *means* to that goal, but neither an end in itself nor the *only* available means. Some students may need personal attention from instructors, others may not. McKeachie, who has extensively examined instructional forms in higher education, suggests that "for some students at some times really personalized education may involve opportunities for independent study, for work in student-led groups or for other types of learning involving *less* rather than *more* individual contact with faculty members." (McKeachie, 1967, p. 22.) High-ability students may benefit from personal contact if the contact involves exploration; low-ability students may benefit from the clarification they can get from the instructor. It might be revealing to examine the likelihood that, in many cases, personal contact with an instructor may actually be detrimental to student learning.

Similarly, a correlation between small-group instruction and measurable results is rarely significant. Large classes may very well provide for individual differences by permitting some students to read rather than to attend lectures, allowing others to do laboratory work, and still others to gain direct experience in field settings. Yet the presence of students in small groups is often viewed as an instructional form having value of itself.

INNOVATION

Particular examples of the influence of instructional rigidity can be found in considering the fate of innovative instructional practices. In the past several years, junior colleges have introduced many instructional changes. A recent book catalogued literally hundreds of different instructional forms and practices in junior colleges all over the country (Johnson, 1969.) Innovation — usually defined as "anything different from the way we were doing it last year" — is strongly encouraged by leaders in the field as a way of "keeping current." This posture is increasingly seen as having value for its own sake. (Cohen, 1969.)

The many successes in this area should not be overlooked, but most innovations in instruction are incompatible with the philosophies and constructs on which junior colleges themselves are based. Although the new media may be internally consistent, the innovators often fail to make lasting over-all change in instructional forms.

Two examples of the ways in which new designs for instruction are warped to fit the existing system can be discerned by considering the fate of televised instruction and autoinstructional programming. These new devices, both introduced during the past fifteen years, have had their potential effects severely reduced by untoward shaping.

Programmed instruction is not a learning aid or an audiovisual device; it is a concept of pedagogy. It demands a determination in advance of where learning is to go, of how it is to occur, and of its specific content. By definition, a program is any replicable instructional sequence which takes a learner from one measured point to another measured point. It is individualized because it allows each learner to proceed at his own pace; it accepts accountability for learning because if the student fails to achieve mastery of the concept being taught, the program has not succeeded and must therefore be revised. Programming in general has been criticized because it seems to violate the structure of certain concepts by forcing them into straight-line, sequential frames. Even so, programs can teach.

The way in which programmed instruction has been introduced in junior colleges betrays the institutions' inflexible view of instructional forms. It is fashionable to say of programmed instruction, "It will take over the drill-teaching function and release the teacher for creative work with the students." (Coulson, 1966.) The expectation that instructors will be released for such activities results from two lines of thinking: first, that programmed instruction can teach only "recall of data," and second, that teachers will be more likely to accept it if it gives them more free time. (Instructors as a group have long excused their lack of creativity by saying they have too much busy-work to do.) (Garrison, 1967.) But both assumptions are in error. In principle, programming can go as far as a teacher in shaping students' responses to any degree of complexity, though the potential variety of learning paths would require a computer to plot. Although instructors may be more likely to accept programming if they think they will somehow be released from their busy-work tasks, it is a fallacy to think they will become, perforce, more "creative." Many instructors may be suited only for routine teaching tasks; extensive retraining or role-differentiation would probably be necessary to change their modes of behavior appropriately. The scholar is scholarly now; the humanist's wit sparkles through the routine chores. The creative instructor needs no machine to release him.

Curiously, then, programming has been accepted but for the wrong reasons. Most autoinstructional programs are at least as effective as the procedures they replace, even though, according to purists, the programs themselves are seldom very good. This innovation can easily be adopted because extensive capital outlay and staff retraining are not required.

Autoinstructional programs are usually restricted to "learning laboratories," however, where they remain as supplements to the classroom. In the few instances when programs have been accepted as total teaching devices, unanticipated problems have resulted. For example: What happens to the administrative provisions for supervising teachers and apportioning their work load? How are marking "standards" adjusted to the fact that the programs are constructed to ensure the success of a large specified percentage of students. And what of the teachers' own need to perform their traditional role? The introduction of the medium at Oakland Community College in Michigan, for example, resulted in instructors gathering groups of students around them so that they could actually "teach" — that is, do what they felt they were being paid for. (Canfield, 1967.)

In permitting students to work at their own rates autoinstructional devices expose the hollowness of many clichés about individual instruction. Students are often forced to continue working at similar rates — for instance, when arbitrary amounts of study time are required — and slow students are given programs to take home so that they can "catch up." Evaluation practices based on subjective observations by the teacher in the classroom cannot easily be employed. Programs are incompatible not only with grade-ranking but with all norm-referenced testing. These kinds of problems have led several investigators to the conclusion that "schools as they are now structured are either unable or unwilling to accept something near total individualized instruction." (Carlson, 1966, p. 28.)

In part, programming's failure to change instructional practices is a result of the teacher's conception of "teaching," a word that can be defined in many ways. "Teaching" has been characterized as "the process of structuring the environment of an individual and organizing his activities so as to produce desired behavior." (W. Trow, 1949.) Another writer calls it "creating a situation in which maximum learning can and will take place." (Gustad, 1964.) But these are the definitions proposed by researchers and professional educators. Most *instructors* seem to define "teaching" as capturing the attention of a number of students and serving continuously as the mediator between them and the information they are to gain. Because programmed instruction does not give the teacher an opportunity to mediate, instructors often attempt to modify it toward the characteristics of regular classroom instruction. Accordingly, programming is almost exclusively used as an instructional adjunct; its logic will not have its way until a new definition of "teaching" can be conveyed to teachers. In Simon's words, "It is a measure of our naiveté that we assume implicitly, in almost all our practices, . . . that something called a 'class' is the best environment for teaching." (Simon, 1967, p. 73.)

The use of television is another example of an instructional innovation that is blithely expected to solve many problems in the schools. The radio in the twenties, the film in the thirties, TV in the fifties, and computers in the sixties — each in its turn was supposed to "revolutionize education." The educational system adopts all and yet remains basically unchanged.

Many junior colleges offer courses either in whole or in part through the medium of television; Chicago City College has pioneered this innovation in offering an entire TV curriculum. The use of television has in a few instances led to true innovation — for example the television monitoring of student nurses in training programs. But most other uses of television are less dramatic; they merely repackage the instructor and his lectures and present them on a small screen at a time and a place removed from his own person.

There is no question that television can "teach" as well (or as poorly) as a live instructor. (Schueler and Lesser, 1967.) Most research indicates that whether students attend regular classroom situations or view television presentations makes no difference in the extent to which they learn the course material. (Becker and Dallinger, 1960.) Comparisons of "regular teaching procedures" with other instructional forms which merely move the regular procedures from the traditional situation to an "innovative" situation ask little more than the question of whether students and faculty prefer familiar forms or new forms. The fact that both the instructors and the students often prefer live instruction says less about the mode of information presentation than it does about their affinity for the familiar.

It is likely that eventually television will be accepted as readily as the live instructor in the classroom situation. But as long as television is used as an, adjunct to ill-defined courses or as a medium for presenting the traditional lecture, its real potential cannot be realized. (Gross and Murphy, 1966.) The question should be not whether students and teachers have a preference for new or old forms, but how all media can be best employed in an educational system dedicated to bringing specified percentages of students to the ability to think, feel, or act in particular ways.

At least tentatively, it seems fair to conclude that intellectual skills related to reflective thought can be taught in traditional *or* innovative situations and that they can be learned. Such abilities can be measured, and significantly better results can be obtained when the development of them becomes the *focus* of instruction rather than a hoped for by-product. (Haefner, 1964.) What seems to be required, however, is a pedagogy that has not even begun to develop. The instructional forms currently in use, coming as they do from the elitist, the mysterious university, and the highly structured public schools, cannot do it. (Kauffman *et al.*, 1968.)

Probably the greatest single contributor to the incongruities noted in this chapter is the fact that "teaching" is too often implicitly defined as something other than "causing learning." This unfortunate attitude has thus far kept the twentieth-century teaching institution from going into the learning business.

The most significant improvements in education must be intellectual, not technological. Theories of instruction will have to be based on the extent to which variant instructional forms cause learning of different concepts among different types of students. To date, there is little study of these issues in the educational literature and even less among the junior colleges themselves. The junior college must not only study instruction, it must *lead* in the development of instructional theory. It cannot do so as long as instructional archaism is dominant.

The single most debilitating misconception about junior college instruction is probably the one which holds that teaching is better at junior colleges than at universities because junior college instructors are not involved in research. This belief is a fallacy in logic analogous to "That animal is a man because it is not a horse," and it begs the crucial question. If the junior college is a "teaching institution," it should be concerned with instructional forms — not with loud advertisement that its instructors are not researchers. As long as such a defensive viewpoint dominates, the rigorous examination of instruction itself and, more importantly of the *effects* of instruction, will remain limited.

The dual influences of universities on the media and of public schools on the organization of instruction still pervade the junior college. Concerned administrators and instructors attempt to create forms better suited to the college's purpose, but the system mitigates their efforts. Eventually, if directed change is to occur, the junior college must stop climbing on every innovative bandwagon that comes along and begin to study instruction itself. Or is this not what a "teaching institution" should be doing?

Chapter Eleven

Status and the Teacher

What attracts a young person to become an instructor in higher education? The particular field of work which one selects dictates, or at least greatly influences, his choice of friends, his recreational activities, the mannerisms he displays, his place of residence, and many other important variables in his life. Many other career choices are open to the competent adult who has attained a Master's degree or some equivalent evidence of qualification that is recognized and rewarded in our culture. What are the elements within a person and within the teaching situation that lead him to don the robes?

THE ROLE

Many studies have attempted to answer this question. (Brawer, 1968.) Demographic variables have been considered along with personality factors in the efforts to find common patterns among people who have chosen to become members of the teaching profession. Most research of this type has demonstrated only that a few traits are held in common by all groups studied. The measuring devices employed in such studies indicate that teachers and teachers in training are about average in intelligence. There are no overriding background characteristics that can be used to predict which people will enter the profession, and the groups studied usually are a cross section of the population entering college. It is very likely that the prospective teacher makes his career choice after observing his instructors and deciding, "I want to be one of them." He chooses to become a teacher because he wishes to play a role similar to that performed by a teacher or teachers, he has known. But the most any study is able to say for certain is that a new faculty member is a person who has accepted a job offer from a college; exactly how and why he reached his decision is rarely revealed. (Allen and Sutherland, 1963.)

The student who plans to be a teacher usually has a limited view of the profession. He has seen faculty members performing as on a stage, seemingly general practitioners in the field of education. The student does not realize that the classroom interaction is only a part of the teacher's job, and that other functions must be managed as well — constructing examination items, serving on committees, selecting media to employ, and so forth. Only rarely are these tasks considered by the prospective instructor.

The issue of role expectation is important because the attitudes, motivation, and life style of a professor are largely shaped, if not before he enters the profession, very early during the formative years in his first teaching position. College administrators seldom claim that they have reduced to exact job descriptions just what they expect of new faculty members, so that the teacher's own role expectations are rarely challenged. The teacher has planned to interact with students (his definition of "teaching") and this remains the focus of his activities on the job.

This selection of a role based on a single uninformed interpretation of the instructor's tasks has led the faculty members of most colleges to become specialists in what is really only a small segment of the field. They are "classroom teachers." Other concerns, no matter how they may be emphasized in education courses, are viewed as peripheral, if only because the elements that encouraged the person's decision to enter the profession did not include them. Candidates for teaching positions still want to view themselves as members of a profession in which they are independent practitioners who specialize in interaction with students in groups. It is difficult to find people who have chosen to teach because they have a bent for the other tasks associated with instruction.

STUDENTS, PAY, AND STANDARDS

One of the factors that apparently attracts prospective instructors is the teacher's strong status position — an intangible but important matter. Whence is the junior college instructor's status derived? — not through indentification with a disciplinary field. Within his institution, he is usually labeled an "instructional staff member" — not "historian," "psychologist," or "physicist." And, despite various efforts by instructors to obtain status through their association with an academic field, many factors militate against such identification — the most important being the fact that three of ten new junior college instructors come from secondary schools, in which they are viewed primarily as teachers, not as members of an academic discipline. (National Science Foundation, 1967, p. 7.)

The scholar-researcher is not sought by the junior college and is rarely found therein. The institution sets its face sternly against the practice of extensive academic research and paid consultation with industry and public agencies — two activities central to scholarly life at the major universities. (B. Clark, 1963, p. 46.) Junior college teachers are told they will be judged on the basis of their teaching. Coupled with the initial role-choice of the new teacher, the organizational climate exerts a force for "teaching" too powerful, in most instances, for a single individual to overcome, no matter how much he wishes to be considered primarily as a member of an academic field.

Another status conflict revolves around the issue of appropriate salaries. As a way of recognizing differences among instructors, merit pay has long been sought but seldom offered on a broad scale, primarily because there seems to be no satisfactory way of determining merit. Here a teacher is recognized as a well-organized lecturer; there, as a masterful classroom manager or discussion leader. Another instructor is a favorite with students outside the class room. Here is one whose students consistently measure better on standardized tests; there, one whose classes are filled with admiring students. And there is also the occasional faculty member who is valued for his ability to represent the campus to the community. Which instructor should get the merit increase? Who has contributed most to the institution? What scale of "merit" can assign extra pay to the satisfaction of all?

The difficulty of assigning differential rewards is not the only factor that makes for rigid salary schedules. The roots of most junior college systems lie in the public schools from which they emerged, and the "unified district" — one in which junior colleges and public schools are under the same jurisdiction — is still found in many states. Equitable or not, the public school's mode of pay is still employed in most junior colleges: salary schedules are based on the academic course credits earned and on seniority. (Mood, 1967.) Here, too, the single-role view held by instructors makes it difficult to effect change.

The preference for classroom interaction is both reflected in and encouraged by current methods of evaluating instructors. In spite of the unanimity with which information-dissemination through personal contact is regarded as the teacher's central function, there is confusion about criteria for determining competence; "teaching" itself is nebulously defined. Most teacher-assessment plans are in reality *people*-assessment devices. Scholastic achievement is only one of many things a "successful" teacher must accomplish. He must also be socially competent and must conform to certain standards of ethics, manners, morals, patriotism, and "good citizenship." But it is impossible to relate such qualities to that ill-defined thing, "good teaching." Teachers may say they would rather be judged by their teaching, but they make no effort to define the concept. They alone are not to blame. Many of the problems of assessing instruction stem from the fact that just what the junior college as an *institution* is supposed to do has never been defined in terms that hold common meaning. Consequently, criteria for effective service within the institution are almost impossible to stabilize. (Cohen and Brawer, 1969.)

It has been claimed that good teaching is not rewarded because of communication gulfs between faculty and administrators and because disciplinary groups exercise greater influence than institutional loyalties. (Gustad, 1961.) But the most difficult barrier to overcome is the impossibility of agreement on the criteria and technical practices of evaluation. The responsibility for evaluating teachers lies basically with college administrators, but in practice "little is done to obtain anything that even approaches sound data on the basis of which reasonably good evaluations of classroom teaching can be made." (Gustad, 1961, p. 12.) Categorically, teacher-evaluation in the junior college is an exercise in futility. In its current form, it certainly cannot validly be used to support differential pay scales.

PROFESSIONALISM

No longer the docile schoolmaster, today's instructor is being heard in academic senates, in active union organizations, and in other ways that indicate his demands for more status and a greater voice in his own destiny. Instructors now commonly view unionism as a combined reaction against low pay and administrative interference. Their militancy may also be considered an effort to break out of the public-school image to emphasize links with the university's academia. But although higher pay may result eventually from union or faculty senate efforts, true professionalism lies at the end of another road than that taken by most faculty organizations. As presently operated, instructors' guilds rarely seek to regulate teachers' functions or to develop rules about matters which fall under the rubric, "professional." Their stance is commonly viewed by administrators and board members as power-seeking unionism. For better or worse, "professional" faculty associations seem to strive primarily toward changes in salary and conditions of employment. The cases in which the real requisites for professional status are advanced as end goals stand out as exceptions.(Stinnett, 1966, p. 80.)

The associations' posture reflects the instructors' condition. Each faculty member would like to be identified as a member of a profession, but as a profession, junior college teaching falls far short of a meaningful standard. The *primary* role of a profession is to perform a service for society or a particular clientele. Its functions are highly formalized. It practices licensing, and is regulated by internally and externally developed rules concerning standards and practice and client-practitioner relations; it has standardized training requirements, and is guided or controlled by a highly organized, protective professional association. (Friedman, 1967.) However, the junior college teacher is not in this situation.

The junior college instructor who "advances" from the secondary school often feels he is permitted to shift his concern from teaching methods to subject matter. He may prepare his classroom presentations more deliberately and be pleased with the reduction of busy-work. Many of the motives that initially encouraged him to enter secondary (rather than elementary school) teaching — the desire to impart subject matter to students with a minimum of interruptions, extra duties, and discipline problems — are given full sway in the junior college. Now he identifies himself neither as a scholar-researcher nor as a methodologist but, because he is in "college," as a "subject-matterist." However, such a change in self-perception hardly gains professional status for an individual. Curiously, the elementary-school teacher may be more nearly a "professional" in the sense that he is engaged in the defined overall task of working with children in whatever areas of intellectual, physical, and emotional development that this entails. Unlike his colleague in the junior college, he is not split between dreams of scholarly affiliations on one hand and a nonprofessional situation on the other.

As a final point touching on the question of professional status, it is well to return to the beginnings of the educational forms upon which the community college modeled itself. As the university evolved, the lecturer became exalted as a scholar — as one who worked with knowledge of a complex and esoteric nature. He alone understood relationships among abstract ideas; he alone used a specialized vocabulary; he knew concepts and theories, and others did not. His role became one of revealing the working of his mind to people who, by their presence, indicated their interest in his thinking. However, he did *not* become a professional instructor. His scholarly pursuits and his lecturing did *not* lead him to specialize in instruction per se.

The instructor who has adopted the singular role of classroom lecturer or discussion leader has difficulty in viewing himself as manager of a total learning environment. Even more difficult to accept is the idea that his value to the community is dependent on the learning achieved by his clientele — a concept only now evolving, and slowly, because the field doggedly resists change — yet that is the stuff of which junior college professionalism must be made.

What are the factors, then, which go into instructors' resistance to change in the direction of professionalism? A genuine desire for genuine classroom interaction — the motive for which they entered the profession in the first place? Perhaps. But the crucial questions are really: What is the *role* of the professor if the subject is presented by a medium other than the professor himself? (Bright, 1967.) What will be his *status* if he becomes a "manager of learning," rather than a "dispenser of wisdom?" How will he spend his time and effort — if he is not needed to fill the role he sought when he entered the profession? Sociological and psychological researchers might well address themselves to such issues. Until they resolve a few of them, Saul Bellow's comment may well be applied to instructors and their reluctance to alter the non-professional patterns of their work:

> When a man's breast feels like a cage from which all the dark birds have flown — he is free, he is light. And he longs to have his vultures back again. He wants his customary struggles, his nameless, empty works, his anger, his afflictions and his sins.   — SAUL BELLOW, *Herzog*.

Chapter Twelve

Research:
Platitude and Tautology

As a way of gaining support for the community college during the early stages of its development, leaders in the movement felt the need to publicize their high hopes. The college was billed primarily as an agency that would take over lower-division university work and provide technical and general education to all who could benefit therefrom. Educators' efforts to convince their constituent communities of the values of organizing junior colleges were rewarded by a rapid institutional growth-rate — one which has not yet reached its peak.

Now that the junior college is fairly launched and has carved a niche in American higher education, calls are being made for research to demonstrate the effectiveness of its programs, to help in institutional planning, and generally to improve the quality of the education received by its enrollees. The Peterson Report (1965, p. 26), a study of California junior colleges, ranked research second only to "Improvement of instruction" as a critical need. The report noted particularly that research should be conducted by the institutions, not for the purpose of "advancing the frontiers" of knowledge but as a way of enhancing instruction.

To date, however, institutional research has not been one of the junior college's strong points — not a surprising fact because the college's roots in secondary school systems and its own insistence on being categorized as a "teaching institution" point away from research as a key function. Junior college faculty members often resist participation in research studies; in some instances they have fled from the university because this activity was required of them. In 1964, only one junior college in five had a formally organized research program (Swanson, 1965), and despite the fact that junior college presidents typically pay lip service to the need for research, they rarely base their decisions on research findings.

Research on broad trends in junior college education is often arranged and conducted by agencies outside the institutions. The American College Testing Bureau, the offices of state directors of community college systems, and university-based researchers frequently conduct such studies. The American Association of Junior Colleges has begun recently to support more deliberate research, by pursuing investigations on its own and by advocating the establishment of research offices in every institution. The Educational Resources Information Center (ERIC) Clearinghouse for Junior College Information, a project sponsored by the United States Office of Education, was established in 1966 with a particular emphasis on the support and encouragement of junior college institutional research. (Cohen, 1967.) Various Regional Education Laboratories and many university-based junior college leadership programs stimulate research on the junior colleges within their geographical areas. All these efforts have been helpful in allowing pictures to be drawn of junior college trends and modes of operation. But research on *instruction,* if it is to have the effect of changing practices within an institution, must be supported by, and conducted in association with, the faculty members of the institution. It is extremely difficult to encourage them to change their modes of procedure because of research findings unless the instructors have been actively engaged in the studies.

Educational research is surely needed, but doing it is not a simple process. For example, in instructional research alone, only a fraction of actual teaching content can be sampled; it is assumed — probably in error — that the same content has been taught to all students. The effects of differential stress on objectives is often not taken into account. There is no existing explanation for the fact that marked similarities in the pacing of instruction appear to be very common. Variations in teaching practices contribute to the differences in results in ways which are largely unknown. It is impossible to control the quality of teaching. And when objectives are clearly defined (as they must be if the assessment of effects is to be undertaken) the possible effects of variations in instructional treatment are minimized. Faced with problems associated with this and other forms of educational research, many researchers simply give up and devote their efforts primarily to gathering data of dubious value.

Junior college institutional research needs considerable upgrading if it is to affect institutional practices. Currently, indigenous efforts are often dissipated in demonstrating tautological hypotheses, in publishing studies which seem to be exercises in public relations, and in producing reports that merely reinforce platitudes. Seemingly contradictory results often stem from inconsistent or ill-defined methodology. Those who design and conduct the studies are frequently unaware of the complex nature of rigorous educational research and seem willing to settle for finding which prove upon examination to have little meaning. Most vitally, studies are too rarely pointed toward particular problems so that action may be taken on the basis of their findings.

Of what value, for example, is the study that discovers "Perseverance is a factor which contributes greatly to the average student's chances for success after transfer"? (Hall, 1967.) How different is this from the discovery that people who drink a glass of milk a day for ninety years are likely to live a long time? Another study noted that "successful programs were marked by . . . support by teachers." (Apsler, 1967.) Other investigations similarly pursue pure circularity of reasoning, often because they define "teaching" as lecturing, writing exams, interacting with students, and other activities in which a teacher commonly engages. Teaching then becomes "doing that which a teacher commonly does" — itself a tautological statement.

The junior college field typically accepts more jargon and platitudes than it should. What are the "needs" that must be "met"? What is "rapport" between teacher and student, and how is it measured? What does it mean when a report says, "Students must be brought to a better understanding of their aptitudes and limitations"? (Hakanson, 1967.) Much junior college research is defensive and seemingly pointed toward public relations. Studies that report findings such as, "Our students do as well in the university as those who entered there" (Roueche, 1967) seem only to say, "We are as good as they." By far the most common type of junior college study compares the grades earned by students when they attended the junior college with the grades of the same students after they transferred to a university. What can be done with this information? Make grading more stringent? Flunk out higher numbers of "less-than-college-level" students? The same amount of effort could better be put into studies that produce potentially useful results.

Contradictory findings are frequently a result of inconsistent methodology. Rarely are attempts made by junior college researchers to repeat studies — use the same instrument on a similarly selected population. Normally each data-collector defines his own sample group, employs homemade instruments, and applies his own interpretations to his findings. Hence, for every study which finds that "junior colleges serve the student who finds work immediately after graduation." (Matteson, 1966.) Another announces that findings on curriculum designed for "specific job preparation indicate a need for a more critical look at the program." (Moughamiam, 1967.)

An overriding problem in junior college research is the fact that the methodology employed in the studies falls almost exclusively into the category of data-collection from existing records. The investigator typically tabulates data obtained from college files or from questionnaires sent to undifferentiated numbers of students and presents his "findings." An examination of more than 1,000 research reports collected by the ERIC Clearinghouse for Junior College Information in 1966 and 1967 revealed few studies in which experimental designs were employed and few in which even rudimentary experimental controls were used. (Thomson, 1967.) Typically, population sampling is not undertaken, hypotheses are poorly drawn (if stated at all), and simple research designs are lacking.

How can institutional research be upgraded? Better training of researchers and higher budget allotments would help, but this would not be sufficient. Research in all areas of the junior college operation suffers not as much from the lack of money or trained people as from the lack of interest in using research to change practices in the institution. A recent survey of institutional research practices found that most college presidents have little knowledge of how research can be used to help them understand and solve problems within their organizations. (Roueche and Boggs, 1968.) Lawyers have a maxim, "An ounce of precedent is worth more than a pound of logic." In education, an ounce of tradition is more influential than several pounds of research data. Not until administrators and instructors realize its value will properly conducted research become a fact of junior college life.

Studies that repeat platitudes, demonstrate tautologies, and employ inconsistent methodologies have served a purpose — building a precedent for further, better research — even though the investigations themselves have failed to meet acceptable quality standards. On some campuses, there is now at least an awareness of the potential value of research and the rudiments of a research office. Too, strong research programs have been built in a few colleges, and where they have, institutional practices have been affected. A notable example is Los Angeles City College's studies of its low-ability students: Special programs were built, assessed, and modified on the basis of controlled experimentation. (Powell, 1966.) Several other community colleges have similarly organized or changed remedial programs as a result of careful research studies. (Roueche, 1968.)

Many districts have budgeted funds for research and, where research has been supported and the right questions asked in the right order, useful findings have been produced. Assuredly — because of the variety of interactions among college environments, concepts and objectives, instructors, methods, and students — proper educational research is difficult to undertake. However, it can be used to good effect in many areas currently untouched.

Part Three

The Conceptual Bridge

> ... Nothing is ever done until everyone is convinced that it ought to be done, and has been convinced for so long that it is now time to do something else.
>
> —F. M. CORNFORD (1923, p. 4.)

Several issues were examined in Part Two: the forces behind the tremendous growth rate of community colleges, the colleges' almost exclusive concern with means rather than with ends, the images projected by the institutions, the pragmatic students, the sources of instructional practices, the inertia of the faculties, and the weaknesses of institutional research. Many incongruities were shown to be based on the fact that the "teaching institution" of today is not in the business of causing learning. Rather, its goals seem to be self-perpetuation, the offering of ever more varied programs, steady growth in enrollments and operating budgets, and the construction of monumental buildings. The community college operates under the pretext of "meeting community needs" — a term few people within the institution attempt to define, except by pointing to the means by which the needs are presumed to be met. It is the twentieth-century effluvium of a stream of education that has flowed from liberal arts colleges and public school systems into the river of American society.

Part Two thus criticized several features of currently operating community junior colleges, whereas Part One posited a paradigmatic college as it could look if certain changes were undertaken. Part Three will present a defined rationale for the changes, comparing the college of 1969 with its counterpart ten years hence, and building conceptual bridges between the two. By citing authority and philosophy, theory and principle, the arguments for change in the indicated directions take on persuasive force.

The model college depicted in Part One is not as radically different from today's institutions as it might easily be. It is not a utopian scheme, nor does it pose as a panacea for all educational ills. It has merely arrived at the point where it can cope with the general-education needs of the kinds of students enrolled in 1969. It has not begun to wrestle directly with the problems of the urban revolution or with the issue of providing appropriate opportunities to people who are not inclined to achieve rewards from "school." Rather, by building on pre-existing forms the paradigm institution has simply attempted to shift its direction toward producing learning, and thus indirectly to affect the broader problems of its community.

The basic difference between the college of '79 and its immediate predecessor is that the institution has achieved a definition of purpose. It has realized that to attempt everything is to achieve nothing, and it has narrowed the range of its goals accordingly. What remains is a community-based institution focused on student learning — differing from the 1969 college in its view of ends and means, in its concern with the effects of its efforts. In 1969, the central thrust was a merging of traditional college forms with the concept, "provide opportunity for all." A pattern of sprawling, amorphous expansion had developed. Conversely, the college of 1979 moves outward from the nucleus of its key instructional task. Learning, a process of continuing community change, is the exclusive goal, which all practices are arranged particularly to fit.

The issues explored in Part Three are crucial because, although the current explosion in numbers of community colleges may spell "success" to many people, the next ten years will be the most significant in the institution's short history. Change will certainly occur; the only real question is whether it will develop out of present practices or be so revolutionary that the entire structure of the community college is radically altered. The college of 1979 can evolve out of existing forms but only if appropriate leadership and critical intelligence — from within the present system — are dedicated to the issue.

Chapter Thirteen

Into the City

WHAT KIND OF CHANGE?

Present-day schools are, among other things, "a form of child care and a *rite de passage* which we take for granted" (Illich, 1968) — a role not always assigned to them. As currently organized, schools are rather recent creations of the industrial state; a people involved with handicraft and family farming had little need for them. The technological and attendant social changes that began in the late nineteenth century changed patterns of work, education, and people's way of spending their time. Accordingly, schools were altered; a variety of new schemes attempted to fit these changes.

But soon after an institution has been developed to serve a particular group, to fulfill a certain function, its perpetuation becomes an end in itself. Tyler (1967, p. 15) has explained it well:

> Most institutions begin as responses to the need of certain clients for services. As years go by, programs are developed that are reasonably acceptable to the clients they have been serving. Then the institution is likely to believe that its program is its raison d'etre rather than the need for its services. When this program-worship stage is reached, the institution seeks to find clients who like the program and can get along with it, and to deny admission to others. After a time, the terminology develops that those not admitted are "poor students," "not intelligent," not of "college calibre." In many cases, as in the founding of the Land-Grant Colleges, new institutions have to be established to serve the clients rejected by the older ones.

Not only is the institution its own reason for being, but those who have not been exposed to it are seen as being automatically less worthy. Young people *must* attend school; they are caught in a "mandarin system" erected by society which makes college "indispensable for business and the professions." (Barzun, 1968, p. 73.) They cannot decline to attend because:

> As much as anything else, schooling implies custodial care for persons who are declared undesirable elsewhere by the simple fact that a school has been built to serve them. . . . Once universal schooling has been accepted as the hallmark for the in-members of a society, fitness is measured by the amount of time and money spent on formal education in youth rather than by ability acquired independently. . . . (Illich, 1968.)

Thus, whereas in an earlier time "higher education *reflected* the status system of the society; today it is a *determinant* of the stratification system." (D. Bell, 1968.)

If the surge toward social equality were not so pronounced now, it might be largely a matter of curiosity that, to a great extent, selection into a social stratum is based on attendance at an institution ostensibly organized for quite different reasons. On the basis of utility alone, one could deplore a college in which education — the gaining of skills, attitudes, and patterns of thought — is secondary to the sorting and ranking of students on a hierarchy of presumed worth. However, a more pertinent problem is that "it is impossible under existing practices to use schools and colleges as instruments to select some for economic advancement without using the same schools to reject others." (Schrag, 1968a.) And many groups share a growing disinclination to accept the built-in modes of rejection on which present-day schools are based.

A basic necessity now for schools at all levels is reconciliation between the institution, which surely selects but may or may not educate, and the changed demands of society in the second half of the twentieth century. A different phase of education has opened in the United States; it brings with it new opportunities for the junior college. Whereas until now making education *available* has been the goal, as that goal comes within reach, a new target is appearing — guaranteeing some form of *minimum educational achievement*. The basic question which the community college must face is, "Do we seek only equality of educational opportunity or do we want also some useful degree of equality of educational results?" (Jennings, 1966.) Continuing to offer only the opportunity to be rejected will surely court public wrath. The "cooling out" function (letting the student know he is not "college material") of the junior college, so well described by Burton Clark (1960), is outmoded.

Educational systems which select but do not educate are not only wasteful and unwise in our society, they are *unnecessary*. It *is* possible to educate. We need not operate a selective system with check-points at every stage — points at which greater numbers of students are dropped off the paths, wiped out as it were. Of course some of those who come through are well educated and knowledgeable, but would they be less so had more of their fellows graduated with them? Current knowledge of learning processes combined with a pedagogy directed toward *teaching* (not judging) can serve to undergird curricula that are accountable for the learning achieved by the students.

In admitting all applicants, in offering curricula in every field and discipline, the junior college has been saying both directly and by implication, "Come, we will teach you to the limit of your ability to learn." The key words in that statement — "teach" and "your ability" — must be carefully considered. If the junior college is to move away from the circularity of reasoning described in Chapter Twelve, it must accept "causing learning" as the operational definition of teaching. To the extent it does, the junior college will drop its archaic "cooling out" and will gain a function and identity more in line with the needs and desires of the larger community. For their own sake and for the well-being of the nation, people must learn. An educational institution that is structured primarily to "keep them off the streets" or to "sort them out" is doing a disservice to its community.

INTO THE CITY

Educators, students, architects, and community groups of all types have pressured for changes in educational institutions. The need for a structure which would move the opportunity for learning more directly into the city is itself well documented. McDaniel (1968) has made a plea for the junior college to be reorganized as a "sidewalk college." In his scheme, the institution would be spread through the town, in store-fronts and in church basements; it would have no athletic teams and few student activities as such, but would be pointedly dedicated to community upgrading through educational opportunities in every city block. Mayhew (1968b, p. 204) sees the urban college sprawled "amoeba-like through large parts of the largest cities, expecting that, as students go from class to class, they will pass through and profit from the variegated richness of experience which renovated cities provide." Others have called for "urban universities" — twentieth-century counterparts of the land-grant colleges. Located in the cities, they would be supported by federal funds and be dedicated to studying urban problems and proposing solutions. Gideonse calls his community-centered institution the "communiversity." He suggests that today's four-year college does not provide a sufficient variety of models to which young people can look, saying that students should be "apprenticing as human beings" to the world, not just to faculty members. In the communiversity, the present categories of students, faculty, and community would fade and *all* would become participants in the learning process. (1967, p. 132.)

Paul Goodman (1968) focuses his attention on the elementary school but again calls for "radical decentralization." He proposes a system of "mini-schools" which would occupy "two, three, or four rooms in existing school buildings, church basements, settlement houses otherwise empty during school hours, rooms set aside in housing projects, store-fronts," suggesting that many problems of mass education could be overcome by that form of decentralization. Birenbaum (1968) calls "the idea of 'campus' " archaic and asks for "new standards to honor *impermanence* and to accommodate the reality of change." And Antioch College, long a leader in educational innovation, has designed a "Beachhead College" to be located in temporary quarters in areas of need and to be built only with the intent of disposing of the site and moving the college elsewhere within five years. (Baskin, 1967.)

Many architectural firms, particularly those which have worked on community college designs, understand the need to transfer the opportunity for learning from the traditional campus into the community itself. A design competition held by Rice University produced plans that embodied such concepts as the "academic street" wherein a "grow it yourself college" would expand or contract along a road. The college would become a series of overlapping and meshing spaces where people live, work, and learn. The street would be "the main hall of the college, not a corridor" — a "museum without walls." The "community's own life-giving forces" would be incorporated into the college itself. (Lacy, 1962, pp. 49, 50.)

Moving the college into the city by establishing miniature campuses and by opening classes in store-fronts is not the only form of architectural change suggested by writers in the field. Others have called for "cluster colleges" (Yeo, 1968), "house plans" (Walker, 1968), and a variety of imaginative structures designed to fit unique site problems (Lacy, 1962). However, a major conceptual distinction exists between the "sidewalk college" and related models and the "cluster college" or similar designs for campus operation. It is the difference between integrating learning with community life on the one hand, and moving the person out of his natural environment into a segregated place of learning on the other.

In the "sidewalk" scheme, education is part of everyday living. It is as easy for a person to attend school as it is for him to window-shop or go to the movies. School is part of the scene; it is on the street where he lives. Community problems are more likely to be resolved because the school is part of the community, not a separate enterprise wherein people are judged and sorted — passed into upper strata or "failed" into a lifetime of menial jobs. Massive buildings which may tend to intimidate the young are not part of the educational process.

Designs for the isolate campus, however, perpetuate the tradition of separation. "House plan" or "cluster college," education is still expected to occur in a particular place. It is not related to work, consumption, entertainment, life, or love — it is a thing apart, an artificial construct of hard desks, sterile walls, and repressive adults. "Youth must be saved," says this approach, "from the sin of base distractions of community by removal beyond the walls wherein salvation in the form of rational knowledge is to be found."

The case for integrating town and gown is being deliberately overstated here, because the idea is apparently alien to most junior college educators. There are compelling arguments in favor of isolate campuses: the college's function as a symbol of affluence to which townspeople can point with pride; the status that comes from being associated (as teacher, administrator, or student) with an institution of massive facades; the honest belief that students learn better if they rub minds without distraction (coed colleges?). But if any post-secondary institution is to experiment with other forms, the community college seems the most logical candidate. To a greater degree than any other academic institution, it is committed to its community and must therefore be immediately responsive to changing demands — easy access, lifelong opportunity, and institutional accountability.

Outside the field of professional education, community groups have called for educational structures which would interact with their environment. The Los Angeles Urban League has sought to open a "street academy" offering tutorial aid and counseling in poverty areas. The "academy" would not be restricted to the usual school hours, but would offer an "action line" service to provide twenty-four hour counseling by telephone. Sixteen such "store-fronts peddling education" were in operation in New York City in the fall of 1968. The East Harlem Block Schools operate nursery and primary classes in store-fronts "as a way of bringing schools closer to the community and of dissociating education from the repressive Gothic fortresses in which it was traditionally housed." They "have discovered no new pedagogical secrets" but are successful probably because they "provide the kind of accountability and responsibility that many parents demand of the public schools but rarely get." (Schrag, 1968b.)

And in the junior college field itself, changes are occurring in cities where extreme community pressures have been brought to bear. The Peralta Junior College District (Oakland, California) has an Inner City Project that includes a Student Service Corps in which students are paid to work in public agencies, an Enrichment Program to provide workshops in the arts at the neighborhood level, Community Development Centers to provide counseling services, and a variety of scholarship projects. (Waits, 1969.) In New York (Knoell, 1967), Los Angeles, and other metropolitan areas, similar attempts are being made to move the college into the city. Still to be achieved, however, is the integration of the various community-service projects with the "regular" college program.

Viewed in the light of the many current statements insisting that education can be brought to bear more effectively on community problems if campuses are spread into town, the paradigm 1979 college campus is a conservative change. It operates in branch centers, each of which offers a full program of study. Each center is complete in itself; thus, the college is far from being a "mini-school" or a "sidewalk college." However, its move toward the city is manifested in several important features. Its students go into diverse neighborhoods in their study of social problems and for their vocational training. They "drop in" at any college center whenever they wish. Too, the college of '79 may soon offer some course units through its audiotutorial instructional mode in drive-in theatres during the daytime hours. The college is building outward from its campuses while maintaining its curricular and instructional integrity.

In their roles as innovative agents in their community of 1979, college leaders may determine that the institution should encourage people to take all their course units at centers outside their immediate neighborhoods. When that happens, the college will offer differential programs in the various centers. But because the college of '79 is based on a core curriculum, it has not yet seemed necessary to move learning away from students' residences. It is first essential for the total population to gain the same interest in learning that it now has for the acquisition of material possessions.

In its use and design of physical space, the college of '79 stands between its bastioned counterpart of today and the plans of those who call for "sidewalk colleges." It represents an intermediate movement, an interim step away from the highly structured campus toward the complete integration of education with other elements of everyday life.

Chapter Fourteen

Preparing the Faculty

FACULTY ROLES

Technology, it is often claimed, will someday release teachers for creative interaction with students. Following immediately thereupon, dull pedants will be transformed into sparkling wits; the only thing holding them back now is the variety of routine tasks with which they are plagued. Instead of continuing to perpetuate this fond and foolish dream, educators would be well-advised to consider the specific role-changes that teachers will need to (or want to) make in the face of technological advancement. A new breed of resident scholars, savants, and creative, feeling people sprung full blown from the brow of the present faculty is not a reasonable expectation. As Goodlad (1967, p. 9) contends, "Simply to say that the advent of the computer will leave the more sensitive and significant teaching tasks to human teachers is not enough. The process of humanizing instruction will not occur by chance."

Currently, each instructor is required to possess "a preposterous array of competencies." (Trow, 1963.) Everyone must be well-qualified in librarianship, psychology, counseling, course-planning, inspirational guidance, and media-construction, because these skills are required for a full program of instruction. The college of today expects all from each instructor, even though it is patently impossible for everyone to be expert in each function — tradition alone demands it. But other occupations have changed in the direction of specialization. For example, although there are still general practitioners, there are increasing numbers of medical specialists. Similarly, there are still general farmers, but there are also farmers who specialize in animal husbandry, poultry, fruit, and grain. In all cases, when technology and the state of knowledge about the effects of particular practices has advanced, specialization has resulted. Why not in teaching?

One can make a strong case for instructional specialization. The experience of other occupations is one argument. The need for a changed focus on institutional purpose is another: the new role of the college as a medium for provoking changes in its clientele and in its community will require specialists in building objectives and evalution devices, in constructing tests, in designing media, and so forth. The junior colleges cannot wait for, or depend upon, outside agencies to perform those tasks; if it did, it would be betraying its charge as a leader in learning. The college must house its own experts if it is to become and remain responsive to changes in its population of students and in its constituent community. But technology alone cannot bring specialization; it may instead, in the short run, generate a new breed of Luddites.

Regardless of reasons for the change, the concept of the "complete teacher" is outworn. The current state of knowledge of the teaching–learning process has long doomed the generalist. Emphasizing specialization, Trow (1963, pp. 140–146) suggests dividing teachers into learning - materials workers, consultants, programmers, monitors, demonstrators, directors, and discussion leaders. He also projects another group of specialists in student personnel services, examinations, and research. Sanford (1967, p. 193), too, suggests that faculty members must become specialists but does not provide the subdivisions. In any case, it is no longer appropriate to say that "the new technology may free the teacher to do the things he alone can do: to inspire creativity, to build interpersonal relationships, to convey the excitement of the pursuit of knowledge and truth" (Rees, 1968); specific direction and specialization is more clearly indicated.

In one or another facet of instruction, specialization will involve, as a desirable concomitant, a changed faculty role. Instructors will specialize in certain activities and as they gain competency in performing differentiated tasks, the stereotype which points toward *the* role of *the* teacher will disappear. If instructors can be selected and rewarded in accordance with their carefully delineated preferences and skills, the result must be greater teaching efficiency and satisfaction. It will not be a golden age — in fact, many currently practicing instructors will object to the new functions — but the new era will come.

In addition to the changed faculty roles, a corollary of specialization in the junior college of 1979 will be professionalism. Professionalization of teaching has been a fitful dream of instructors for generations. It has been fought for in several ways — for example, in coercing governing boards to spend more money to increase salaries and to reduce the size of classes. But these activities have not brought instructors any nearer to professionalism than has the phenomenon of their leaders' pounding tables and *demanding* they be recognized as professionals.

The difference between the professional and the non-professional is not in training and income but in the broad agreement on, and acceptance of, the professional's role in society — the acknowledgment of his expertise in a specific area. The engineer, the lawyer, the dentist, is listened to on his own subject; people consult him about their buildings, their court cases, their teeth. But not so the teacher. He is seldom consulted on matters relating to learning and the process of instruction. The responsibility for organizing the schools is not in his hands. A major reason for his being left out is that he fancies himself an artist, weaving the threads of his subject area together with his knowledge of human functioning in order to form a tapestry in which something of value happens to students fortunate enough to be involved in the process. To that extent, then, the likelihood of his being listened to as a professional in instruction is forfeited in exchange for the artist's freedom to express himself. Well and good; teaching may indeed be an art, and any school may have a number of artists within it. But they should not, then, expect to be consulted as professionals who operate within a body of transmittable knowledge and who, alone, are fully competent in their own realm.

The current situation of instructors is analogous to doctors' including in their hospital rounds such activities as taking patients' temperatures, dispensing medication, and serving meals. Because instructors are so involved in routine tasks, they do little that might not be as well performed by a literate housewife or businessman after a few weeks' training in learning routines and in reading some materials used in the classroom.

(Popham, 1967.) That statement could not validly be made about any other "profession"!

But although teachers' groups and others have called for help in performing routine tasks, they often stop short of seeking aides who can meet with students and help them learn. The faculty commonly insists that it alone can "teach," in spite of the fact that much evidence is accumulating to indicate that peer tutors can do at least as well. One sometimes wonders whether small classes are for the students or for the instructors; in a recent study, the category "Personal Relationships" was selected by students as that which contributed the *least* to their learning. (McCully, 1968.) Students may, in fact, "feel more comfortable when more anonymous" (Simon, 1967, p. 72); they should at least have the option of working with peers.

Teacher aides are moving into the junior college but, in common with so many other "innovations," they are being introduced for curious reasons. The New Careers Program and other federally funded projects designed to make employment available to the urban poor are encouraging junior colleges to prepare auxiliary personnel for work in educational institutions. (Pearl and Riessman, 1965.) Junior colleges are well suited to the task—many already train paraprofessionals in medical sciences, engineering, and other areas. One interesting difference between preparing instructor assistants and other semi-professionals is that, under the programs' impetus, trainees are frequently being hired for permanent work within the training institutions. (Coppock, 1968.) Thus, it is not the professional associations but the federal anti-poverty funds that are inspiring change in the use of manpower in education.

In the model college of '79, instructors manage aides who perform not only routine clerical tasks but who tutor as well—a scheme not as "innovative" as it sounds. For example, when a student was admitted to Joseph Lancaster's schools early in the nineteenth century, a monitor assigned him his class and taught him along with a few other pupils. When he was absent from class one monitor ascertained the fact, and another found out the reason. The monitors conducted recitations and had charge of school supplies. (Salmon, 1904.) However, such extensive uses of peer-group teaching were largely neglected in the first two-thirds of the twentieth century.

Three responsibilities in particular differentiate the instructor of 1979 from his 1969 counterpart: he specializes in one or another institutional practice; he manages a corps of paraprofessionals; and he has abandoned much of his parochialism and works in liaison with agencies, groups, and individuals within the community. The instructor is a specialist in one of the forms previously incorporated into the undifferentiated "teaching role"—test construction, lecturing, replicable media construction, etc.—and he is hired and assigned accordingly. Aides relieve instructors of the routine clerical tasks performed by their 1969 counterparts, and they help them in tutoring. As part of the 1979 teachers' work, they engage in community studies, design follow-up examinations of the students on a continuing basis, and test media for other institutions.

The college of '79 specifies the faculty's role and pays most for the scarcest skills. For example, planning and conducting long-range student follow-up studies is essential to the purposes of the college. In order to attract people who can do that necessary task adequately, the college rewards with a higher rate of pay those instructors who work on the "evaluation" team. Another group that is paid well compared with others is made up of individuals who suggest new and revised curricular objectives. Skill in constructing objectives is a quality that has always been difficult to find among people in the teaching profession, despite the fact that objectives need continuous review in order to ensure their relevance to the purposes of the institution and of the students. A third group of specialists constructs and analyzes test items. Skilled classroom managers are at least as valuable to the college as are other specialists, but because of the self-selection and role perceptions which still prevail, faculty members with these capabilities are in a surplus. Overall, specialization has resulted in a higher level of performance and in greater individual satisfaction.

The instructor–researcher or the "teacher empiricist" (Popham, 1965) is also represented at the college. These specialists design and help implement research on the short-term effects of different types of instruction. Answers to general questions about what approaches work best with particular students are still being sought by university-based scholars using complex research designs, but simple classroom experiments are conducted by the college staff. Although the findings are not always generalizable, they are an aid to instructors and students at the college itself.

In the broadest sense, the instructor in the college of '79 is a social scientist, and the college provides him with an administrative housing. The greatest concentration of disciplinary expertise in the community is represented in the college faculty. Instructors' skills are not dissipated in the supervision of student clubs, various kinds of non-professional community service, repetitive clerical tasks, and other functions irrelevant to teaching. Rather, the staff as a whole is engaged in a continuous effort of hypothesis-making and testing in the field of teaching and learning. Instructors in the college of 1979 have disavowed the naïvete of their predecessors who refused to propose concrete learning objectives for their communities. Their prime activities are defining the desired results and devising learning paths which will move students to those ends.

FACULTY PREPARATION

Before role-differentiation and professionalism can be brought to the level posited here for 1979, teacher recruiting and preparation practices must be somewhat altered. Today, instructional experts are not widely available. The special preparation of community college instructors typically approximates the training in "methods" of secondary-school teacher programs; it may come close to the university scholar's total lack of teacher-training. (Cohen, 1968, p. 21.) Teachers uniquely qualified to cause learning are not often found, one reason being that most training programs are not designed to prepare instructional specialists. This deficit has been duly noted by community college leaders who perennially call for particularized programs, some going so far as to recommend development of separate institutes — a "Master's College" (Dawson, 1968), for example, or a "Community College Institute" (Singer, 1968). These teacher training schools would be operated exclusively by and for community colleges, providing degree-granting programs and refresher courses for college instructors.

However, the impact that such institutions could make is disputable. Historically, advances in professional education have come about through regulation and quality control provided by members of the profession. But teacher-training has been at its best when it is combined with the type of broad learning experience available at a liberal arts college or university; a return to the "normal school" would seem to run counter to tradition. Impatience and frustration on the part of junior college leaders is understandable though, because for the most part, their institutions' needs have been ignored by universities. Fortunately, there are some notable exceptions — programs that are leading the way toward specialized preparation for service in the community college.

As a way of coping with demands for college teacher-training, several universities are in the process of introducing non-doctoral graduate-degree programs. Favorite titles are "Candidate" or "Master" in Philosophy. The Assembly of the Academic Senate, University of California, has recommended the "Candidate" degree which "formalizes the all-but-dissertation status of the Ph.D." (Wortham, 1967.) It is patterned on a plan initiated by the Midwest consortium of Big Ten universities. (University of California, 1967, p. 45.) Yale University has reintroduced the Master of Philosophy (Walters, 1967) and several other institutions, including Boston University and Carnegie Institute of Technology, are also considering the establishment of a recognized degree for college teachers. In addition, the Master of Arts in College Teaching has been introduced on many campuses.

Arguments rage over whether or not the non-doctoral degrees will be recognized and accorded appropriate status. Junior college leaders are concerned lest the glacial rates at which university graduate schools change their procedures will allow action to be taken within the near future, if at all. Gleazer (1967), for example, fears that "programs of this kind may turn out to be only thin overlays on substantially unchanged graduate offerings."

The doubts expressed by several educators appear to be warranted, especially because the format of the college-teacher programs, the institutes in which they are housed, the nature of their offerings, the name of the degree awarded, and other considerations typically debated all skirt the real issue. The attitudes and motives that lead a young person to decide to enter junior college teaching dictate his future activities more than does the pattern of courses he takes; the rewards offered by employer colleges are considerably more influential than the title of the degree he holds. Not until the function of the junior college and the role of the teacher upon whom a prospective instructor models himself change will there be a significant difference in instructor's behavior. Teachers must enter the profession for different reasons and be rewarded for different activities if their work is to be significantly affected. (Brawer, 1968.)

Change is slow in American higher education. The academic discipline of professional instruction has not yet "arrived." Its theories are weak, its practitioners are few. What passes for teaching is a curious amalgam of showmanship, intuitive insight, vague principles, a few tested procedures, and much faith. Any specialized teacher-preparation program must focus on defining and advancing instructional concepts if it is to have long-term value for the profession. But because reward structures and emphases in community colleges are not often so oriented, the influence of even the most enlightened pre-service programs remains minimal. The issue is circular: few training programs have been built particularly to bring people to the point where they can predictably and efficiently cause learning, because junior colleges have not demanded that type of expertise. Few colleges seek specialists in instruction because their leaders have not been so oriented. The situation is not likely to be drastically altered at any time soon.

This being the case, even in 1979, the paradigm college takes responsibility for orienting its own teachers toward teaching. It attempts to change the role expectations of prospective instructors by having students serve as apprentices to instructional specialists. Student aides learn there is more to teaching than lecturing, and they modify their expectations accordingly. If they choose to enter teaching as a career, they do so with a more accurate view of the profession than they would have gained had they not already served it.

Newly graduated instructors work with teams in specialized areas. Deliberate training, differential rewards, and the practice of holding instructors accountable for the learning achieved by their students exercise powerful influences. Experienced teachers are given periodic retraining in short courses operated by the college. The college does not expect its teachers to have been prepared as instructional experts in the university. It begins where most Master's degree programs end, and prepares people to serve its unique purposes.

The college has developed its own preparation program because teaching is its main function; it cannot wait for other institutions of higher education to recognize and appreciate its concrete goals. It accepts prospective teachers' subject-area expertise as certified by the university, but deliberately trains them to teach in ways that fit its own needs. It does not seek the "total" instructor because it needs specialists. In keeping with its commitment to instructional leadership, the college prepares instructors by focusing their attention on student learning, on the *effects* of their efforts.

Chapter Fifteen

From Sorting
to Teaching

The archaic, yet persistent, use of schools as devices to sort people is well documented. Current norm-referenced testing and curve-based grade-marking practices are the most visible — but not the only — manifestations of that inclination. Most junior colleges perpetuate such activities, many of them guarding the use of marks as zealously as if a commandment to assign grades had come down from Sinai along with the other ten. And norm-referenced testing, basically a sorting mechanism regardless of the attempts to ascribe other values to it, is used in the colleges almost exclusively. If a "teaching institution" would truly serve, it must view such practices as obsolescent aberrations and abandon them forthwith.

There are many arguments against ever using norm-referenced testing. It hampers instruction by putting students in competition with each other and with their instructors. It also propagates testing procedures of dubious worth. For example, the difficulty-level of items on norm-based examinations is often manipulated so that a "better spread" of scores is obtained. In many cases this is done without the test writer's awareness that he may be changing the nature of the behavior being appraised and thus invalidating the entire instrument. (Tyler, 1967, p. 14.) How many instructors have made a second test more "difficult," often by increasing the ambiguity of items, when the first test was mastered by a majority of their students? A "good" test item is one which is answered incorrectly by a substantial number of "poor" students; a "good" test is one which has a wide range of scores, thus casting students into "better" and "worse" categories. Test construction specialists not only condone, they support, such practices in their efforts to help instructors apply the curve of normal probabilities to their examinations, hence, to their classes. (Wood, 1967, p. 82.)

Marking is similarly defended. The "grade-point differential" — the difference between marks earned by a student at the junior college and the marks he earns when he transfers to a four-year institution — is the most widely used index of a college's worth. Remove that and most institutions would have few standards on which to judge their success. Defenders of the practice seem unconcerned that only a minority of students actually transfer, and that marks are only one indicator — a relatively poor one — of the learning attained.

Feasible alternatives to grading practices are not easily found. Those that are suggested usually fall into one of two categories: first, that marks be replaced either by letters written by faculty members who appraise each student's total progress; second, that examinations be given when a student is ready to demonstrate that he has mastered a particular segment of subject matter. In this case marks would be distributed according to scores on the tests. (Rami, 1967.) "Pass/fail" is receiving much attention, however, as disenchantment with the marking system sets in. Sanford (1967, p. 100) suggests:

> It would not be surprising if within the next few years distinguished undergraduate institutions were to give all their courses on a pass/fail basis. It will be recognized, in time, that what students need for their education is not grades. . . .

Several junior colleges are trying variations of "pass/fail" in certain courses. However, the incompatibility between a dichotomous marking scheme and norm-referenced testing poses a major problem. Pass/fail is an either/or system — the student mastered the objectives or he did not. Norm-referenced testing, designed to rank students according to the degree by which their scores deviate from the group's average, does not fit the binary approach. It can be used, but then, why sort at all? If a score above a minimum cutoff point means "pass," there is no need for normative testing.

Colleges will more likely find "pass/fail" accepted by students, faculty, employers, and transfer institutions if they change their testing practices from norm-referenced to criterion-referenced examinations. Criterion-referenced testing employs a group of test items related to a specific learning objective with the intent that the students achieve a minimum score. When they have done so, they have fulfilled all that is required of them. They are not sorted or ranked in competition with their fellows but are simply credited with performing a task at a pre-set level of competence. Criterion-referenced tests currently are used primarily for purposes of determining whether or not particular instructional designs are effective. But they are essential to a credit/no credit system of student marking, regardless of the instructional medium.

When criterion-referenced testing is employed, objectives may be evaluated *in advance* of instruction. Post hoc judging of student worth is mitigated. Everyone, students and instructors alike, may discuss and agree in advance on appropriate criteria. Instructors may commit themselves to bringing specified percentages of their students to certain levels of achievement. The institution that employs a credit/no credit marking system is taking a step toward becoming an institution that accepts accountability for the learning achieved by its students, one that is committed to bringing specified percentages of them to a minimum level of learning achievement.

Criterion-referenced testing is another example of a practice, not actually strange or new to American higher education, which could feasibly be employed much more widely without a traumatic change in the educational system. It is really the procedure upon which "credit by examination" qualifying schemes are based. It is used not only for courses in college but is also widely employed in adult education and in giving students credit for extramural experiences — military service, for example. A recent bibliography published by College Entrance Examination Board reviewed hundreds of studies reporting on the various uses of "credit by examination." (Flaugher *et al.*, 1967.) Criterion-referenced testing is thus by no means an alien concept, though for a variety of reasons its use in most American colleges has always been peripheral.

In the college of '79 there is no grade-marking, and there are no norm-referenced tests. When a student has demonstrated his achievement of the objectives for a single unit, he is given credit for that unit and proceeds to the next. The objectives may call for him to attain a particular score on a criterion-referenced test, or they may involve his writing papers, giving talks, participating in laboratory exercises, or performing certain tasks away from the college itself. When he has demonstrated his achievement of all objectives in the core curriculum, he is awarded his Associate in Arts degree. Testing and the objectives themselves thus becoming teaching devices, for when a student's attention is focused on the ends rather than on the means of instruction, learning is demonstrably enhanced (Tyler, 1967), and the odious practice of judging as a substitute for teaching is absent.

DROP IN, DROP OUT

When institutions define their degrees so as to make clear what each graduate must accomplish, and when, at the same time, each student follows his own path, long or short, to any given degree, colleges and universities can, with no sacrifice of educational standards, accommodate a flood of newcomers whose interests and abilities are widely different.
— ELIZABETH PASCHAL (1968, p. 235.)

"Dropout," a word typically applied alike to students who fail to complete a semester or who fail to register for the next series of courses in a particular curriculum, is often coupled with the word "problem," to form a term which suggests something that must be "solved." Depending on one's view, a student who drops out has either failed to "achieve his potential" (play the game according to the rules) or has been let down by schools which have neglected to provide an "experience appropriate to his needs." In either case, the "problem" exists.

The penalties for the student dropout are often severe. In many colleges, before readmittance will be granted, a dropout must submit justification for having broken the straight-line, year-after-year pattern of attendance. The difficulty of gaining admittance to college at all, unless particular requisites are met, is well known. Guardians, in the persons of admissions officers with responsibility for keeping out the unfit, man the gates at many two-year, most four-year, and all graduate schools. And woe to the prospective student who applies with marks on his transcript that indicate he withdrew before completing a course at some point in his school career.

Why so? Why, despite pronouncements to the contrary, is our society"... not geared to the idea of *second chances?* The possibilities of leaving school after graduation, knocking about or working for several

years, and then going on to graduate or professional school are few."
(D. Bell, 1968). Perhaps it is because there is but "one ladder of educational success" from nursery school on, and anyone who fails to climb it all the way to the top "is *ipso facto* a dropout and a failure." (McClellan, 1968, p. 15.) Why must every student go through every course in every program in which he enrolls? The position is difficult to justify logically.

Many writers in the field of education deplore the "dropout problem" and seek ways of keeping students in school. However, others seek institutional changes that will accommodate students who desire to come and go at will. They call for new institutions

> ... far more flexible than the college and university as we now know it. For example, students should have easy access in and out so that, sure of admission, they can attend part-time or drop out temporarily to work or to have some other kind of experience. Every student who "finished" such an institution would understand that he had to go on learning, and that from time to time he might return to his school to do so. (Sanford, 1967, p. 191.)

The student "must be able to leave and return at various stages of his career and maturity without penalty." (Worthen, 1967.)

This mood and vision of how opportunity for education should be structured is furthered in the popular press as well. The *Saturday Review* insists:

> We must make it possible for anyone—be he a Ph.D. or a fifth grade dropout—to continue his learning full-time or part-time at whatever level he is to begin. This means ... abandoning the idea that any educational system is finite, either as to time or place. The central enterprise of this society will be learning. ... It should, by definition, be impossible for any person in America to drop out of the educational system, even though he may be a dropout from one or several specific institutions within it. (April 20, 1968, p. 53.)

The general idea of the second chance is fairly well established in the junior college; in fact, institutions often pride themselves on enrolling students who have been rejected by four-year colleges. (O'Connell, 1968, p. 5.) And schemes which make it easy for anyone to attend—Saturday class scheduling, for example—are tried on occasion. *No junior college, however, has developed an organization so flexible that a student can enter, leave, and return at times of his own choosing without penalty.*

At best, he must break at the end of a semester or other arbitrary time block or be subject to receiving a "Withdrawn" mark, often with attendant untoward consequences.

Many arguments in favor of freedom to drop in and out of school may be found. Bruner and other cognitive theorists suggest that the student be allowed choice in learning when he chooses, because "mental growth is not a gradual accretion." Rather it moves in spurts and rests like a staircase with sharp risers. (Bruner, 1966, p. 27.) The concept, "readiness," has also been described and related to students' entrance and exit at will. But our current state of knowledge of how learning occurs is limited to the fact that no known test validly assesses "readiness" to learn or subtleties of individual learning styles. Students cannot be assigned different learning tasks at various times with assurance that the proper choice has been made. Nor can students themselves, except in isolated cases, reliably predict when and how they will master particular concepts. The best we can do now is to allow as much freedom of choice as possible regarding the means of instruction to be applied at a particular time in an individual's life.

The "dropout problem" is both pedagogical and administrative. Pressure to change the present structure will not be applied by administrators who find it convenient to begin and end human intellectual processes according to the calendar. Nor will it be advanced by instructors who seek primarily to "cover" particular blocks of material. It is as easy to justify talking about a subject for four months as it is to advocate discussing it for four days or four years. Why change? Many junior college courses currently offered have built-in sequences that lend themselves well to stopping and starting at times other than the end of the semester or quarter. In fact, instructors must often cut or fill so that they can fit their courses to allocated blocks of time. But the current ludicrous picture of thousands of students and instructors beginning and ending their formal educational experiences at the same time persists. Rarely is an attempt made to justify the practice on grounds that have any validity in the learning process. The student who starts or stops out of phase is a paper problem, one compounded by a tradition of starting and stopping schools along with the seasons.

It is relatively simple to erect a system that would lead to flexible scheduling patterns and, at the same time, effectively eliminate the "dropout problem." Computerized scheduling systems have been in use for several years. Programs are available to generate master schedules and concomitantly produce lists of students requesting specified courses, enrollment projections, class lists, checks to see that students have met course requirements, transcripts, library circulation control, and many other administrative conveniences. The challenge is to use the available information for reevaluation and reshaping of the educational enterprise itself.

At present, computers in the same school are typically fed with mutually exclusive systems. The pay-roll office may be using one set of codes and files; the registrar's pupil-record office another; an alumni office uses still another; the business manager and contracts officer may employ even others. But the movement "is toward the design of centrally planned and managed systems that meet the needs of research, instruction, and administration." (Bushnell and Allen, 1967, p. 219.)

If all offices' codes, files, and records were integrated, one computer teletype system could register students for courses, providing automatic feedback if course prerequisites had not been met. Students could also receive information about their past records and use the terminals for routine advising assistance—requirements for certification in various fields and admission demands of other schools, for example. The same system could be used in many types of research studies in which follow-up or other data on students were needed. All is readily available within the current state of the computer art.

Dropout is no problem if students can come and go at will. In order to allow free access to classes, however, time blocks must be shortened so that students can move from unit to unit and section to section in two- or three-week periods—not the three- or four-month segments of today's college. The concepts now presented in most courses can be fit into shorter time spans, with courses, or at least course units, begun and ended every few weeks. Another prime requirement for ready accessibility is the specific definition of where individual course units begin and end. Such a direction implies that deliberate learning objectives must be specified within a framework of defined outcomes, concepts to be treated more fully in Part Four of this book.

Administrative management of individualized student entrance and exit can be arranged. The student's single identification card could allow his access to library materials, register and enroll him in course units, and provide him with a complete transcript at almost any time. (Gerard, 1967.) Such a design is now available through an all-electronic system that can function with any on- or off-line computer system. Each student receives one all-purpose card; the computer does the rest.

Many features of the college of '79 require integration of the separate administrative segments of today's institution. The computer can maintain a merger, but college personnel must first be willing to put materials and ideas together with the hardware. Student attrition can be effectively eliminated as a "problem" if entry and exit to the institution or to any of its instructional units is so easy that, by definition, everyone can drop in or out at his own volition without penalty. The "problem" even now is one for the college to solve by changing the traditional practices that have created it.

A VARIETY OF INSTRUCTIONAL PATHS

The need to "individualize" instruction is a shibboleth in American education; "Break the lock step!" is the rallying cry. Yet true and complete individualization is impossible unless an environment can be created which is totally receptive to each learner on each day. Obviously, we do not know enough about human learning to design such an instantly flexible environment. And the state of instructional technology has not advanced to the point that schools could provide it if such knowledge *were* available. Individuals change daily, hourly. Their approaches to situations with which they are confronted display more differences than similarities. They differ within themselves as well as among each other. The learning strategies they employ vary greatly, depending, for example, on whether they are called upon to juggle abstract concepts, perform tasks on the basis of stated principles or to make multiple discriminations among undifferentiated phenomena.

The design of instruction — individualized or not — is a complex process. Which among the many possible modes of instruction leads to what learning for which students? For *any* students? Variations of these questions are as old as education. Differences in environments, students' learning styles, instructional methodology, levels of tasks to be learned, and interactions among all relevant characteristics have seemed to be beyond comprehension or control. Not only do different students need different instruction, but "choice among existing practices cannot be made from data demonstrating the greater effectiveness of one over another." (Oettinger, 1968.) Recently reanalysis of the data from almost 100 comparative studies of different college teaching methods found no shred of evidence to indicate any basis for preferring one method over another. (*R & D Perspectives*, 1968.) These are central problems in instructional design. Only one principle is clear above all: Conventional boundaries of methods that are chosen without regard for varied learning styles cannot lead to true individualization. Allowing flexible time periods for individual students to complete the same cycle is not enough.

It seems reasonable to expect that different students need various forms of instruction to learn different concepts, but we do not yet know why. Certain principles have become apparent. Research seems to indicate "that some students can learn quite well through independent learning efforts while others need highly structured teaching-learning situations." (Bloom, 1968.) The advantages of tutoring have been linked to the likelihood that a good tutor will find the path best suited to his pupil for the concept with which they are dealing. And group study procedures have been shown to be helpful when "the students could cooperate and help each other without any danger of giving each other special advantages in a competitive situation." (Bloom, 1968.)

In speaking about the relative value of one method versus another, Philip Jacob (1957, p. 8) determined that:

> Some students react very negatively to a more permissive teaching technique. They feel frustrated and uneasy without more direction and authority exercised by the teacher. Consequently, they may actually learn less and be less profoundly affected by a course taught in this manner, than by a more formal, definitely structured approach.

But such principles, stated most often as negatives ("We know what does *not* always work"), fall short of providing the type of information needed by instructional planners who can but attempt to make a variety of paths available. Lecture and discussion sections, live and machine media, permissive and highly structured environments — all must be employed because today the learner alone can (hopefully) know when and in what fashion he is ready to learn a particular body of concept. (Bruner, 1966.) Therefore, although even he is often unconscious of his readiness to learn, the student must be free to move in and out of instructional situations at his discretion and without penalty; furthermore, these situations must be varied. As McKeachie (1968) has summed it up: "At present we do not know much about which students best achieve which goals with which experiences, but I would bet that the mere presence of several alternatives would result in educational gain."

Any attempt at individualizing instruction requires that there be different ways for people to learn (Glaser, 1966b); but we need to know much more about the phenomena of learning before separate paths can be *prescribed* for students. Hence the variety of instructional sections in the college of '79. Students may pick that which best helps them *at that time.* They (and the college) *know* when they have learned because criterion tests are administered at frequent intervals. And they can drop in and out at will. The college offers as much flexibility and individualization as is feasible given the current state of the instructional art.

Chapter Sixteen

Integrating College Curricula

Junior college programs are often maintained with little regard for their interrelationships. Each time a curricular program is begun, much justification is made for its introduction as part of the college's total offerings. But then, as the program matures, it acquires its own reason for being, gaining apologists and a set of vested interests along the way. In time, the program's rationale is so belabored by its advocates that it often becomes thoroughly warped. Eventually, the college becomes a loose conglomeration of curricula, many of which have long outlived the purposes for which they were initiated.

An institution dedicated to "meeting community needs" in whatever form they appear finds it difficult to turn down any request to begin a program. Similarly, it is almost impossible to eliminate a type of offering unless enrollments fall so low that economy forces the change. Yet there must be some focus, some better reason for maintaining a program than, "It is, therefore it should be."

If the college is truly to serve its community, it can best do so by seeking ways of shaping its functions toward a common cause. The rationale developed in this book is that of the college as a learning institution, directly accountable for student change. That purpose is itself subordinate to the college as an agency of community transformation. The college of '79 is a mechanism of instruction, a leader among the community's educational agencies and an aide in defining objectives for community endeavors. Accordingly, it must integrate all its activities toward those ends. It cannot abide programs which *are* because they *were*.

In the junior colleges' move toward leadership in a learning society, community services and occupational programs are two examples of functions which can be maintained but which must be transformed. As currently offered, they are often disruptive—not part of the "transfer" curriculum, stepchildren of the colleges. To be effective, they must merge and blend with the colleges' overall purpose. They should not continue to exist apart.

COMMUNITY SERVICES

As an element in the total curriculum, community services stemmed from an idea that everyone connected with the community college would look around, find educational gaps, and help fill them. They would survey the community's desires, build responsive programs, and generally upgrade the districts in which they were located. The extent to which this has happened is open to question, though community-service programs are well entrenched today. Do they actually serve the segments of society which are most in need of being served? The current focus on means rather than on ends and the absence of built-in evaluation procedures make this question difficult to answer. Often, community-service leaders will say, "Here is a program in which many are enrolled; ergo, it fills a community need."

In a sense, it is difficult to justify the worth of most community services except as a form of public relations, although they are viewed as "essential elements" in the college program. (Harlacher, 1968.) There are, however, notable exceptions. Harlacher has documented many outstanding attempts by junior colleges to build imaginative curricula outside the traditional realms of instruction. He has found "aggressive multi-service outreach programs" designed to extend campuses throughout the entire college district through the use of "extension centers, empty stores, portable units located on vacant land, mobile units," and other community facilities. (1968, p. 14.) In addition, he lists in-plant training, consulting services, programs for the disadvantaged, and cooperative efforts with other educational institutions among the community services developed by junior colleges.

If community services follow some of the directions suggested by Harlacher, they may lead the junior college toward becoming the community-integrated institution of 1979. However, if the colleges continue merely to provide space for hobby courses, the community's performing groups, and miscellaneous workshops, institutes and conferences — listed as "community services" mainly because they are allowed to be held on the campus — then the worth of community-service programs is in doubt.

VOCATIONAL CURRICULA

Like community services, vocational programs are well entrenched in community junior colleges. Large-scale federal funding is available for occupational curricula, and junior colleges have not been remiss in obtaining their share of the grants. Indeed, the availability of these grants may be a major explanation for the continuation of many outmoded programs. The number of students receiving training for manual trades in a junior college is often pointed out with a pride almost as great as that attaching to the number of students who transfer to four-year institutions. Yet the vocational–technical programs stand on one side of a deep chasm which separates them from the "college level" offerings. In spite of periodic calls for integration, the twain shall never meet in today's community college.

Arrangements for technical training are essential in every city, but is it necessary or even particularly desirable that they be presented on a college campus? Most junior college administrators insist they should. The offering of vocational–technical courses in campus facilities has been common for more than forty years (Coons, 1968, pp. 24–25), and it seems likely to continue. Even when community college leaders project their visions of future colleges, they often envision industry feeding support into campus-based laboratories (Cosand, 1968, pp. 143–144) — not colleges that reach out toward their communities. One model community college of the future even has the institution housed in an isolate campus along with miniature factories where students are prepared for occupations. The college is a city in microcosm. (Yeo, 1968.) But this plan and others like it are built on perpetuating the tradition which demands that the young be *removed* from the community so that they can learn. An alternative view holds that vocational education only *pretends* to educate when it creates "a spurious facsimile of the factory within a school building." The "medieval tradition in which men are prepared for the 'secular world' by incarceration in a sacred precinct, be it monastery, synagogue, or school" is the model. (Illich, 1968.) It is such a familiar form that many educators are unaware of the feasibility—not to say the desirability—of alternatives.

Instead of creating a miniature world within the walls of the campus, why not a subsidized transformation of the industrial plant? Partnerships between schools and industries have already sprung up in many places. Often, when junior colleges have not led in these endeavors, industries have taken it on themselves to effect the liaison. In Detroit, the Chrysler Corporation "adopted" a predominantly Negro school and now offers the students "work experience, job application guidance and training, and assistance in finding employment." (*Saturday Review*, June 15, 1968.) Similar phenomena have appeared in other cities in which needs are particularly acute; are they indicative of a trend that will move technical training *out* of the college?

Current moves to offer total vocational education within industries primarily attempt to lessen disaffection between the unemployed and the larger community, but they are rooted in sound pedagogical practice and an understanding of twentieth-century technology. The right thing is happening, though for reasons that are incidental to the purposes of junior college planning. The simple fact is that "some of the skills now taught in the schools could be done better by local industries, business firms, and professions." (Gray, 1968, p. 224.) Integration can and should be effected.

Formalized puberty rites are almost nonexistent in America. However, as part of the phenomenon of enforced, prolonged adolescence, students have been kept from full participation in society. They have been put away, kept in custody, for periods of time ranging up to twenty years —a practice that has been accepted by the large community as being necessary to keep them out of the work force. Hence the community uproar when students, complaining of the irrelevance of school, take steps toward direct social involvement. (K. Clark, 1968.) It has become apparent that many students are unwilling to wait until they have been "certified" as adults to take action regarding the world around them.

But our current refusal to let students participate *responsibly* and *productively* in society "is no more civilized than our custom of dispossessing the older generations." (Bicker, 1967, p. 64.) The distinction between "learning" and "working" has become increasingly blurred as technological obsolescence has made retraining a continuing necessity; "vocational" and "academic" have lost much of their original meanings. The distinction between "student" and "citizen" is similarly outmoded—

young people themselves have broken down those barriers. The integration of roles takes place continually.

By providing an altered focus, the junior college can help effect a merger of the process of working, learning, and becoming involved in community life. Students can be apprenticed or can serve as volunteer aides to workers in all areas — in hospitals, factories, service enterprises, and in the schools themselves. This practice is not child labor dictated by economic necessity; rather, it is an attempt to bring young people into early participation in society and to integrate all their experiences both in and out of school. "Academic" programs can have "technical" components; "vocational" curricula can have "college-level" requisites. In any case, the distinction among these terms is so vague that they serve no defensible operational purpose.

There is no reason why students must be viewed as somehow living apart from the mainstream of community activities. Work, learning, and social activism are interrelated within the world outlook of a single individual; they can so be viewed by educators. While they are attending school, all students can be earning money, experience, school credit, and self-confidence in work programs whether or not they are enrolled in formally defined trades curricula. Concurrently, they can be active in community affairs, for student participation in the community can readily be developed. Such programs might involve students' working voluntarily with civic agencies, participating in the processes of operating programs, or doing research and writing reports on actual problems. "The key points would be relevance of the activity to community needs and contribution to student development. ("Patterns for Change," 1967, p. 67.)

Currently, there are many college courses with specific requirements that students participate directly in community life. Social science instructors frequently require that students do volunteer work in clinics. For decades Antioch College has had a work–study plan according to which students receive credit for jobs in their areas of interest, which they pursue off-campus for major parts of the year. Merrill College of the University of California, Santa Cruz, plans to send its students to do unpaid field work for months at a time "with migrant workers, . . . in a community development project or a primary school in Upper Volta [Africa] or Peru." (P. W. Bell, 1968.) According to Feldman (1967) of the Ford Foundation:

> The urgent need is a systematic approach that meshes a number of programs, now separate, in general education, vocational education, manpower development, adult education, and on-the-job training. . . . An educational system that fences

off the vocational aspect of life in a compartment called vocational education, separate from the mainstream, . . . and serving only one student in ten is an anomaly, if not a fantasy.

The concept is not unique; it is being continually rediscovered.

Dual offerings, isolate functions, and the building of shops and
laboratories on college campuses only serve to further a spiritual and
physical separation between student and society. Junior colleges need
now to take a lead in helping other community agencies — including industrial plants — participate in providing opportunity for young people
to learn of their ways of functioning. This is not vocational training
offered as a thing apart, but a program of deliberate educational sequences
offered by and within all forms of social enterprises — private or public,
for service or for profit.

In the college of '79, community services are not a separate function
— the college *is* a community service. The college staff helps other
agencies design programs that do not fit into the core curriculum framework. There are no "extension" classes or "mobile units"; the college
centers open and close in response to population shifts. Special short
courses are not needed because the curriculum is itself a series of short
units. If a learning objective cannot logically be built into a unit of a core
course, it is delegated to another community group that employs the college staff to help in the initial planning of instructional sequences. The
college's community entertainment functions such as its sports events
have been dropped. The college is in the learning business.

Community service, that distinctively American contribution to
higher education (Wellman, 1968, p. 8), is also represented by college
staff members who serve on various types of community planning committees. They participate with governmental and private groups involved
with matters of zoning, finance, public health, recreation, and other
aspects of community life. The ends-orientation they bring helps these
groups focus on the outcomes of the proposed endeavors. Thus the college personnel, in addition to offering disciplinary expertise to the committees, aid in defining objectives for the entire community. Students and
staff; vocational and academic; learning, working, and public service —
by conscious intent, all have blended into the city.

TOWARD A LEARNING COMMUNITY

An argument cannot be well documented for a community college's
doing primarily that which it alone can do best. Although a few writers
in the field have suggested that each institution focus on certain programs,
most argue for "comprehensiveness" — implicitly defined as anything for

which the schools can receive financial support. Blocker (1965, p. 271) has said, "A more healthy situation would be for the college to define its educational roles, to make clear that it can sustain only a limited number of programs," but his statement is not typical. Most writers list the functions of the institutions — transfer education, occupational education, adult education, etc. — and maintain that junior colleges should strive in all their endeavors for something called, incomprehensibly, "excellence."

One or another form of curricular change is frequently undertaken in the junior college — often under the guise of "innovation." However, most such efforts are devoted to altering offerings for the "terminal" or "remedial" student. Students classified as low in ability need special counseling, tutoring, "block" programs and interdisciplinary courses (Roueche, 1968, pp. 126ff.), according to the usual thinking, but the "transfer" curriculum is "dictated by the university," hence sacrosanct in format. The feeling seems to be, "Prepare students for transfer by offering university parallel courses. Try something, anything, with the 'less-than-college-level' group, but follow slavishly the specialty preparation and survey curriculum laid down by Big Brother or risk being labeled 'other-than-higher' education." The fact that *it is just possible the university does not have all the answers to undergraduate education* is not often discussed in arguments over junior college curriculum revision.

Ostensibly pragmatic and not bound to tradition, a junior college should adopt a plan of curricular development that it can justify and defend as it own. This plan should be not only for the "non-transfer" or occupational (meet-the-job-needs) programs, but for *all* offerings. The failure to accept that responsibility dooms the institution to suffer according to the whims of political and economic fortune. "Let's do it because everyone else is" or "because we can get paid for it" are frightening statements. Yet they are frequently uttered by, or may be inferred from the actions of, a community's educational "leaders." Can any college worthy of the name afford to settle for such purely expedient self-justifications?

If the curriculum is to be built indigenously by each institution (and it is difficult to conceive of a valid contrary position), there must be a consistent base from which to work. What lines of inquiry should be taken? Whitehead's cyclic view of learning? Newman's divisions of God, Nature, and Man? Tyler's way of arriving at value statements? Dewey's pragmatic, ever-evolving approach? There are many potential avenues, several of which are eclectic. Which may best be advanced?

The field of higher education suffers for lack of theory. Postulates abound, but rarely are they tied together in such a manner that broad hypotheses might be generated and tested. The literature is filled with wholesale assumptions, but there is no fully developed theory. (Mayhew, 1966, p. 38.) Unfortunately, as Goodlad (1968) points out, the "political–rhetorical demands of gaining acceptance for new constructs use up available energies.... The field ... desperately needs bold working hypotheses." Upon what, then, may the junior college build its curriculum?

Important elements in curriculum change include feasibility, practically, and an image or view of purpose. A *feasible* answer to questions of curriculum development may be found by beginning with the institution as it exists now, and as it might evolve. The colleges *are*. Relative to other forms of higher education, their modes of operation are in flux, but definite patterns are apparent. There is little value in advancing philosophical solutions that have no chance of being incorporated into practice.

Junior college leaders often refer to their institutions as being community-centered. As such, they reason, colleges should draw data from their constituencies and plan programs accordingly. This form of practicality is philosophically defensible, and because it represents a pattern of thought widely held, it is more likely to lead to institutional change than would a plan that required execution by people of alternative vision. Hence, it is feasible.

Unfortunately, however, definitive plans are rarely employed in practice. Information is gathered haphazardly — usually through surveys taken at infrequent intervals — and it seldom sheds light on the effects of the programs themselves. Data pointed toward gaining knowledge of numbers of students who plan to enroll, numbers who intend to transfer, numbers who seek job training, and so on are gathered assiduously. They are used for planning buildings and parking lots and, on occasion, for organizing occupational curricula, but seldom, if ever, are they employed in plotting general studies. Rare exceptions may be found, but most often the type of information gathered cannot be used in course and curriculum structuring.

Suppose a community junior college deliberately and honestly set out to build a program on the basis of the realities of its social context. The staff would first be forced to understand that it could not meet all community needs because no one institution could possibly realize that goal. The failure to reach this conclusion would doom the enterprise from the start. Next, the college would have to determine which forms of education could as well be presented by other agencies. A realistic look at this question might lead the college to abandon many programs currently deemed essential. What of courses for the university-bound? Would anything other than a "parallel" program be accepted by four-year institutions? Universities in some states have already agreed to accept the junior colleges' determination of a student's having met lower-division requirements; the policies of four-year institutions elsewhere will simply have to be tested. Indigenous junior college planning would be a first step.

What innovative procedures might be employed by the community college? An institutional research thrust of a magnitude not yet attempted by any educational enterprise would be a basic requisite. Rational curricular decisions would have to rest on deliberately designed, continuing, carefully controlled research conducted by and for the institution itself. The staff members would be forced to accept the responsibility for collecting data about their students and for using the data in particular, predetermined ways. For example, information gathered in regularly obtained alumni-reaction and student-opinion polls would be employed as input for altering procedures. Standardized test-score comparisons would be made, not for purpose of inter-institutional comparison but for changing course objectives and acceptable criterion levels. Experimentation in instructional forms might lead to a greater efficiency of techniques. Curriculum committees could involve non-professional people from the community. But the entire effort would have to rest on a particular rationale, a view of values, or it would lead quickly to irreconcilable issues. There is no such thing as an absolute, unchanging individual and social imperative beyond the level of physical safety and self-perpetuation. Eventually, even practicality — itself a value system — leads to value choices.

Assuming a community-centered approach to be both feasible and practical, an image of a community remains to be developed. The junior college as a medium designed to transform its constituency is a minimal requirement. The construction of a college that "will serve the educational needs of every young man and woman [has] no operative value as policy." (McClellan, 1968, p. 10.) All attempts to build programs on the rationale, "to provide opportunity" quickly reach a dead end. If information about community needs is to be processed and transformed into program determinants, a view of what the city should be like is essential.

THE COMMUNITY

An image of a learning community, one in which all are engaged in increasing everyone's abilities, is not yet widely understood despite the fact that moves are being taken to make education available to all. Education is being sold now as a property — if you have it, you are wealthier than a person who does not. Young people are told, "Go to school and you will earn many thousands of dollars in your lifetime. You will possess culture. You will thus own more than your fellow who does not attend. You will move above him." The touchstones of a community based on property values, on a view of the world as containing a finite number of goods, are being used to sell education. According to this system of assumptions, property owned by one man cannot be used by another except by the owner's leave. If one has it, another cannot—there is one less thing in the world available to him if someone else owns it.

Normative scales in the schools are built on a similar model. A student knows more than another—hence he is better equipped, more likely to attain rewards, has achieved more. Scores are reported on the basis of how far a person deviates from the group mean. The "above average" students go on to higher learning, better jobs; the "below average" are shunted onto alternative tracks. Unfortunately, the model demands that half the students be below average, and, accordingly, less worthy. It is as though there is only so much "goodness" to go around.

In addition to the fact that there is growing evidence to indicate the "lower" half's unwillingness to play the game any longer by those rules (Are riots a form of criticism of the eductional system?), *the model proceeds from a fundamental error about the nature of knowledge and from an unproved view of innate human variability*. Knowledge should not be put into the category of a staple economic good. If it is construed as a form of wealth similar to energy, land, and mineral resources, it is debased. Such a view leads to a desire for acquisition, a form of competition for a finite store of goods; it breeds antagonisms, not learning. A set of data may be called a resource; it may be stored, retrieved, classified, handled, and managed like any other stock. Analytical knowledge, however, is uniquely human; it is basic to the process of transforming data into action, raw bits of information into decisions.

A community in the business of gaining knowledge is a desirable and feasible image. "Knowledge" here means a view of interrelationships among people and information. Knowledge differs in kind from property because one man's possession of knowledge does not diminish the knowledge of another. To the contrary, if one knows and another does not, *both* are the lesser for it. If one teaches another, both gain. Unlike possessions, knowledge is not finite but an infinity of patterns. The more people there are who understand, the better the community is for it. When one person gains knowledge, the holdings of all are increased proportionately. This is a pervasive, fundamental distinction, one which must be kept in view if the junior college is to become a medium for community transformation.

The opening of post-secondary education to all was based on the fact that few jobs were available for high school graduates and that repeated retraining had become necessary for the worker who would keep up. The next step to be undertaken is the transformation of the view of what education *itself* is. The educator who would look on education exclusively as the logical solution to the problem of technological unemployment misses much. Electronics and instant data-transmission, coupled with a rising demand for social equality, have changed the quality and style of life in every community, although curriculum builders continue to act as though they had not. The junior college must stop its attempt to provide a vocationally oriented education for yesterday's society. For regardless of the terms employed, when education is seen as a possession that makes one human better than another, it is vocational in nature.

A new image is essential, one that views a community as a group of people engaged in a process of continuous learning.

Chapter Seventeen

The College Transformed

Institutions ought to be more parsimonious in their claimed
objectives. Colleges and universities are not churches, clinics,
or even parents. They are devices by which a limited number
of skills, insights, and understandings are communicated to
the young in the belief that their possession somehow aids the
individual to become a more effective human being.
— LEWIS B. MAYHEW (1968a.)

BUILDING A CORE CURRICULUM

The college that would serve as a medium to help transform its community needs a curriculum different from those currently in vogue. Yet in
order to be feasible and practical, the proposed changes cannot completely

break with precedent; few junior college administrators would accept such a departure. A form of liberal, general education would meet all requirements. It is feasible because current staff members understand it (at least rudimentarily); it is practical because it stems from a fusion of the liberal arts tradition with current individual and social needs; and it could be structured so that it would serve present communities while helping in the process of community transformation. In addition, it would appeal to many simply because it is innovative.

The community college has never really tried general education. In this context, "general education" is not what is typically pursued in today's community college, even though the words appear among the requirements for most curriculum programs. It is *not* a distribution requirement — six units of English, six units of American studies, etc. — which is often used to lend a "collegiate" tone to what are actually occupational or remedial programs.

A first requirement for the institution inclined to make an attempt toward building a form of general education would be to decide on a definition of the concept. Many interpretations are available; the one that is employed in this book sees general education as that which leads a learner to acquire a sense of social integration, an awareness of himself, and a sense of his place in the matrix of society. He is led to gain value structures on his own through learning of the values held by his contemporaries and historical predecessors and through viewing the culture milieu in which they live and have lived.

General education requires more than exposure to blocks of knowledge arranged by discipline. It must be an interdisciplinary institutional thrust, one that is built on principles of integration, and effect on individuals. It is interdisciplinary for two reasons: first, because "continually new organizations of knowledge require a capacity to draw from several existing fields cutting across the departmental divisions that have grown up around advanced specialties" (Sanford, 1967, p. 20); and, second, because the hard problems of life do not conform to the way academic disciplines have sliced up knowledge and human behavior. It is institution-wide because if departments cannot agree on a core curriculum, it is very unlikely that general education experiences will arise out of the uncoordinated work of individual instructors. People need training in conceptual analysis and in the standards of judgment. (D. Bell, 1966, p. 181.) And they need to gain a capacity for making value judgments — one that can be learned in an institution which is itself founded on judgments of what a community can and should be. General education does not strengthen student values by particular methods of teaching but through its being offered by instructors and institutions which themselves have taken particular definitive positions. (Jacob, 1957, p. 8.)

The type of general education that is frequently favored by advocates — and the type least often found in the community college — is predicated on the belief that there should be a direct relationship between the end behaviors sought by the curriculum designers and what is taught. The objectives of general education — whether a course, a segment of a course, or an entire program — should be made explicit and then deliberate attention given to those experiences demonstrated as being effectual in achieving the purposes. If the goal is to "gain facility in critical thinking," then the course or program should include specifications of what people do who "think critically." Not surprisingly, students enrolled in general education courses, specifically designed to train for critical thinking, do better on measures of that quality than those enrolled in conventional courses. (Fahey and Ball, 1960.)

The same Commission which stated the case that led to the post-World War II expansion of the two-year college argued thus in favor of general education, saying,

> The purposes of general education should be understood in terms of performance, of behavior. . . .
>
> The habit of making this approach to any situation can best be developed by leading the student to apply it at every opportunity in his life on the campus, in solving problems both inside and outside the classroom. (President's Commission, 1948, pp. 50, 57–58.)

Can the community college continue to ignore the concept or, worse, persist in paying it lip service?

Among the many compelling arguments for creating a general education curriculum in the junior college, one stands out — young people of every community need it and they are not likely to get it anywhere else. The one institution to which all can turn, which is available to everyone, is the community junior college. Of all forms of freely available education, it alone can devote itself to the task of leading young adults to the ability to think abstractly, logically, rationally. Vocations, specialties, disciplines can all be taught by other groups. To the extent it dissipates its energies in those peripheral functions, the college fails its community.

Unfortunately, when they speak of a need for "general education," most writers either fail to view ends because they are so busy examining means, or they look on the ends from a philosophical point of view that is difficult to translate into specific program objectives. Rather than as a means of instituting defined change in the community, general education is usually considered another "opportunity" — a curricular offering on the same smorgasbord table with other programs which the college "provides." And if its ends are noted, "general education" is too often vaguely perceived as a means of somehow "preparing total personalities." The utilization of a general-education core curriculum for all students as a deliberate force for community change is rarely considered.

As a concept, general education staggers through the history of the community college. Its feeble state is a serious matter, reflecting many colleges' abrogation of the responsibilities most of them were created to fulfill; this is the result of a failure of confidence and purpose. When general education is not included in a two-year curriculum, the lack may be based on any or all of several assumptions, for example:

(1) College faculties cannot define an appropriate common intellecual experience for students; instead they should delegate that responsibility to others — perhaps to the secondary schools.

(2) The years after secondary school must give exclusive priority to helping students master some specialty. There is no time to offer a broad education to the members of the social strata attending the community college.

(3) The rate and type of psychological developments between the ages of seventeen and twenty-one are not compatible with exploring the forms of human thought. It is the wrong time for young people to establish the habits of critical thinking.

If these statements were true, they would destroy the very basis of the junior college as a unique institution with its own distinct functions.

There is a variety of reasons for the lack of general education. Most relate to the fact that it is much easier for the academician to deal with ideological questions than with organizational difficulties. Many problems associated with establishing general education courses and programs are actually institutional and administrative dilemmas which are confused with arguments about intellectual content. (M. Trow, 1968.) Such problems can and should be overcome.

The college of '79 bases its offerings on a general education core not only because of logic or persuasion but because its image of its community has led it to believe that general education is most appropriate. Thus it builds on a dual rationale: first, that general education is needed, and the college is best suited to provide it; second, its own research efforts have indicated that its community is best served when all citizens have participated in a shared experience. There is common ground for dialogue. Most people are aware of, and tend to act on community problems. *Science, Social Science, Communications,* and *Humanities* make up the core, the means through which people are led to think and feel. They are not ends in themselves.

In the college of '79, students confront situations and work through problems in which value issues are at stake. They are required to take and defend positions on community issues, not alone through bibliographic searches and the writing of papers but by working with people and groups who are attempting to cope with existent problems. In contrast to "role playing," these then become *real* situations of concern to students. They have focus and purpose, and students are required to get firsthand information and to take action.

Students work in hospitals, laboratories, factories, and social agencies. They campaign for candidates of their choice and collect and distribute funds, not as "student activities" but as part of their general-education curriculum requirements. Integration of learning and experience is not merely hoped for — it *is* the program, one which can be articulated into a "coherent intellectual structure that is rationally defensible." (D. Bell, 1968, p. 405.) Students do not take courses that merely talk about community issues. They are in and of their city, helping it to define its goals, moving it toward becoming itself a center of learning.

THE COLLEGE TRANSFORMED

The college of '79 is an example of an institution that has heeded some of the many calls now being made for alternative types of institutions. At present, despite variation in locale, modes of selecting students, and curricular emphasis, "We have as the ideal for colleges and universities variations of only one model. That model is the versity and its variations are the miniversity, the university, and the multiversity." (W. Martin, 1968, pp. 20–21.) No matter how inappropriate this model for the community college is, it exists and is typified in such dimensions as departmentalization, faculty role-orientation, teaching methods, and testing and marking procedures. Regardless of how the junior college attempts to serve its community, it is too often locked into archaic forms by its view of itself as a truncated "versity."

Junior college educators like to speak of the "excellence" of their institutions and of the fact that they are performing tasks different from those undertaken at the university. They say they "teach" as well as or better than instructors at the four-year institutions, and they claim to serve their communities more directly by providing vocational training. But their view of excellence is still tied to the university model. Their claims of value rest on the same *type* of education that has been handed down from the medieval university and the colonial arts college. When the nature and values of this supposed special brand of excellence are not spelled out, they tend in practice to center around what is rewarded in prestige or money. There are no evident alternative criteria of success for the college or its students.

Why this keying on a single model of "excellence"? Why the inability to design alternatives? Do the inconsistencies represent cultural lag, ignorance of the forms different institutions can take, or a formless striving for a prestige which cannot be attained? The deficiencies of educational institutions are being pointed up in a variety of ways, yet despite repeated calls for new approaches, few junior colleges have responded. Will they await a crisis occasioned by withdrawal of financial support, civil disorder, or some other disaster which closes their doors? The philosophical pose of "providing opportunity for all" is belied by existing organizational patterns. And, if opportunity *were* provided for all to enroll in short-sighted, out-dated curricula, what would be really gained?

Colleges must become more distinctive by deciding what they want to do and can manage well, and what they should leave to someone else (Keeton, 1968); but calls for cluster-colleges, house plans, and various modes of structuring student experiences focus on *means* rather than on institutional *ends*. The college that views such means as ends will not be a maximum force for change in its community. To transform a city, intricate and active engagement in education beyond campus boundaries is a minimum first step. The integration of the student's work and learning experiences is a second. A third is institutional commitment to becoming accountable for learning. All must be bounded by a vision of a changed community.

The key to the mode of organization of the college of '79 is in its definition of specific objectives to be attained by its students and its acceptance of accountability for their being achieved. Learning objectives are, in a sense, interim objectives which must be attained if the larger goal of community transformation is to be reached. The college defines ends: for its students in course units; in the core courses and in the programs; and for its community by active participation in master planning. It assumes leadership in helping other agencies (governmental, industrial, social service) plot goals for the community at large. Society desperately needs the types of expertise to be found among people who are dedicated to causing learning.

The college staff has stepped out of the tradition which suggests that esoteric learning and the search for truth are apart from direct involvement in community life. In effect, the college has marked off a ground and determined to define ends for itself and the community that supports it. Every facet of its organization interacts with the main questions, "What are we trying to do?" and "What should our community be like?" Excuses labeled, "We would do it but funds aren't available"; "Our students are not real college material"; and "We gave them the option, sorry if they were unmotivated to change their behavior" — these have been abandoned. Defining ends and using instruction to move people toward them are the college's main purposes; it does not allow its staff to escape that responsibility.

The college defines ends for its students because, by so doing, it can phase in their education toward its image of the learning community. It holds itself accountable for their learning because this, not sorting, is the function of a college. It continually assesses the effects of its own endeavors because only thus can it modify its processes with any degree of validity.

Community service in the college of '79 is not a grab bag of short courses and entertainment activities. It is a process of leading the total community toward defining goals for itself. What medical facilities are needed in the city? The college designs a survey and its students help conduct it. Are zoning laws in need of revision? The college and its students help plot trends. What is an appropriate level for recreational facilities? What types of neighborhod action committees are desirable? Staff and students alike, the college is involved. What does a community need that a college can uniquely provide? Custodial care of the young or help in defining social goals? The college has a ready answer.

The ties between the schools of today and the college of '79 may be found in such commonalities as the fact that both operate on campuses, offer courses, have defined curricula, and employ as instructors trained adult members of the community. Even the differences are more in degree than kind. Instructional goals are comparable, but in the college of '79, they have been refined into specific objectives. Community services have gained direction and focus in the staff's assistance in community planning. Instructional services have been extended as faculty members help industrial and other groups set up training programs (similar to consulting activities practiced by university professors). Nothing is so at variance that feasible transition steps cannot now begin.

There is no assurance that integration of learning activities with other facets of community life will lead to a "better life," but something must be tried. What is being done now is not working. The community college is stretching its bounds, opening branches, and adding programs, but because archaic forms dictate current functions, its impact is minimal. When all is attempted, focus cannot be brought to bear so that much of anything is achieved. More and more tasks must eventually lead to splintering and reforming, or the institution will become static, paralyzed by its own attempt to accomplish inchoate goals without the requisite inner vision.

The college of '79 is not the only way to structure an institution that differs from existing models. Another possibility is a college in which there are no formal courses or grades; instead, students are allowed to participate for a year in a variety of experiences. In this institution, the junior college's custodial function would be acknowledged and justified by demonstrating that an older student is better able to achieve "college-level" success than is a recent high school graduate. The desirability of a break in the straight line, sixteen-year sequence of classroom education can be well documented — the best evidence for it lies in the examination of the post-war college experiences of the millions of students who had their formal schooling interrupted by service in the armed forces during World War II. Why not a college built on the custodial model? Would it then be other than "college"? Would that matter?

What is being proposed in this book, however, is a junior college with a focus on learning, on instruction as a discipline. The model represents a turning away from vaguely defined ends, a feasible alternative to a plethora of activities leading no one knows where. Instruction is the core; the city is the campus. The curriculum has been cut to four courses, but the community is well served. There is a two-way flow between college and city; all relates to instruction as a central process. The college in the city and the focus on learning are manifestations of a thrust toward a learning community. The junior college is one, but not the only, medium enhancing the transformation.

Forward-looking junior college educators may wish to adopt some characteristics of the college of '79 and not others. The core curriculum may appeal to those who recognize that curricular boundaries cannot be stretched infinitely. Others may want to reduce peripheral functions and focus on demonstrating the effects of instruction through research as a way of better serving students and of gaining long-sought identity. A different form of community service, one constructed on a type of outreach, may appeal to still others. Any of the separate features may be introduced into existing schools. One which *all* should try, however, is the process of defining outcomes. No other single change is likely to have such pervasive consequences.

Part Four

Defined
Outcomes

Chapter Eighteen

The Concept

A model institution built on and committed to a specific educational form is depicted in Part One of this text. The underlying rationale for that pattern is a defined-outcomes approach to curriculum and instruction — an encompassing concept suited not only to the college of '79 but to many other types of educational situations. In fact, the use of defined outcomes has something to offer any instructor or administrator, regardless of whether or not his whole institution is pointed in that direction. One need not be part of a college of '79 to work toward specific ends.

In every college, some educational policies are accepted, and others are rejected or ignored. Selections are made within a philosophical context whether a philosophy is explicitly stated or can only be deduced. Each choice — even a determination *not* to adopt a consistent rationale — is a value-laden decision. In Birenbaum's words (1968, p. 55), unless an institution "simply doesn't think about what it teaches (and many don't), then it must make choices, the consequences of which are not neutral."

A philosophy is a view of ends, of ultimate objectives. However, since most schools make little conscious effort to construct goals which stem from the consideration of predictable outcomes, philosophical timidity or vacuity is the prevailing norm. The most recurrent criticism made of American college and university programs is that they lack definite aim. (Stecklein, 1960, p. 268.) A form of this aimlessness is apparent in efforts as broad as state master plans that fail to postulate the effects of the institutions they propose to build, and as narrow as the frequently directionless classroom activities of a single instructor. The ends are too often left in the void.

To the degree that a college fails to maintain a consistent viewpoint regarding the purposes and directions of its efforts, its practices vacillate with the changing wind of fashion. And the directionless college influences its community only as much as the changeable zephyr affects the undulations of the sea. Educational reforms very rarely cause — rather, they result from — altered social perspective. (Hutchins, 1968, p. 126.) The irresolute institution cannot lead.

There are many forms of educational goals that can be classified so that purpose may be discerned. For example, *structural* goals refer to the organization and housing of the schools; *process* goals are concerned with the people served and the programs designed and operated to serve them. Goals which refer to *effort* expended can be used to apportion finances or allocate staff time for various uses. The degree to which these common kinds of goals are attained can be readily assessed. If an objective requires that a particular number of buildings be constructed with certain pieces of equipment in them, it is achieved when the physical plant is so expanded. Similarly, process outcomes may be appraised easily; there are many examples of state college systems in which predetermined numbers of students are enrolled and of individual colleges which have admitted certain percentages of their constituent populations — thereby fulfilling projected goals. Relative effort may be assessed by examining the counselor–student ratio, teacher–student ratio, proportions of funds allocated to certain functions, and similar matters.

But assessment of attainment is only peripherally related to a school's educational philosophy. Goals inevitably reflect values; underlying all are assumptions of worth. If a system's goals can be grouped exclusively under the headings of "process," "structure," or "effort," then the system must particularly value those forms. The extent to which such goals are attained thus becomes a measure of the system's "goodness." It is readily apparent, however, that "structure," "process," and "effort" are severely limited categories through which to view the purposes of education. There is no guarantee that a structure or process actually brings about the learning toward which it is ostensibly pointed. There is little evidence to suggest a positive correlation between the amount of institutional effort and student learning. Yet effort, process, and structure are the ends consciously sought by most educators who in so doing ignore, or at best assume, the problematic connection between those ends and what should be their ultimate aims — student learning and community change. In short, those who hold exclusive views of the *means* of education as the *ends* of their efforts are victims of a philosophical sterility that is in fact the most pervasive shortcoming in the junior college field today.

Defined outcomes is an ends-oriented concept. It means that the college spells out in advance — and accepts accountability for — the changes it expects to produce in its students, and often in its community. According to this concept, schools are media designed to cause changes in people and communities, and they are also uniquely qualified to define the direction of those changes. Thus the school is at once a setter of ends and a medium designed to move people to achievement of those ends. Strict adherence to such a rationale affects all institutional practices and influences the work of everyone connected with the college.

In an institution using a defined-outcomes approach, goals are stated in such words as: "The student will learn to . . ." rather than "The college will provide . . ."; "The community will become . . ." rather than "The college offers opportunity for . . . ." Instructional designs require that: "The student will be able to . . ." rather than "The instructor will discuss . . . ." One approach depicts *ends*, the other *means;* one defines *product*, the other *process.*

Defined outcomes is, then, a philosophy and a set of principles. It is *itself* a process that guides institutional activities through a focus on ends. Structure and effort are viewed but only as they serve to enhance learning and community change, not as ends in themselves. Because it is basic in instructional design, the concept of accountability falls within the defined-outcomes rubric. Without accountability there is little to prevent instruction from becoming aimless activity in which staff members engage for various purposes that stem from their own predilections. With it, instruction becomes a set of sequences that *must* lead learners to certain capabilities or attitudes — otherwise the sequences are changed methodically.

No peculiar definitions are included within a defined-outcomes concept: "Learning" is seen as changed capability for, or tendency toward, acting in particular ways; "education" is a consequential (as opposed to a theoretical or formalistic) process of changing; "instruction" is a deliberate sequencing of events so that learning occurs. All are common-language definitions to which most educators adhere. A major difference between defined outcomes and other philosophical views, however, is in the degree of specificity demanded and/or tolerated.

In order to make a defined-outcomes concept operable, objectives must be specified in terms of what will happen to students, and instructional sequences designed to lead to those ends must be devised. However, the implications of the approach go far beyond the specification of objectives, implications which reach out in time and space beyond the single classroom or school term. Some effects are foreseeable, others are not. The dynamics of a social system mandate that change in one part brings known and unknown changes in others; but the implications of failing to change are no less pervasive. If the community college accepts defined outcomes and instructional accountability as its basic philosophy, change will occur. If it does not, change will occur nevertheless. The choice for the institution is not between changing and not changing but of taking on the task of methodically causing student learning or consciously rejecting it. It must do one or the other.

If learning—human change—is to be fostered by the schools, it must have direction, purpose, and design. Schools now find it difficult to justify their endeavors merely in terms of providing opportunities for students to engage in activities for reasons unknown. Schools have always had vague goals; those goals must now be refined so that they can be better understood by all people concerned with higher education. Instruction in the college environment is supposed to lead students to become responsible citizens, to have them gain spiritual and moral values, to help them acquire appreciation of their cultural heritage. Before any attempt can be made to determine if these attitudes and values have been learned, they must be defined. And central to the definition is the behavior exhibited under specified conditions by the students involved—behavior that translates into specific instructional objectives.

Without objectives, the community college may or may not continue to persevere. Perhaps it will continue to aggrandize itself by trumpeting the virtue of its structure and its processes. If on the other hand, concrete objectives are specified, the extent of the resulting change cannot be predicted, because no community college has wholly structured itself upon a defined-outcomes approach. However, the dynamics of change in American society and the underlying philosophy of the community college seem to demand that at least some of the institutions make the attempt.

Chapter Nineteen

Specific Objectives: History, Definitions, Examples

If an institution is to be organized totally within a defined-outcomes framework, certain practices in administration, student affairs, instruction, and other common activities are essential. One of these is the specification of instructional objectives in terms of student learning.

"The student will understand the differences between democracy and authoritarianism." "The student will be able to write effective compositions." "The student will appreciate fine music and recognize its relevance to his life." These statements — and hundreds of similar genre — may be found in college catalogs, course syllabi, textbooks, instructors' manuals, and other paraphernalia associated with the practice of teaching in the junior college. They represent *generalized outcomes* of the educational process. Hence, in a defined-outcomes approach, they are *goals* from which specific objectives may be derived.

Similarly classified as goals are statements such as, "The student will understand (appreciate, relate to . . .)" because they point to *constructs*. They represent assumptions about the student's state of mind. Although the terms are often used as though they had clear referents, it is actually impossible to get agreement on the constructs alone. Each one must be translated into overt behavior before the extent to which the surmised quality is present can be determined; each must be refined into one or more objectives.

When does the student "understand"? Any of several measures may be devised to answer this question. For example, we may be satisfied that the student understands when he says he does; we may accept that he understands if he was in the room when the principle was explained by someone who does understand it; we may say that he understands if he answers questions he could not answer if he did not understand; we may assess the way he conducts his affairs and then postulate the degree of his understanding. In each case, and in others that might be mentioned, a different degree of confidence may be placed on the measure of the student's understanding. Each statement is itself an educational goal. The goal may require that students say they understand, sit in a room, answer questions, or arrange their lives in particular ways; these are defined outcomes.

The difference between generalized goals of the sort mentioned and specific instructional objectives are that objectives restrict to observable phenomena the definition of what is to happen to the student. They allow only for statements which particularize students' actions, to be performed under certain conditions with certain degrees of accuracy. Objectives thus move defined outcomes as a general philosophy into a concrete sphere and allow for several considerations regarding teaching and learning which cannot be determined from the rationale alone.

HISTORY

Even though the practice of specifying instructional objectives in terms of student behaviors has not been widely accepted, it has a long history. It was proposed by Thorndike at the beginning of this century and has been found since in many forms of education, both in and out of public schools. In the early 1930's, the University of Chicago experimented with "credit by examination" and "advanced placement" and realized quickly that it was first necessary to determine what competencies were to be demonstrated by students.

The definition of particular learning outcomes has been well established in military and industrial education programs since World War I, but the deliberate specification of objectives has never enjoyed great popularity within the realm of public education. Many reasons may be advanced for this situation, not the least of which is the fact that specific objectives are not evidently needed unless schools are operating within a defined-outcomes rationale. Without the philosophical base, objectives seem purposeless. It is not necessary for them to be specified in order that an assessment of structure, process, or effort be completed.

Several other reasons may be advanced for colleges' failing to specify objectives. When an effort is made to write objectives without a total institutional commitment, attempts to translate general school goals into specific student behaviors typically suffer from triviality. Even the Eight Year Study, a massive project that attempted to develop objectives for programs of general education, was criticized because of the apparent superficiality of the objectives it examined. It attempted to break down goals like "Understanding of cultural heritage" and "Appreciation for democratic processes" into such behaviors as students attending concerts, reading books, and voting. Furthermore, though it was difficult enough to find causal relationships between school programs and actions taken by students in subsequent years, it was even more difficult to make deliberate recommendations for program modification based on the results of the study. (American Education Fellowship, 1942–43.) Values, which are easily stated, are extremely difficult to define and translate into behavior. And even when they are defined it is almost impossible to relate value structures to specific educational programs. (Jacob, 1957.) The difficulty is both cause and effect of the philosophical vacuum in which the schools labor.

Nevertheless, specific objectives for school programs have remained a fond hope of instructional theorists. The concept's current modest vogue is a result of several forces which have impinged on the schools in recent years. These include the attempt to construct replicable media which would supplement live instruction; the incursion of industry into the educational process; students' and communities' refusal to accept schools unquestioningly; and the rise of mass media as an educational force so powerful it is as yet only dimly understood.

The programming boom of the early 1950's was one force that pointed up the vagueness of educational ends. A prime requirement for any replicable instructional sequence is that it lead to one or more deliberate objectives. By definition it is impossible to plan an autoinstructional program without first specifying the outcomes desired — the behavior toward which the program must lead the learner.

Programs were sold — oversold — fifteen years ago. They were to individualize instruction, make every student his own teacher, make operating the schools more economical, release teachers to do creative tutoring, and so on ad absurdum. Programming failed to achieve the ends its most vocal adherents claimed it would, but it helped turn attention once again to what instruction in the schools was actually supposed to accomplish. In fact, until programming appeared and was forced to defend itself, relatively little attention was given to the extent to which the schools were actually meeting their pronounced objectives. It was contended that machine programs could not teach pupils to be "creative," for example, but few had thought to ask whether the traditional procedures had produced this effect — or indeed what "creative" behavior was. (W. Trow, 1963, pp. 139–140.)

Another intrusive force was the educational "package" designed, constructed, and put into practice by industrial corporations operating outside the schools. In the late 1950's, industry began to seize on media of demonstrable relevance and effect, and to develop not mere texts (as it had for generations) but complete instructional programs, and in some cases entire curricula. Total instructional sequences were produced outside the schools to do many specialized tasks of education. During the 1960's, Job Corps, Head Start, and other governmental projects were built and operated extramurally. Curricula — complete with packaged tapes, films, workbooks, and tests — were designed and offered for sale in and out of the schools. Instructional designers in the employ of publishers concerned themselves with the analysis of tasks, the characteristics of students, and the process of moving learners from one to another state of subject-matter competence. Their efforts made deep inroads on what historically had been the domain of the schools.

Students have pressed in their own way for the form of honesty represented by specific objectives. At least in part, student "activism" and "dropout" are related. Both represent a growing tendency on the part of the young to refuse to accept uncritically the paths and patterns set down for them by their elders both in and out of school. They often become militant and demonstrate their disaffection by vociferous demands or by withdrawing from the entire enterprise. Simultaneously pleading and protesting, they say, in effect, "We want to know why we are here, and you do not seem to be qualified to tell us."

Attitudinal changes in youth may be related to the impact of the mass media. Perhaps Marshall McLuhan (1964) exaggerated only slightly when he said, "A child interrupts his education when he goes to school." In contrast to television itself and to promises flaunted by advertisers employing other media, schools operate largely on a pattern of delayed gratification. The student must listen to the lecture today so that he can pass the test tomorrow, so that he can pass the course next week, so that he may complete the program and obtain a degree next year, so that he may obtain a job and "the good life" some years hence. That theme is antithetical to the immediate rewards offered by all the educational forces beyond the walls of the classroom. With short-term, specific objectives, learning tasks take on an immediacy that students are not now finding in school.

DEFINITIONS AND EXAMPLES

Objectives are the link between the concept of defined outcomes and the practice of instruction. The process of specifying objectives is applicable to any area, field, subject, discipline, body of knowledge, or desired teaching outcome. It is applicable whether an institution is expected to provide liberal, general, technical, or eclectic education. The ends specified may refer to appreciations, understandings, attitudes, skills, and awarenesses. A rule of thumb: if an educational purpose can be defined, it may be cast in the form of an objective.

A distinction must be made here between goals and objectives. Of course, they are both statements about the purposes of action. But in this context a goal is a basic aim — a value-construct, the achievement of which can be assessed only in inferential terms. An objective, on the other hand, is a concrete criterion of achievement, measurable in terms of overt behavior. In educational practice, both are necessary.

To ask an instructor to abandon sight of the goal in order to concentrate on an objective is to invite triviality and purposelessness. (Tyler, 1964.) Conversely, exclusive focus on goals with no attempt to refine them into objectives leads inevitably to aimlessness and a failure to understand—hence to realize—intent. Objectives act as a communication device; they are stated in terms which have common referents; goal statements refer to the society's values and assumptions about the aims of education.

The relationship between goals and objectives is logically tenuous, because there is no way to span the gap between spiritual values and physical realities—between mental constructs and overt behavior. What behavior, for example, can guarantee a student's appreciation of Elizabethan literature? Even if he checks new books out of the library every day, he may be doing it to impress his girlfriend. Similarly, though the achievement of a proper objective is easy to ascertain, there is no way to guarantee that the individual student's attainment is the result of any specific instructional experience. Nevertheless, objectives may act as testable hypotheses about differing instructional methods, providing the criteria by which learning is concretely measured. It is the goals that suggest which of these hypotheses will be formulated and tested.

Objectives may be classified in various ways. They may call for simple "recall" or "recognition" to be demonstrated by the student or they may require complex behaviors. They may ask for manifestations of what is typically called "attitude change," or they may point to evidence of "skill." But classification aside, regardless of the type or "level" of behavior specified, the form of the objective remains constant. The same pattern may be used to define objectives in any sphere. Similarly, regardless of the time expended or the instructional designs required for a learner to attain an objective, the way the objective is written remains the same.

A specific objective must meet certain requisites. First, it must derive from a goal — the attainment of a student's state of mind presumed to underlie the designated behavior or action. The objective itself must then be written so that it includes three parts: a *task* (activity, behavior), to be performed by a learner under a particular set of *conditions* or circumstances, to a specified degree of accuracy — a *criterion* or standard. The student's learning objective is stated as though it pertained to one learner only ("The student will . . ."); the specification of numbers or percentages of students who will in fact display the designated ability or tendency is a teaching objective.

Several taxonomic schemes have been devised to classify objectives according to various hierarchies. Currently, the most popular is proposed in Bloom's *Taxonomy* (1956); this system defines six categories of objectives in the Cognitive Domain, each with several subcategories. (The Domain refers to the mind-set inferred from the overt action specified in the objective.)

The hierarchy postulated by the *Taxonomy* is one of relative complexity; it assumes that each more complex task depends on a prior ability to perform a specified task of lesser complexity. The categories range from "knowledge" (recall of data) through "understanding," "application," "analysis," and "synthesis," to "evaluation" — considered to be the highest order of task in the Cognitive Domain. An example of an objective at the simplest level:

Task: Given a list of any fifteen items from the attached list of one hundred, the student will match them with a given list of definitions.
Conditions: No references permitted; time: twenty minutes.
Criterion: One hundred per cent accuracy.

The task required is simply that the student match terms with given definitions. Note that there is nothing contained in the objective itself which suggests that he must have learned those terms in class — he may have known them when he entered. The objective simply states exactly what he must demonstrate an ability to do and does not include—although it may certainly imply—a statement of instructional procedures required to move him to that state of mind. An objective at a more complex level would be:

> Task: The student will prepare a paper in which he elaborates on the concept of ———. Paper will include explication of the following points ——— and will be submitted in accordance with prescribed fcrm.
> Conditions: Outside of class, using all necessary references.
> Criterion: Eight of possible twelve points included; no deviation from form.

In this objective, the student must not only know terms, he must be able to apply them and weave them together in an original communication. That complex task obviously requires prior or concurrent mastery of lesser abilities.

A point often overlooked in the specification of objectives is that each one must be attained on an "either/or" basis. The objective itself should include no provision for partial attainment. What is often called the "quality" of a response is usually a response which more nearly approximates a model of desired communication; a response of lesser quality is one that deviates from the model. If the objective is stated properly, there should be little ambiguity about determining whether or not it has been attained. The latter point holds even when objectives call for tasks to be performed which must be judged "subjectively." For example:

> Task: The student will write a composition which I, on the day I read it, deem to be imaginative and creative.
> Conditions: Outside of class, using any necessary references.
> Criterion: The instructor's determination.

In this case, the instructor has made his own determination of worth an integral part of the objective. The form of the objective has not changed — there is still a task to be performed under a certain set of conditions with a specified degree of accuracy — but the criterion has gained a different referent. Instead of a pre-set scale against which to assess the response made by the student, the instructor has kept the scale in his mind and agreed to judge only after the results are in. It is still a specific measurable objective and, incidentally, one which calls for a rather complex set of abilities — not the least of which is guessing how the instructor will react to the work.

Another classification scheme for objectives postulates an Affective Domain (Krathwohl *et al.*, 1964), with scales ranging from "awareness" through "responding," "being committed to," "organizing," and "being characterized by." However, this classificatory scheme has not been as widely employed as the Bloom taxonomy primarily because most objectives actually specified in schools call for students to learn cognitive skills. Instructors typically have difficulty in translating "affect" into overt activities to be performed by students. In large measure, the difficulty stems from the fact that action taken on the basis of attitude, to be genuine, must be voluntary; hence, "affective" objectives do not lend themselves well to measurement in the classroom. Even so, objectives may be set to measure students' behavior outside the classroom. For example:

> Task: The student shall read three books of contemrary fiction before the end of the course.
> Conditions: His own volition.
> Criterion: He shall do it.

Similarly, they may be written so that their attainment occurs at a later date:

> Task: When he transfers to a four-year institution, the student will major in ————.
> Conditions: Voluntary.
> Criterion: He shall do it.

The goal from which the objective stems is that the student be so stimulated by the course or program for which the objective was written that he "becomes characterized by" a feeling for the discipline. The depth of his commitment is evidenced by the fact that he has become willing to devote several years of his life to its study. Another example of an "affective" objective:

> Task: Prior to each general election over the next ten years, the student shall campaign for a candidate by working in his office, or by distributing campaign materials.
> Conditions: Voluntarily.
> Criterion: Not less than forty hours per election.

The goal from which such an objective stems would be that the student recognizes and acts on his responsibilities as a citizen. It is little more difficult to gather evidence of students' attaining these types of objectives than it is to assess their performance on classroom quizzes.

In many courses, it is desirable to plot objectives in sequence — according to the taxonomies or other models — so that abilities prerequisite to the performance of more complex tasks may be checked along the way. Thus, before asking a student to produce a research paper, it might be desirable to check his knowledge of terminology, understanding of concepts and principles, ability to apply rules, ability to analyze readings in the subject area, understanding of library usage, and so on. Each subordinate ability can be specified in an objective, and the attainment of such interim objectives can be assessed. In that way instruction can be deliberately planned. The instructor can require that each lesser ability be attained before a student enters the instructional sequence designed to lead him to more complex tasks.

Learning objectives may be further classified as "process" and "product." A process objective is one that requires a student to master and employ a particular pattern of approach to certain situations. For example:

> Task: When given any pair of two-digit numbers to multiply, the student will employ the ——— method.

A "product objective" would simply require the student to come up with a solution regardless of the method employed.

In the term "process objective" the word "process" may be misleading. The confusion is particularly apparent in the current emphasis on "discovery learning" in the elementary schools. One kind of event has to do with learning *by* discovery (process); the other event has to do with learning to discover or to make continuing inquiry (behavioral states). One is a learning method, the others are mental sets which are manifest in the ability to make discoveries and the tendency to inquire. The objective is a desired behavioral state; the process of attaining that state is that which is promoted and guided by an instructional sequence. (Glaser, 1966a.) States of mind can, of course, be written as goals and then translated into objectives.

Regardless of how they are classified or interpreted, objectives function variously as building blocks for curriculum, statements of particularized purpose, beginning points for planning instruction, communication devices between instructors and students (as well as other interested people), and hypotheses against which varied instructional forms may be tested. However, care must be taken lest objectives become trivial — it is easier to write objectives which demand simple recall than to specify the order of complex activities. On the other hand, tasks that demand a high level of analytical sophistication must not be specified to the exclusion of objectives which assess prerequisite abilities. In such cases, the likelihood of students' failing to attain the complex abilities may be increased.

Nothing in the formulation or communication of objectives demands that all instructors use similar sets. The process itself does not require commonality of purpose between sections of a course, between courses, or between programs. Whether or not instructors use objectives in common is a question of a different sort — one that depends upon the orientation of the school or of the instructors concerned. Whether or not objectives are communicated to students in advance of instruction is similarly a different type of question. In the case of objectives which demand voluntary, outside-of-class performance (such as those which specify students' attending community events), objectives should not be communicated to students in advance lest the voluntary condition be subverted. Speaking generally, however, there may be no better way for students, instructors, and the community at large to view the true ends of education than through perusal of the specific objectives of the institution and of each segment within it.

Chapter Twenty

Shaping Instruction

Education is a branch of knowledge, an applied science dedicated to the realization of certain ends that most citizens deem to have social value. As such, it should be concerned with ways of *deliberately* effecting changes in its clients. (Ausubel, 1953.) All facets of the system should point toward just that goal.

But philosophically, American education has failed to accept the implications of the premise that learning does not just happen, that it can be and is shaped by conditions external as well as internal to the learner. Some hold that learning can be caused — predictably and demonstrably, but others act on a view that considers almost exclusively the learners' innate tendencies. The fact that the precise nature of learning *objectives* is open to question should not be allowed to cloud the issue. The root cause of a dilemma and much controversy within educational structures is that some believe learning can be methodically effected, while others — those who primarily seek better sorting devices — do not.

INSTRUCTION

Within the framework of education as a formal process is the discipline of instruction. Instruction is the application of treatments in a sequence designed to move people from one set of tendencies or competencies to another — in other words, to cause them to learn. If a set of experiences is *not* designed to do that, it may act as an "educational opportunity" in some broad sense, but it is not instruction per se. Because it has no definitive ends, it does not fit the definition.

Instruction is effected by ordering a subject — any group of skills, facts, or ideas — and making its constituent parts apparent. It is a process of leading the learner through a series of statements and restatements of a problem in order to increase his ability to "grasp, transform, and transfer what he is learning." Ordering stimuli is important to instruction because "the sequence in which a learner encounters materials within a domain of knowledge affects the difficulty he will have in achieving mastery." (Bruner, 1966, p. 49.)

Instruction generally, then, is the deliberate manipulation of a learner's environment. Conditions external to the learner are altered, structured, and shaped in order to bring about desired change. Learning may (and often does) occur even in a haphazardly manipulated environment; however, it has not resulted from instruction. Instruction occurs only when there is pattern and reason to the changes in conditions. Patterns may be arranged with respect to any of several principles — sequence, repetition (allowing for learners to practice the desired end behavior), or in accordance with logical categories. In every case, some rationale must be employed in instructional design if it is to be other than a set of unintentional experiences.

Instruction must have ends, outcomes, objectives, or it cannot be designed. Thus the specification of the desired end actions taken — or evidence of attitudes to be acquired — by the learner is a first step. Although the ends point to the means within the instructional process, ends also may *become* means because, when objectives are set, the conditions of learning are inevitably altered; the activities of instructors and learners are affected by the objectives themselves.

If there were some superordinate agency preparing objectives and testing students on their attainment without communicating the objectives or the results to instructors and students, objectives might have little influence on classroom processes. But in American higher education, instructors are at once setters of ends and designers of means. This holds true in all cases except those in which an instructor is assigned to a group of students and told to monitor their progress through a set of programmed texts. In such circumstances, the texts in fact become the instructors; the "teachers" become proctors.

Because of the way American junior colleges are organized, ends and means are designed by people who typically work in isolation from each other. Accordingly, ends may be broad or narrow, valuable or worthless, depending on the orientation of each individual. Means may or may not be related to the ends desired. In short, because of the nature of the system, the relationships between ends and means are often uncoordinated and instruction is a haphazard enterprise.

As compensation for aimless instruction, much seeking and searching behavior is exhibited by both teachers and students. Instructors seek ways of maintaining students' attention, of explaining and reifying "content," and of assessing the extent of student learning. Students seek instructors whose approach feels comfortable, whose methods of presentation, style, sequencing, and pacing fit into integrated wholes. Instruction and the learning process are far from being exact sciences, and much of what happens to students and to instructors in the classroom is *ad hoc;* it is introduced, warped, changed and iterated to fit the moment. The direction of the change may be the result of dynamic interactions between instructors and students; however, it should not be directionless or unpremeditated.

Specific objectives can serve to bring order—but not rigidity—into the instructional process. When long-range objectives are set, and also objectives to be attained by the end of a course built to support them, direction is inherent. The instructor working within such a framework can build—for himself or in association with his colleagues—interim or intermediate objectives that guide activities in bits as large or as minute as he wishes. Objectives may be used as lesson plans with attainment-checking noted on a daily or even narrower basis. Or, depending on the concepts to be learned and on the instructor's tendencies, a unit may be treated as a unified whole with the objective being held as a constant to be assessed only at the end of several class sessions. Much flexibility in the use of specified objectives is possible.

Variance in approach might also be taken into account by students in their own search for compatible courses. Some students might find that for them, interim or short-term objectives have a liberating effect. They would be drawn along with each requisite ability carefully checked on a daily basis. Such students might rebel against being plunged into a two-week or longer unit in which they would be required to sort relevant clues for themselves. Other students might find that small steps specified by instructors were a distraction. Their tendencies would lead them to listen to lectures or participate in discussions by letting their thoughts range freely over the principles or concepts being treated. Short-term objectives — with their attendant frequent testing sessions — would represent an annoyance for such learners. By arranging a variety of instructional designs (one possible pattern was outlined in Chapter Three), the college can allow students to choose. Thus, this approach considers individuality of learning style but only within an instructional framework.

Currently, instructional plans are often somewhat less than deliberate. Not only is the student ignorant of how instruction is designed, but the instructor himself is often unaware of his pattern of procedure. Because of this, instructors must make frequent adjustments. Accordingly, their preferences for small classes may be based on a firmer reason than their oft-expressed desire to "know each student as an individual." As McKeachie (1968) outlined it:

> One of the real advantages of small discussion classes over large lectures or television is the amount and specificity of feedback the teacher receives about who is responding how at a particular time . . . . [The teacher's] ability to plan optimally for student education depends upon continuous feedback from the students. As classes become larger, the opportunities for such . . . moment to moment shifting of one's educational strategy are reduced.

Thus the common plea for small classes may well be related to instructional strategy rather than to a cult of personality.

In some cases, instructors constantly modify procedures in accordance with student responses. Modification may be, and often is, unconscious — part of the "art" of good teaching. When used as short-range, deliberate checks on student understandings, specific objectives can aid in moving a portion of the "art" into the realm of the consciously managed; they can thus point to instructional designs which are themselves means leading to broader objectives as ends. Objectives then become part of the process of shaping perceptions and manipulating the environment — the process which is itself instruction.

Interim objectives or short-range, subordinate tasks should not be viewed necessarily as describing the individual routes all students must take in gaining the relatively complex end objectives. In a situation in which short-range objectives are specified, a single learner may skip one or more of the steps because of previously learned generalizable skills or because his own mode of approach allows him to seize on complex tasks without going through intermediate steps. But for most learners, some less-complex tasks can help in moving toward mastery of the desired terminal objective. The assumption on which interim objectives are plotted is that many learning difficulties may be ascribed not to "motivation" or other unseen constructs, but to the fact that tasks prerequisite to the end ability had never been mastered. Objectives thus become links in the instructional process itself. For the learners, they are guideposts; for the teachers, they provide short-term knowledge of results.

NEEDED STUDY

Although there have been few attempts to examine the effects of objectives on instructional processes, experiments can be devised. However, researchers must be aware that objectives act as both means and ends. Short-range experiments, limited by the rigors of classical design, are not easily fit to the use of objectives in instructional programs because, once outcomes have been defined for an experiment to test the effects of objectives on teaching and learning, the conditions of the instructional process have been changed. Nevertheless, the effects of the use of objectives should be studied in order to shed light on research problems like the following:

—Communicate objectives to students; control with randomly selected groups of students not given objectives; use the same instructor. Is there a difference in learning?

—Have selected instructors define objectives, conduct classes. Rate them by trained raters. Is there a difference between perceived performance of instructors who have specified objectives as compared to that of a control group of instructors who have not?

—In situations where objectives have been specified and communicated to the students in advance of instruction, are the students less inclined to drop out of the course? That is, having perceived the end goal early in the course, are they more likely to stay?

—After participating in a course in which objectives were clearly specified and communicated, does the student tend to perform better in subsequent courses in the same and other areas in which objectives are specified? Does he tend to perform better comparatively in traditional instructional situations?

—After having participated in a series of courses in which objectives were specified, does the shape of a student's scores change on a test of general cognitive skills as compared to a matched partner who has taken his courses in the traditional fashion? Does his overall score on a general-skills test improve?

—Can psychological tests identify students who will achieve more in classes in which objectives are specified and those who prefer to "experience" and thus order their own learning patterns?

—When objectives are specified and communicated to a student in advance of instruction, does it tend to place a ceiling on his learning? Would he have achieved more had the program objectives remained vague or not been communicated to him?

—When objectives are specified and communicated by an instructor and accepted by the student, does the student's achievement in other courses taken concurrently become higher? That is, has he been set free to attend to his other studies?

The operations described are commonly subsumed under the term "research," but in a college operating under a defined-outcomes rationale — the college of '79, for example — they would be included as part of the instructional process itself.

In order to give the specification of objectives a fair test, colleges are needed in which outcomes are defined, follow-ups are made, and instruction is so arranged that objectives are the core of the instructional process. Needed, too, is a breadth of commitment that the field has not yet seen; this means not simply talk about specifying objectives, but a whole college that is structured around them. Consensual commitments to overall junior college functions and philosophy now exist in most institutions. There are even commitments to certain media with entire colleges structured around audio-tutorial or around dialogue instruction. However, before we can tell the effects of specifying objectives — in a sense the unification of ends and means — we need a junior college committed to the process.

The empirical validation of propositions is necessary to turn an applied discipline into a science by deliberately associating its means and ends. Given the current state of junior college education, however, it is more likely that individual instructors will specify objectives for their courses than that a whole institution will be committed to test the value of defined-outcomes instruction. And the individual instructors will be motivated more by rhetoric than by scientific dedication. Innovations, especially those of such potential far-reaching effect as specific objectives, are rarely introduced or maintained on their merits.

Objectives should be used — whether or not experimentation is conducted — if for no other reason than for their demonstrable effects on instructional planning. Currently, the form is applicable to a wide range of educational situations. In an individualized instruction system, each student may get his own set of objectives and proceed at his own pace. In those institutions that insist on maintaining grade-marks as a student-sorting mechanism, differential objectives can be set for A's, B's, etc. (Burns, 1968.) The same is true for lock-step programs in which students achieve or drop off a defined track at specified intervals. Eventually, objectives can form the heart of an approach to instruction in which the institution brings predetermined percentages of its students to the ability or tendency to act in particular ways, as in the paradigm college of '79. In any event, objectives are so basic to instructional design that they must eventually be used in some capacity by all instructional planners.

Chapter Twenty-One

Objectives
and
Learning Theory

Educational theories are attempts at explaining the process of teaching and learning; objectives are specifications for defined behavior changes. Nevertheless, many ties may be found between the definition and communication of specific objectives and those broad areas of learning theory subsumed under the two headings, cognitive theory and stimulus–response theory. In addition, objectives relate to various concepts and strategies which are on the way toward becoming a theory of instruction.

Because it is not the purpose of Chapter Twenty-One to examine learning theories in detail, they will be sketched only for purposes of identification. Cognitive theory includes elements of dynamism, general organizational patterns, and gestalt theory. Stimulus–response theory is that which is usually associated with classical and operant conditioning, rote learning, and associationism. Cognitive theory recognizes elements of general consciousness, insight, and intuitiveness which cannot be explained by known connections among learned events, whereas stimulus–response theory views the mind as changing in reaction to connections built up through series of trials and associations.

Certain principles are held in common by both blocks of theory, but variations in acceptance of particular concepts set them apart. Principles emphasized within cognitive theory include the conceptions that: the organizing features according to which the problem is perceived by the learner are important learning conditions; knowledge must be organized in sequence from simplified wholes to more complex wholes; learning with understanding is more permanent than learning by rote; feedback from environment to learner is a necessary test and confirmation of correct knowledge; goal setting by the learner is important in his motivation; and divergent (inventive) thinking must be nurtured along with convergent thinking. Stimulus–response (S–R) theory stresses that: the learner's role be active rather than passive; reinforcement and frequent repetition are important learning devices; practice in varied contexts must be allowed; and innate human drives, conflicts, and frustrations must be recognized and accommodated. (Hilgard and Bower, 1966, pp. 562–564.)

OBJECTIVES AND S–R THEORY

Instructional objectives are essential within stimulus–response theory. A specific instructional objective is at once a stimulus to learning and a pattern of response to be exhibited by the learner when he has completed the process. When a learner is presented with an objective, the instructor has already outlined for him the nature of the desired response. When the learner has accepted this desired response as worthy of his attention, the objective thus becomes a stimulus to his learning.

Demonstrating that phenomenon is rather simple. A student who is told, "On Tuesday you will be asked to answer *these* types of questions which require *these* types of answers," has been given both a suggested response pattern and a stimulus to learn (assuming, of course, that he both understands and accepts the assignment). Students themselves seek such direct stimuli by asking, "What will be on the examination?" "Will we be held responsible for that?" They ask that the patterns of the responses expected of them be made clear in advance; the responses thus shape their study activities.

A set of specific objectives, prepared by an instructor and distributed to students at the beginning of an instructional unit, answers the questions they usually ask on their initial contact with a teacher: "What must we be able to do in order to succeed in this class?" Students have been conditioned throughout their school careers to seek appropriate response patterns from instructor's actions and from textbook emphases. But when objectives are specified, the expected responses are thus communicated in a direct fashion, and the traditional lines of questioning are subverted. Instruction then must include convincing the students of the relevance of the objectives — the expected response patterns — to their lives. The effects of the stimuli are related to the degree to which the objectives are accepted.

Intermediate objectives — those specified as leading to still more complex abilities — relate directly to stimulus–response theory. When a student is asked to perform a complex task, the asking (the stimulus) is more powerful if the attainment of prerequisite abilities (the intermediate objectives) has been previously assessed. (Gagné, 1965.) Unless the prerequisite task is demonstrated, the communication of the objective calling for the more complex behavior is a weaker stimulus. According to theory, the response pattern is already organized in the learner; the objective provides a focused stimulus. In the vernacular, the intermediate objectives are springboards from which students can jump to greater heights.

Stimulus–response theory suggests that the mind changes as a result of connections between series of trials and associations; series of objectives can provide clearly defined connections. Overt shaping patterns may be constructed so that the direction of the overall learning is made apparent. Stimuli and responses are present both in each objective and in series of objectives which fit together in sequences.

The "active response" principle of S–R theory is another feature built into an objective-based mode of instruction. Each objective calls for an overt response to be made by the learner — the more objectives, the more active responses. Although any instructional scheme *may* demand periodic active responses on the part of the students, one which is based on specific objectives *must* include regularly observed student actions.

Experimenters working within the framework of stimulus–response theory have made much of the principle of reinforcement, which holds that if a learner's response is rewarded, it is more likely to be repeated. Objectives can themselves serve as reinforcers when learners check their own responses against the specific objectives they were attempting to reach. Each objective can simultaneously reinforce responses and stimulate further response. If concrete rewards are attached to successful attainment, reinforcement can be made extrinsic to the objective. However, when the end is clearly known, attainment can be its *own* reinforcing device.

OBJECTIVES AND COGNITIVE THEORY

Specific objectives relate as well to cognitive theory. Knowledge of the form of expected responses presents a model to the student. His perceptions, the cues he takes from his environment, are shaped by his view of the task with which he is to be confronted. When he knows what he will be called upon to do, his attempts to sort relevant from irrelevant experiences are aided. He is afforded the opportunity to alter his own perceptual structure, the filter through which he views his world. (Miller *et al.*, 1960.)

The teacher who manipulates a learner's environment in accordance with the laws of logic and cognition is actually influencing the learner's perceptions just as though he were manipulating the actual perceptual approach. (Gage, 1965.) A simple demonstration of the phenomenon of selective perception may be arranged by telling students who have been in a room for many hours over a period of weeks to close their eyes. Then ask, "How many light fixtures are on the ceiling?" It is unlikely that any of them will know. Say to them, "Tomorrow you will be quizzed on the architectural features of this room." Immediately their attention is directed not only to light fixtures but to doors, windows, room size, etc. They begin to perceive what they had never "seen" before. Specific objectives have a similar effect on students' perceptions of lectures, readings, and other media through which learning occurs. Their attention is diverted from the irrelevant and focused on that which has meaning for the task at hand. Put another way, this is the "organizing feature" so important in cognitive theory.

What are the links between cognition and action? According to cognitive theory, a person's actions are controlled by the way he organizes his perceptions (images) of the universe. Changes in such images are effected by executing plans for gathering, storing, or transforming information. One imagines what is coming and builds plans (strategies, tactics) to meet the eventuality. (Miller *et al.*, 1960, p. 16.)

Specific objectives help learners create plans because they are particular guides toward expected actions. They help create models for thinking because they are themselves models. When a student asks, "What is to be learned in this course?" the information he receives must somehow be fitted into the conceptual scheme he already possesses. When the requirements of the situation do not fit the student's current scheme, however, he is forced to alter it or extend it to accommodate new information.

A rotation of learning tasks that calls for the assimilation of new information into students' existing conceptual schemes is a suggested teaching strategy. Cognitive theory postulates that prolonged assimilation of facts without a corresponding reshaping of the conceptual schemes with which to organize them is "bound to retard the maturation of thought." (Taba and Elzey, 1965, p. 528.) Students who require more "concrete thinking" than others may be exhibiting just this type of learning problem.

Students may have cognitive "preferences," particular ways of organizing their learning plans. If students are to succeed in school, their preferences must fit the nature of the tasks with which they are presented, the type of instructional sequence through which they pass, or the instructor's own cognitive preferences (expressed in ways of which he may not be aware). The cognitive aspect of teacher behavior — the logic of what teachers say to students — has not been studied to the extent that programmers, for example, have focused on the cognitive structures of their programs. Some instructors may prefer to deal with details and to neglect general ideas, while others tend to discuss generalizations and consequently overlook details. If the exact tasks to be performed by students are specified, the study of cognitive features of instruction will be facilitated.

Cognitive theory suggests that learning proceeds from simplified wholes to more complex, integrated wholes. Each objective is itself a simplified whole; when put together with others it may become a part of a more complex structure. The terminal objective for a course or curriculum should represent the complex whole toward which the entire sequence is designed to lead. Gestalt theory, itself usually associated with cognitive theory (Bigge, 1964, p. 51) suggests that learning strategies are formed on the basis of perceptions that combine pieces into patterned structures. A person learns a task as a meaningful whole rather than in a piecemeal fashion, through insight rather than association (Hall and Lindzey, 1957, p. 297) with insight "possible only if the learning situation is so arranged that all necessary aspects are open to observation." (Hilgard and Bower, 1966, p. 241.) When objectives are specified, patterns of thought through which learners may be led are opened to view. Theoretically, insight is made more feasible. Hilgard and Bower (1966, pp. 241–242) explain this phenomenon in classroom terms:

> Skilled teachers are well aware of differences between situations in which understanding is arrived at easily and those in which it is achieved with difficulty — even though the same ultimate steps are involved and the same end stage reached. In the favored arrangement the problem is so structured that significant features are perceived in proper relationship, and

distracting or confusing features are subordinated. Some mathematics teachers make problem solution difficult to grasp because they go through derivations step by step without an overview of where the steps are leading or what the articulating principles are. They teach the necessary operations, but the final insight eludes the students because of the manner in which the proof is arranged.

One more principle in cognitive theory that relates directly to a defined-outcomes mode of teaching should be mentioned. The law of closure holds that "The direction of behavior is toward an end-situation which brings closure with it . . . . In a problematic situation the whole is seen as incomplete and a tension is set up toward completion. This strain to complete is an aid to learning, and to achieve closure is satisfying." (Hilgard and Bower, 1966, p. 235.) When objectives are specified, closure may be experienced only when the objective is achieved. If objectives are not specified, the risk is that the only satisfying closure for the student is in his obtaining a grade-mark and leaving the course; there is no other way for him to know that he has attained the desired end behavior.

Both cognitive and stimulus–response theories have their adherents in schools. Although most instructors are unconscious of their modes of proceeding and ascribe their successes to "art," elements in their instructional practices may be classified with one or another — and often both — theoretical groupings. Specifying objectives is a tool which fits within both theories and which enables instructors to move back and forth from student-learning results to instructional designs, with theory serving as the bridge.

The specification of objectives can help to bring theory and practice more into line with each other — an essential because, "a sound theory of learning must eventually be validated by its influence upon the arts of practice. If educational practices cannot be improved as a result of research investigations of learning, something is [very] wrong with that research." (Hilgard and Bower, 1966, p. 542.) And in practice, evidence is accumulating that students learn more in situations in which objectives are specified in advance. Instructors learn, too. The process of examining criteria by which actions are to be assessed leads to a focus on ends. By virtue of engaging in this process, recent graduate school products, who are often guilty of confusing the certitudes and achievements of their disciplines with reality on a cosmic scale, may be led to bring their knowledge more appropriately to bear on the business of causing learning.

Chapter Twenty-Two

Effects on Instructors, Students, and Institutional Practices

EFFECTS ON INSTRUCTORS

The typical classroom instructor is little concerned with learning theory. Major curricular decisions rarely fall within his scope. He is not involved in broad-scale instructional planning, let alone in defining desirable behaviors for the members of the community in which his institution is located. He is concerned rather with his own classroom and his own instructional processes. To him the specifying of objectives has a limited — but very significant — range of applications.

The instructor who specifies objectives lends direction and purpose to several areas of his activity. He has a frame of reference within which he can build and test hypotheses regarding his practices and his effects; his planning of instruction takes on different dimensions; classroom interaction between him and his students is changed; and he gains a heightened awareness of what he is trying to do. But he must go through the process himself; he should not be handed objectives with the injunction, "Go teach to them."

When an instructor bases his practices on defined objectives, he gains a different perspective upon his courses. The context of questions about whether to spend more or less time on a specific bit of subject matter has altered; he now sees his subject as a vehicle by which students can learn to think in particular ways. Course content and coverage become less sacred. The instructor has committed himself to bring his students to specific abilities. Is it really necessary to "cover the text?" What if some students have not learned that which was supposed to have been taught — must he continue "covering content" or can he double back repeatedly until he is satisfied that a minimum percentage of students has learned what he hoped he was teaching? The instructor who has specified objectives is in a better position to answer these questions because he has set particular ends and he knows whether or not they have been reached.

Instructional methods, too, take on a different dimension. When an instructor knows clearly whether or not anyone has learned from him, he can change his techniques on the basis of particular referents. Does he get better results when he lectures? When he conducts class discussion? When he shows films or plays tapes? He has provided himself with an entire basis for experimentation in the relative merits of instructional media. He can communicate with fellow instructors on the value and worth of his objectives, his sequences, and his methods. The time he spends in attempting to teach one task or a group of tasks can be compared with that spent by others who are attempting to teach the same abilities but who are using different methods. By specifying objectives the instructor moves in the direction of becoming an experimentalist, a specialist in causing learning.

When an instructor specifies objectives, certain questions become pointless. What is "student-centered" instruction, and how does it differ from that which is "teacher centered"? The entire process is designed to cause students to learn or it has no meaning. "Are the students applying concepts outside the classroom?" If the teacher's objective is that students gain an attitude of continuing inquiry as manifested by certain aspects of their behavior outside the class, the instructor can easily assess his results. Common euphemisms such as "remedial," "terminal," and "college level" lose their meanings. "What can the students do when they enter the course? What can they do when they leave?" These are revealed as the *real* questions.

For the instructor who has specified his objectives, the assigning of grade-marks can be related to specific student accomplishments. Marks take on particular meaning as the bridge between course content and student learning is made apparent. What does an "A" mean? It means that a student has performed *these* tasks under *these* conditions with *this* degree of accuracy. An "A" is less likely to indicate that a student has appeared for class every day and has matched some vague standards determined by the instructor only after the results were in.

The instructor who plots his objectives sequentially so that each leads to broader aims is not likely to make the error of asking students to achieve some complex task without first ensuring their ability to master the simpler elements contained within it. Once he has structured clear objectives, he finds in many cases that his assessment devices have also been refined. He can quickly see the difference between an objective that asks for a complex behavior and a test item that demands but simple recall. It becomes possible for the instructor to sort out deficiencies in instruction before too much time is lost. As he plots objectives and test items, he is led to avoid a pattern of lecturing for several weeks, administering a complex test, and then discovering that the basic vocabulary he has been using was beyond the ken of many of his students.

Once he sets objectives, the instructor is virtually forced to find appropriate instructional media. Students who are learning in a situation in which objectives have been specified and communicated to them in advance of the course refuse to tolerate shoddy media — and that includes irrelevant lecturing. In many cases the instructor must create his own materials.

Postlethwaite (1965), a pioneer in the development of an audio-tutorial system for teaching botany, noted that as the media he constructed proved more relevant to the purpose of the course than did his lectures, students, of their own volition, stopped attending the lectures and went to the laboratory where directly relevant materials were available. Students knew clearly what they had to learn; materials in the laboratory tied in directly with their objectives where the lectures often did not. Eventually, a sort of reverse Gresham's law developed in which the "hard" media drove the "soft" lectures out of circulation.

Instructors' classroom activities change along observable dimensions when they are attempting to teach for specific outcomes. In one study, supervisors, told to rate teachers on their apparent classroom effectiveness, perceived as more effective those teachers who had been required to cause students to learn in particular directions. (McNeil, 1967.) In addition, teachers viewed supervisors' suggestions as being more relevant and helpful, because the suggestions were seen as means to help the teachers bring about learning rather than as ends in themselves.

Most instructors will say that they always work toward causing student change. However, an explicit requirement that instructors teach for higher student scores on a specific standardized test produces a change in the behavior of the teacher. Teachers act differently when they are charged with causing learning. In some cases pupils show greater gain in desired directions when the teacher's reinforcement (his own success) is contingent upon such gain. (Wittrock, 1962.) Experimental evidence is yet meager, but it seems that when instructors are required to teach toward specific objectives, student learning is measurably affected. The instructor acts differently. Perhaps he reduces the number of irrelevant intrusions or attends more to deliberate instruction. Or perhaps greater student learning is a result of the phenomenon of "the self-fulfilling prophecy" — when and if an instructor is determined that his students learn, they learn.

What is most important from the instructor's point of view is that when he lays out objectives, he is forced to define, to justify, and to defend what he is trying to do in all facets of his work. It is no longer possible for him to hide behind the "normal curve" of probable student achievement. He is committed to certain minimum levels of student learning in advance of his instructional efforts. By making definite commitments, he cannot manipulate the classroom as though "teacher" and "learners" were abstractions. He is forced back on himself and must answer the constantly posed question, "What am I trying to accomplish?" The answer comes back in the form of another question, "What are my students doing now that they did not do formerly?" He no longer says, "I opened up the subject for the students. The more able learned — I'm sorry about the others." He becomes conscious of his content-selection process and reviews continually the reasons for using particular types of materials and teaching patterns. His activities move on to a different plane.

Throughout recent years, many writers have commented on the depersonalized aspects of American higher education. (Kean *et al.*, 1967.) Much of the criticism is directed toward institutionalized procedures that tend to maintain screens between administrator, instructor, and student, and force them to mistrust each other. Classrooms *are* ridden with secrecy, with failure in communication. Even the simple task of specifying in advance what an instructor must do to please his supervisors remains in the realm of hearsay and post facto determination. What the student must do to satisfy the instructor is often played as though it were a game of, "I've got a secret. Guess what you have to do to pass this course." When objectives are written down, the veil is removed.

Much of what happens to an instructor when he specifies objectives can be summed by saying that he learns "what he is about." The teacher who lectures for several weeks and then says in effect, "Write an essay in which you sort out the relevant clues," may be saying in reality, "When I see your essays, I will know who I am and what I think." The process of asking the student to write a composition for which rules and guidelines have *not* been defined cannot be excused as a part of instruction. What can the instructor do to help the student *after* he reads the compositions? Teaching and learning, a process of interaction between instructor and student, must be based on common ground. The instructor who specifies objectives reveals himself to his students before he asks that they reveal themselves to him. And what better way to dispel skepticism and distrust!

Most published discussions about the effects of objectives on instructors are extrapolations drawn from a few research studies and reports of personal experiences by instructors who have engaged in the process. Much information is speculation and must remain so until the process becomes more widespread than it is at the present time. It seems safe to say, however, that objectives clearly specified and communicated in advance can serve to bring to the teaching–learning process dimensions of honesty and understanding that have long been sought but despaired of as being improbable under current practices. It is also likely that the instructor who engages in the practice may find himself in a corner from which all exits labeled "They are poor students; they don't want to learn; they didn't know what I was talking about" are closed. In the corner is a mirror, and the reflection says, "What are you *really* trying to do?" Many may not like what they see.

EFFECTS ON STUDENTS

The evidence of the effects of different institutional practices on students' attitudes, habits, and abilities is incomplete and often contradictory. Information is not easily collected. It is difficult to establish causal relationships between structure (physical plant, organization) and process (courses, teaching methods, counseling) on the one hand, and student change on the other. Students select certain colleges — why? How much of student change arises from off-campus influences? What types of students do best under what instructional modes? College goals are vague and capable of varying interpretation — what forms of learning are really being sought? Empirical investigation suffers as a result of a host of such ambiguities and enigmas affecting study design.

What would happen to students if all learning objectives were clearly specified — whether by them, by the college staff, or by the two groups working together? Although a few experimenters have addressed themselves to the issue (Dalis, 1969), little more than speculation based on theory and logic can be mentioned at this time. Few college courses, fewer complete programs, and no whole colleges are organized to achieve sets of specific objectives. Most of the research that seeks knowledge regarding institutional effects sets objectives toward which students must strive or deduces objectives from media being employed in existing curricula. But because of the varying interactional effects of media, student tendencies, and objectives themselves, clear evidence of the consequences of a defined-outcomes approach must wait until it has been tried in a number of contexts.

Many effects may be presumed. Under current practice, students know that instruction is designed to lead somewhere — but where? To say only that long-range ends are being effected by trivial tasks is meaningless, and students are well aware of the triviality of most short-range objectives. They often ask, "Why bother?" and unless they have a fair idea of global ends, they may be disinclined to participate. Would their motivation be affected if deliberate objectives were posited?

The kinds of statements found in course descriptions seldom directly influence students' progress. "To provide a clear understanding of the backgrounds of English culture, traditions, and language" or similar statements typically locked in the dean's files or in the catalog seldom elicit more than a brief glance from a student. "What papers are required? What reading? What texts must I buy? How many tests are given?" To the extent the student thinks of the course, these are the questions toward which he directs his inquiry. Generalized course or unit descriptions are deemed unworthy of his scrutiny.

Without being aware of it, students are thus forced to focus on the *media*, not the outcomes of a course. The implication is that students will turn course experiences to ends of their own devising, and that any activity selected will be satisfactory or not to the extent it keeps them involved in something called the "learning process." But the student may not get that far. His involvement and concern with mundane classroom activities are not the ends of instruction — at least not for the student. On the other hand, when objectives are clearly specified, sequences and patterns become apparent and directions can be plotted. Objectives then serve as *reasons* for study. Students who are given the opportunity of planning for the performance of particular tasks may have a decided advantage over those who are expected to engage in ill-defined activities for unknown reasons.

Student guidance may also be improved when a college uses a defined-outcomes approach. Once laid out in sequential, communicable fashion, course outlines can be used to help counsel students. Students may be asked, "Is this what you want to be able to do?" And "Are you able now to perform *these* tasks that are requisite for entry?" The ideal of the individually patterned curriculum may be brought closer to realization. The ability to plan ahead is a necessary characteristic of the integrated person; the opportunity to plan his program in accordance with desired outcomes must be offered to the individual student. That planning can be done with more reasonable deliberation if the actual abilities to be gained are indicated to him as part of the process.

Presented with objectives for the first time, students exhibit intriguing behavior patterns that point up the inadequacies of ambiguous goals. First, they ignore the course outline and look at the instructor in an attempt to determine what he *really* has in mind. Next, they check through the outline seeking *media* lists. Even after a quiz in which the instructor carefully points out how all items relate specifically to objectives, students are incredulous. Habituated to the "educational" guessing game played in the lower schools, they repeatedly search for the "catch." As the course progresses, students often come in one by one, speaking with amazement about the fact that the instructor had been honest with them about the required tasks. A few often go a step further and remark that they were released for *thinking* about the subject matter. They realize that by communicating exactly what they were to do, the instructor removed a screen, a veil of secrecy, from between himself and them.

In many instructional situations, students themselves could very beneficially participate in setting objectives in advance of the course. The actual writing of objectives thus can be part of the learning process. Too, students' acceptance of objectives as being worthy of their attention may be enhanced. As students work with instructors in building specific ends for the course in which they are involved, they learn to focus on the consequences of their actions. That alone is an important activity, one which can be itself a valid goal.

Failure in school often means a student has failed to cope with the mechanics of education. So-called learning ability is likely to be related to the knack of finding one's way through a procedural labyrinth. The means of education do more than effect the ends, they *become* ends. If a student is selected, placed, promoted, and graduated by examinations, from his point of view, the object of the education system must be to pass examinations. (Hutchins, 1968, p. 74.) If he is accepted as a participant in setting educational objectives, one of the goals of the system as he sees it then becomes the defining of ends. If the ends he helps select are directly related to social and individual needs, both short- and long-term, his attention is drawn to the relevant, to the *why* rather than simply to the *how* of his actions. This would seem more valuable than a process that asks a student to attend to pre-set means and to find his own ends within them.

Although there is little available evidence about the specific effects of objectives on students, there seem to be potential similarities between these and some biasing effects long recognized in experimental psychology. In psychology, the influence of the investigator affects the outcomes of the experiment in ways both defined and unknown; the more obvious include the fact that an experimenter, having derived a hypothesis, seeks data to support it. He may continue to seek confirmation by applying different statistics, reorganizing the conditions of an experiment, changing subjects or experimental paraphernalia until required information is obtained, and so on. On the other hand, his attempts to confirm the hypothesis may be as subtle as his smiling at certain interviewed subjects and not at others, or unconsciously selecting particular populations to use and taking other unintentional steps to influence the direction of results. Such activities lead to what has been called the self-fulfilling prophecy. (Rosenthal, 1968.)

Because some expectation of how research might turn out is virtually a constant factor in scientific experiments, it is difficult, if not impossible, to avoid bias completely. Thus it may well be with most classroom instruction. The psychologist experimenter applies different statistics to his data in an effort to help them approximate his expectations; the instructor changes grade-marking patterns. The experimenter reorganizes the condition of the experiment; the instructor changes the classroom situation. Experimenters find different groups of "guinea pigs"; administrators group students according to "ability." And what in experimental psychology is comparable to the phenomenon of an instructor's shuffling and reshuffling papers turned in by students to make them conform to a normal probability curve? What can approximate his making examination items more difficult (more ambiguous, often) when his students achieve an extraordinarily high score on any pre-instruction test? When a teacher expects a "normal distribution," he gets it; when he expects learning, he gets *that* — sometimes with results as dramatic as greatly increased I.Q. scores. (Rosenthal and Jacobson, 1968.) What does he do differently when he actually commits himself to having 90 per cent of his students achieve his objectives?

Psychologists and behavioral scientists suspect that when little is expected, little is achieved. (Hutchins, 1968, p. 15.) However, they are unaware of the specific mechanisms — conscious and unconscious, intentional and unintentional — that affect success or failure in directions expected. If there is a consistent phenomenon of "self-fulfilling prophecy," how does it operate in the schools? Studies have identified certain obvious factors. One group of investigators observed differential cues presented to students by teachers. Instructors allowed more time for "bright" students to answer questions and displayed facial expressions indicating obvious displeasure at remarks made by "dull" students. But there are probably a great number of less apparent cues picked up unconsciously by students. If expectations are somehow communicated to non-human experimental subjects (Rosenthal, 1968, p. 51), what must be the magnitude of the effect on students when an instructor genuinely expects them to learn? What when he expects them to fail to learn?

A changed view of students — one which perceives them all as possessing the ability to learn in a variable but functionally equal manner — might prove to have far-ranging consequences. (Boyer and Walsh, 1968.). The differences among them — in quickness of apprehension, richness of home experience, level of emotional maturity — could then be accommodated. Telling students what they will be able to do at the end of a particular unit may be the most significant single thing an instructor can do to effect learning. Put simply, the single most effective way to help a student achieve within the present school system may be to tell him exactly what he is going to accomplish and to convince him that the instructor is committed to his learning to do it.

EFFECTS ON INSTITUTIONAL PRACTICES

The junior college that would adopt a practice of specifying objectives for its curriculum and instruction within the framework of a defined-outcomes rationale must anticipate changes in several pre-existing organizational patterns. The college's institutional research office, for example, currently collecting data on which administrative decisions are made and writing proposals for funding, would have to devote most of its efforts to assessing the effects of instruction. The role of department chairmen and deans would change from that of personnel administrators toward that of instructional managers. Curricular prerequisites would be revised. Patterns of courses which students must fulfill would give way to specification of abilities they must possess. Student assessment for the purpose of improving curriculum and instruction would be emphasized more, and measurement for the evaluation and differentiation of students, less. Relationships between the junior college and the university, other educational institutions, and employers would come to include reviewing and criticizing each other's defined objectives.

Under a system of specified objectives, the commitment of institutional resources must be undertaken in a fashion different from the current practice. When specific outcomes are used as a referent, gaps in the structure are made evident. There may be some goals — perhaps those seen as important by the community at large — toward which the institution is mistakenly not directing its efforts. There may be overlaps — several curricular programs leading toward the same ends. Specific objectives, spelled out and communicated, can help identify those areas and make allocations of resources more practicable.

Under the current system, gaps and overlaps are difficult to assess. Does all follow in sequence? Does the student who passes *Math I* have the requisite skills to enter *Math II?* Can the student who goes through *Remedial English* enter *English I* with a reasonable chance of success? When instructors specify the minimum skills to be achieved by their students in a single course, instructors in subsequent courses know more precisely what entering abilities they may expect. Thus, courses and curricula may be carefully plotted.

Under a defined-outcomes approach, course outlines become documents of great utility. In addition to catalog type data on subject content, they include lists of objectives. One outline is maintained for each course. It is distributed to students when they enter, used by instructors, shown to accreditation committees and interested groups at other institutions, and used by counselors in advising students. In short, *courses* are built, not mere lists of activities vaguely specified.

In the college that undertakes to define its effects, the assessment of student capabilities takes on a different dimension, too. Whether students' entering abilities are determined by individual instructors, by departments, or by institutional testing services, several matters must be considered. For example: the extent to which the individual has already acquired the responses which the college expects to teach him; the extent to which he has acquired the prerequisites for entering the curriculum; and the extent to which his antecedent learnings will facilitate or interfere with new learning under varying instructional conditions. Of course the measuring of such factors will require testing and interviewing programs of much more depth and complexity than those found in today's institutions. (Glaser, 1966a.)

On the other end of curricular design, arrangements must be made to collect long-range follow-up information about students who leave the institution. If instructors are to write objectives that assess the achievement of such goals as, "The student will gain appreciation for poetry," they must be able to obtain feedback about the extent to which their objectives have been attained. Within that goal, any of several objectives may be written; for example, "The student will purchase at least three books of contemporary poetry within the two years after leaving the course." Or "The student will write and submit for publication at least one poem within one year after leaving the course." Objectives may also state ". . . or give similar evidence that he has gained an appreciation for poetry." In all cases, the instructor must know whether or not his objectives were achieved so that he may modify them or his instructional practices. Easily measurable behavior on the part of the students may be taken to indicate the achievement of a rather complex ability or a significant change in attitude.

Because similar objectives may be specified for "transfer" and "terminal" courses alike, the gulf between academic and vocational divisions of the institution is narrowed. When courses are designed to cause specific changes in students, the artificial gap now found among institutional divisions is reduced. Although content and coverage of courses in two curricula may vary, the complexity of a task specified in an objective can be noticeably similar. Thus "standards" can cross disciplinary lines, and a scheme of classifying objectives might be used to compare the "level" of courses, sections of courses, or whole curriculum sequences. The hierarchies employed in assessing the relative complexity of objectives need not be as elaborate as those postulated by Gagné, Bloom, or other learning theorists. For the college's purposes, it may be sufficient to classify objectives according to those calling for the performance of a single task in a prescribed situation and those specifying employment of a particular skill in *any* class of situation. In any case, objectives in courses can be classified in a more structured fashion than that currently employed.

Currently, in most instructional situations, objectives are more vague and variable than media. Instructors use similar methods and materials from one term to the next, but the "standards" of the course fluctuate in accordance with changing student populations. If a student does not perform well relative to his fellows within an allotted time, he "fails." Standards are usually created and modified in relationship to the capacities of the students enrolled, not to external criteria. The institution that introduces a system of specific objectives will likely abandon the marking curve and move to a "pass/no pass" pattern. There is no degree of relativity within a single objective, hence no need to distribute student accomplishments along a continuum. Students achieve in relation to the objectives themselves; data about their achievement are used to modify instructional media, not to differentiate students.

The institution operating with outcomes clearly defined will probably develop much of its own instructional material. Students progress toward common objectives at varying rates, and the demand for individually prescribed materials will grow. Because it is impracticable to provide a tutor for each student, many replicable materials will be needed. In addition, students will more readily serve as tutors to other students when the pressure of grade-marking is removed. The institution will move into the learning business.

Junior college educators may despair of the apparent complexity of organizing an institution for the purpose of causing predictable learning, but a framework for most of the necessary innovations exists now. Most institutions have research directors; their activities must only be differently assigned. Agencies with responsibility for relating college courses to those offered at high schools and transfer institutions exist; the content of their conversations can change from comparing vaguely described course content to relating evidence of course outcomes. Transcripts, catalogs, and counselors' manuals can be rewritten to show specifically the objectives attained by students who have received credit for particular courses. Existing mechanical media can be applied on the basis of demonstrated effect rather than on whim or salesmanship. And the supervision and management of institutions can be related to learning outcomes as well as it can to history and tradition.

Chapter Twenty-Three

Reactions and Criticisms

Resistance to the idea of specifying learning objectives in precise terms has been voiced on a variety of bases, ranging from a belief that it is unfeasible to a contention that it is immoral. Some arguments against the practice have merit. Others can be credited only insofar as they apply to all institutional education. Frequently, objections seem to be based on a combination of unwillingness to do the necessary work, genuine reasoned antipathy to the process, and a feeling of elitism manifest in such statements as, "Hold *me* accountable for *their* learning? They don't belong in college anyway! In *my* *d*ay, we had to *work* for what we got!"

Many critics of the use of objectives in junior colleges associate it exclusively with programmed autoinstruction and let their revulsion against "machines" of all types carry over. (Arnstine, 1964.) Such criticism seems unwarranted because, although the specification of precise outcomes is a necessary condition of programmed instruction, programming is not the only way to teach toward objectives. Instructors may use the process in a free-wheeling classroom or in a school with no rooms, programs, or hardware at all.

Other critics suggest that learning the specific precludes learning the general — that when objectives are specified, the unseen ends of instruction are discounted. There is no evidence, however, that students' broader horizons are narrowed by being taught in a situation where instructional outcomes have been precisely defined. In fact, a contrary thesis may be drawn: When objectives are set, the student is released to learn more. Critics of the process of building a floor under learners may be excessively concerned with ceilings. Wanting to teach everything, they fail to determine whether or not they have taught anything. Lumsdaine (1968) has concluded that "Most instructional lessons, films, television lessons, and college courses try to teach more than they possibly can . . . ."

As an instructional goal, "thinking" must be given top priority. However, the difference between "thinking" and "problem solving" or other forms of overt activity is more semantic than real. The word "thinking" is often used as if it were the real end of education, but the word "too often serves as a pedagogical smokescreen masking the absence of well-defined instructional goals." (Ericksen, 1967, p. 89.) Logically, it is difficult to relate the presence of goals to an absence of thought. When a student solves a problem as the objective suggests he will, his thought has not been diminished in value.

GENERAL VERSUS SPECIFIC

Defined objectives are often criticized because they outline specific sets of ends toward which all students must be led. By contrast, the argument runs, general goals allow for many forms of behavior. It is not proper, however, to draw a distinction between vaguely defined goals and specific objectives; the important line lies between having *no* major explicit goals — hence no concerted control of instruction, content, or structure — and *some*. If outcomes are specified at all, the *degree* of specificity should not be cause for question.

Individualization should not be an issue either. There can be as many sets of separate, measurable objectives as there are students in the school. It is not necessary, or even especially desirable, to design sequences that will lead all students to the same abilities and behavior. The ability to draw inferences, make generalizations, and gather data to test hypotheses is valued in a democratic society. Such learned capacities can be cast in the form of specific objectives — a separate set for each learner, if need be.

Furthermore, content and instructional method used to lead students toward defined objectives can often be varied — for instance with the objective: "Given some data, a student can state one or two types of problems in terms of social-science concepts or previously learned generalizations." Contrast that objective with one that states, "Given the name of an early American settlement, the student will state the form of government instituted in that colony before 1700." The second objective may well be rejected, not only because it demands mere recall but because it specifies the *content* that a teacher must use to teach it. The first example is no less specific, but it is not bound to any specific subject matter. Many critics would probably rate it as worthy a goal as the suggestion that, "The student will be able to solve problems of his own devising." (Raths, 1967.)

A genuine concern that, because it is easier to operationalize, the trivial would be emphasized in defined objectives to the exclusion of the more valuable — this is a criticism less of the process than of the people who use it. (Popham, 1968.) True, trivial objectives may be easy to specify but, once specified, they are open to view and correspondingly easier to reject. If objectives toward which the instructor is *actually* striving are clearly stated, solidly based criticisms may be made by both the instructor and his colleagues. If objectives are hidden behind grandiose phrases, they may not be easily identified, much less analyzed. Instructors are, by nature, idealistic; they consider course content as a vehicle for noble ends. But specific ends are no less worthy.

WHO WILL DEFINE THE OBJECTIVES?

The process of setting up objectives and course sequences is preeminently a faculty responsibility. Administrators can supervise the activity and make assistance available, but instructors must implement the process. If teachers refuse to spell out ends and to accept accountability for their being achieved, the enterprise will not succeed — this in spite of the vigor of administrative pronouncements about educational "innovation." Board policy statements, massive purchases of hardware (often misleadingly classified as "new media"), and frequent publicity releases notwithstanding, if instructors feel a certain percentage of students must fail, that percentage will fail. Moreover, if instructors do not want to work toward specific objectives, they will actively subvert any deliberately designed instructional process. It is the teachers who make the system stand or fail. Accordingly, it is essential to examine carefully reasons why few instructors currently specify objectives for their students.

Some of the reasons why instructors seem to prefer vague aims may result from a fear of converting their exalted calling into a mundane practice. Typically, teachers do not enter their profession for the purpose of causing learning but for a variety of other reasons — for example, a desire simply to perform before, or to interact with, the young. Perhaps many "back" into teaching because there are few other places in society where people may be gainfully employed while dabbling in an academic discipline. When *ends* are defined, teaching becomes more of a job and less fun.

Does specifying and inducing learning in particular directions fall into the category of menial labor in the mind of the teacher? The instructor who chooses to enter the teaching profession may view his move as a step up in social class. In his mind, the planned production of learning has the appearance of mixing mortar or tilling soil. Focusing on ends suggests using one's knowledge for assembly-line purposes; it turns the marvel of the human mind into base coin. Accordingly, the instructor acts as though his status depended on his refusing to accept defined objectives.

A more acceptable excuse for teachers' failures to define objectives may be simply that they do not know how. Few junior college teachers have been "prepared to teach" (Brawer, 1968, p. 37) and even fewer have been exposed to activities in which the writing of objectives was a main function. Graduate school professors rarely use objectives in their own courses. The texts used in teacher preparation occasionally mention that objectives should be specific but they do not often discuss how they should be written. Never having been required to engage in the process or exposed to other instructors who used objectives, the teacher has no frame of reference upon which to draw. Preparation, not mere exhortation, is a minimal necessity. If objectives are to be more than trivial, special training is required. The instructor who has not had such training cannot be faulted for his failure to develop a proper set of objectives.

A belief pervades the field that instructors will be rated by the extent to which their students achieve the objectives they specify; if so, they want no part of the practice. This is understandable because as a group instructors are traditionally hostile to being "evaluated." Their repugnance is certainly justified — the entire history of faculty evaluation approximates the sordid! Gustad (1961) put it mildly when he said, "To call what is typically collected or adduced to support evaluative decisions 'evidence' is to stretch the meaning of that honored word beyond reason." A strong case can be made for abandoning all current practices of faculty evaluation. (Cohen and Brawer, 1969.) However, if a school's faculty and administration decide that evaluation *is* necessary, assessing instructors on the basis of the learning achieved by their students would certainly be a more valid practice than any of the schemes presently in use.

Specific objectives, then, are something new for most instructors, representing a break with tradition for members of a most conservative group. To ask teachers to define outcomes is to suggest that they run counter to their predilections without offering them many overt rewards for doing so. And it is a rare instance in which teachers receive recognition for causing learning, primarily because institutions in which they labor are not rewarded for causing learning.

In general, instructors and college leaders hesitate to define and hold themselves accountable for achievement of instructional objectives because it is far easier to be a "good teacher" or "good college" in a protectively ambiguous sense than it is to define and bring about learning. Before the practice can become widespread, a new definition of teaching must be conveyed. (Carlson, 1966, p. 130.) Until *teaching* is seen as methodically *causing learning*, it will continue to be viewed only in terms of the instructor's actions — not in terms of the results he produces. And until they are expected to show evidence of having caused learning, "good colleges" will be known only by the number of their buildings and the degrees held by staff members. "Good teacher" and "good college" depend upon particular definition of terms. As long as the terms are defined in one way, teachers and institutions will not act in another.

Many powerful external forces act to dissuade instructors and institutions from specifying objectives. In most states, school finance is based on "Average Daily Attendance" or another formula similarly founded on the premise that if the body of a student is in proximity to the body of an instructor for a specified number of hours, something beneficial will happen. As long as money is appropriated on that basis, instructors will not likely find it necessary to specify objectives. However, if institutions received financial aid on the basis of learning achieved, specific objectives would be perceived immediately as a necessity.

A truly significant intrusion by industrial and governmental educational agencies may be necessary before junior college staff members recognize the enormity of their refusal to define and hold themselves accountable for the learning achieved by their students. Their reluctance is not evidence of a recent national malaise but of a persistent long-standing conservatism in American education. It may be laid less to genuine criticism of the defined-outcomes approach than to inertia and failure to recognize the dangers of not changing.

MORALITY

The argument is sometimes raised that it is immoral to manipulate students toward set ends; however, "the institution called a school is specifically charged with just this task." Instructors and governing boards are "required by law and oath to see that the youngsters in their charge learn quite definite patterns of thought and action as prescribed by the adult society." (Komisar and McClellan, 1965.) If required objectives are immoral, then so are all American school laws!

Questions regarding the morality of determining ways of thinking to be attained by another person thus lead to criticisms of the broad purposes of all educational structures. The meaning in Bennis' contention that "There are probably more similarities than would be expected between forms of 'acceptable' social influences, such as psychotherapy or teaching, and 'unacceptable' forms, such as brainwashing" (1966, p. 83n) is not widely recognized. If it is immoral to preset the ends of instruction, then it must be immoral for one person to interact with another at any time for the purpose of changing his behavior. This would include parent and child, husband and wife, friend and friend, as well as teacher and student. In this context, setting objectives *is* immoral.

Parenthetically, morality is rarely brought up when certain other forms of socially acceptable education are under discussion, as, for example, when a junior college attempts to "educate" its community to vote favorably on a bond issue or a tax override. In such cases, the objective is clearly specified — a positive mandate backed by cash — and the methods follow — public information releases, speeches, and conversations that present the college in a favorable light, along with deliberate deemphasis of such unattractive news as student disaffection. If it is moral to manipulate or shape an entire community, is it less moral to move a single student toward predetermined ends?

Teachers sometimes balk at setting objectives in advance of instruction because of their verbalized commitment to the value of spontaneity in the classroom. They seek, rather, "some unplanned, free, creative encounter between teacher and student, in which activities emerge because of their spontaneous appeal. And . . . whatever learning results comes as a genuine surprise to student and teacher alike." (Komisar and McClellan, 1965.) Spontaneity and freedom in instruction are desirable, even delightful, concomitants of the teaching role. Rigid structures ostensibly have no appeal for the creative teacher — and what teacher would characterize himself as being other than creative?

But the morality issue intrudes here, too, albeit in a different way. If instructors truly believe they should not define the direction of their instruction, if they believe it is for the student to decide what is relevant, then "teaching" can be characterized as some type of human encounter without definable meaning. However, the instructor must then abandon all pretense at judging students because *judgments on the basis of nebulous or shifting criteria are the ultimate immorality.* If students and instructors shall be allowed free play, then admission requirements, selection procedures, probation and suspension practices must be discarded along with all goals, whether precise or ambiguous. Human encounter for no reason other than whatever spontaneously happens is a noble aim, but it is not "teaching" in any sense of the word even though, "In our ceremonial moments, we educationists are all suckers for such a view of instruction." (Komisar and McClellan, 1965.)

Teaching — causing learning — is actually a most moral enterprise. In the schools it involves an adult shaping the perceptions of a youth in a fashion such that a student's life and well-being are enhanced. Spelling out the desired ends of that enterprise cannot be considered immoral lest the counter charge be made that the field of public education is actually a vague association of people with no goals for themselves or for anyone else — people who are content both to reflect and to perpetuate uncritically their society's lack of a coherent philosophy.

Epilogue

Our economy and technology do not direct us; they give us a very wide range of choice. The future of the nation and of our educational system is whatever the American people decide to make it, whether they are guided by habit, or wisdom, or fear, or caprice, or good will, or sheer desperation. More than ever before in our history, the task is not so much to guess where we will most likely be, but to decide where we would most like to be. — ROBERT BICKER (1967, p. 61.)

Education and instruction are much bigger than schools. Schools are only a convenient means to more important ends, means that may no longer be relevant several decades from now. — JOHN GOODLAD (1967, p. 15.)

This book has drawn a picture of a college that is a leader in the educational affairs of its community. The college has defined objectives and accepted accountability for learning achieved by its students. Its programs have coalesced around a core of instruction suitable for, and available to, all citizens. Students come and go at will; their activities take them to all parts of the city. Instructors, acting in a professional capacity they never before knew, serve as educational consultants to the community. The college focuses on student learning and community transformation.

Is this college desirable? Feasible? Or is it a dream of an institution that will never be built? In part, the answer depends on the situation of all institutional education in 1979. The next decade could find humane studies centering outside traditional educational structures; the university abandoning the pretext of general education and devoting all its efforts to research, and industrial laboratories building more of their own instructional systems. In such a climate, the college stipulated in this book could flourish.

All features of the college of '79 need not be housed in the same institution but all are needed. Easy access, instructional accountability, courses that take students to all parts of the city, teachers as professionals in instruction, research on learning processes — all are long overdue. The need is so pressing that if currently operating colleges do not provide for alternatives to traditional structures, the *best* that can happen is that other agencies will soon arise, compete for funds, and usurp functions assigned to, but never wholly accepted by, American higher education. (Gleazer, 1968a, p. 131.) The junior college will then have failed to seize the opportunity it had and will become only a vestige of an irrelevant educational form.

This book has argued the case for a defined-outcomes approach to junior college curriculum and instruction by presenting a model of a college built on that rationale. It has spoken in favor of change but failed to consider how change will be stimulated. How will it happen? Through a revolution that destroys current structures? Through forced changes dictated by severely reduced community financial support? Or through the leadership of educators with courage and direction? "How" remains an intriguing question.

Competition, a fascinating potential spur to action, is on the horizon. Will *it* be the trigger? Suppose, for instance, a group appeared at a junior college governing board meeting and made the following proposition:

> We represent the XYZ Learning Corporation. Our instructional specialists have developed and tested certain materials

over the past few years. We have tried these procedures on a variety of populations and feel we can *guarantee* learning along certain dimensions.

Here is a list of specific objectives in the areas of mathematics and communications (we have objectives and programs in other fields as well). We will set up our organization anywhere in your district and take any 1,000 normally functioning young people you send to us. For each student who learns to solve *these* types of problems as measured by *these tests* and to write *these* types of papers in accordance with *these* models, you will pay us $100. If we cannot produce these results within three months with at least 80 per cent of the group, you owe us nothing. No untoward effects will accrue to the learners — you may administer to them any attitudinal tests of your devising.

Suppose, after further elaboration and inquiry, a member of the board turned to the college president and asked, "Your budget last year approximated $2,000,000. Just what did we get for our money?" And, assuming a tenacity not often displayed by board members when speaking of educational matters, suppose he pressed further and said:

Unless you bring us evidence within six months of the nature and extent of the learning achieved by at least a significant proportion of your students, we will seek legislative authorization to use tax funds to be paid to private corporations in accordance with learning contracts. We will set up a public commission to monitor those contracts and, incidentally, we will reduce your budget by an equivalent amount each time we enter into an agreement with a group that guarantees learning.

Don't bring in grade point averages or vague goals capable of an infinity of interpretations! We want concrete evidence that our students are *learning* — demonstrably and predictably.

And if the board were persistent and the president strong of heart, the college might very quickly set itself on a track leading toward the learning institution so badly needed, but so rarely found, in American education. Shall we move *now* — before the mainstream of instruction in this country runs completely out from under what we quaintly call our "educational" institutions?

Bibliography

ALLEN, LUCILLE A. AND ROBERT L. SUTHERLAND
    1963   *Role Conflicts and Congruences.* Austin: University of Texas.

AMERICAN EDUCATION FELLOWSHIP
  1942–43   *Adventure in American Education.* 5 volumes. New York: Harper & Row.

ANDERSON, LESTER
    1960   "Colleges and Universities — Organization and Administration," *Encyclopedia of Educational Research.* New York: Macmillan.

APSLER, ALFRED
    1967   *The Teaching of the Social Sciences to Non-Transfer Students at Community Junior Colleges* (Final Report, U.S. Office of Education; March).

ARNSTINE, DONALD G.
1964 "The Language and Values of Programmed Instruction," *Educational Forum* 28 (Part I, January; Part II, March).

AUSUBEL, DAVID P.
1953 "The Nature of Educational Research," *Educational Theory* 3 (October).

BARZUN, JACQUES
1968 *The American University*. New York: Harper & Row.

BASKIN, SAMUEL
1967 "Patterns for Change: I. The Field-Study Center of 'Beachhead College,'" in *New Designs for Liberal Arts Colleges*, George W. Bonham, ed. Yellow Springs, Ohio: Union for Research and Experimentation in Higher Education.

BECKER, SAMUEL L. AND CARL A. DALLINGER
1960 "The Effect of Instructional Methods Upon Achievement and Attitudes in Communication Skills," *Speech Monographs* 27 (March).

BELL, DANIEL
1966 *The Reforming of General Education*. New York: Columbia University Press.
1968 "About the Reforming of General Education," *American Scholar* 37 (Summer).

BELL, PHILIP W.
1968 Provost, Merrill College; quoted in *Los Angeles Times* (July 29).

BELLOW, SAUL
1964 *Herzog*. New York: Viking Press.

BENNIS, WARREN G.
1966 *Changing Organizations*. New York: McGraw-Hill.

BICKER, ROBERT
1967 "After the Future, What?" in *Inventing Education for the Future*, Warner Z. Hirsch, ed. San Francisco: Chandler Publishing Company.

BIGGE, MORRIS L.
1964 *Learning Theory for Teachers*. New York: Harper & Row.

BIRENBAUM, WILLIAM
1968 "Cities and Universities: Collision of Crises," in *Campus 1980*, Alvin C. Eurich, ed. New York: Delacorte Press.

BLOCKER, CLYDE E., ROBERT H. PLUMMER, AND RICHARD C. RICHARDSON, JR.
1965 *The Two Year College: A Social Synthesis*. Englewood Cliffs, New Jersey: Prentice-Hall, Inc.

BLOOM, BENJAMIN (ed.)
1956 *Taxonomy of Educational Objectives I*. New York: David McKay Company, Inc.

BLOOM, BENJAMIN
    1968   "Learning for Mastery," *Evaluation Comment* 1 (Center for the Study of Evaluation of Instructional Programs, U.C.L.A.; May).

BOYER, WILLIAM H. AND PAUL WALSH
    1968   "Are Children Born Unequal?" *Saturday Review* 51 (October 19).

BRAWER, FLORENCE B.
    1968   *Personality Characteristics of College and University Faculty.* Washington: American Association of Junior Colleges.

BRIGHT, R. LEWIS
    1967   "Research in Educational Technology," *Educom* 2 (December).

BRUNER, JEROME S.
    1966   *Toward a Theory of Instruction.* Cambridge, Massachusetts: Harvard University Press.

BURNS, RICHARD W.
    1968   "Measuring Objectives and Grading," *Educational Technology* 8 (September 30).

BUSHNELL, DON D. AND DWIGHT W. ALLEN
    1967   *The Computer in American Education.* New York: John Wiley & Sons, Inc.

CANFIELD, ALBERT A.
    1967   Vice-President, Curriculum, Oakland Community College; private communication (July).

CARLSON, RICHARD O.
    1966   "Programmed Instruction: Some Unanticipated Consequences," in *Studies of the Use of Programmed Instruction in the Classroom* (Technical Report No. 1), Robert Glaser, *et al.* University of Pittsburgh R and D Center.

CAUDILL, WILLIAM W.
    1965   "Planning Space for Higher Education" (Paper presented at the Conference of California Junior College Association, April 12).

CLARK, BURTON R.
    1960   *The Open-Door College: A Case Study.* New York: McGraw-Hill Book Company.
    1963   "Faculty Culture," *The Study of Campus Cultures.* Berkeley: Committee on Personality Development in Youth of the Social Research Council.

CLARK, KENNETH B.
    1968   "Learning From Students," *Antioch Notes* 46 (November).

COHEN, ARTHUR M.
    1967   "ERIC and the Junior College," *Junior College Journal* 38 (November).

1968 *Focus on Learning: Preparing Teachers for the Two-Year College.* (In collaboration with Florence B. Brawer.) Occasional Report No. 11 (Junior College Leadership Program, U.C.L.A. Graduate School of Education; March).

1969 "Is Innovation Relevant?" *CTA Journal* 65 (January).

COHEN, ARTHUR M. AND FLORENCE B. BRAWER
1969 *Measuring Faculty Performance.* Washington, D.C.: American Association of Junior Colleges.

COLLINGWOOD, R. G.
1939 *An Autobiography.* London: Oxford University Press.

COMMAGER, HENRY S.
1960 *Education in a Free Society.* Pittsburgh: University of Pittsburgh Press.

COONS, ARTHUR G.
1968 *Crisis in California Higher Education.* Los Angeles: Ward Ritchie Press.

COPPOCK, PATRICIA
1968 "An Introduction to the New Careers Program," *Occupational Educational Bulletin,* Vol. B, No. 10 (American Association of Junior Colleges; July 1).

CORNFORD, F. M.
1923 *Microcosmographia Academia; Being a Guide for the Young Academic Politician.* Cambridge, England: Dunster House.

COSAND, JOSEPH P.
1968 "The Community College in 1980," in *Campus 1980,* Alvin C. Eurich, ed. New York: Delacorte Press.

COULSON, JOHN E.
1966 "Automation, Electronic Computers, and Education," *Phi Delta Kappan* 47 (March).

DALIS, GUS T.
1969 "The Effect of Precise Objectives Upon Student Achievement in Health Education." Unpublished dissertation, University of California, Los Angeles.

DAWSON, J. D.
1968 *Research Study of a Proposed New Masters College for the Preparation of Junior College Teachers.* Yellow Springs, Ohio: Union for Research and Experimentation in Higher Education.

DIXON, JAMES O.
1967 "Personalized Higher Education: Ideas and Issues," in *The Individual and the System,* W. John Minter, ed. Boulder, Colorado: Western Interstate Commission for Higher Education.

EDUCATIONAL POLICIES COMMISSION
1964 *Universal Opportunity for Education Beyond the High School.* Washington, D.C.: Educational Policies Commission.

ERICKSEN, STANFORD C.
  1967 "The Teacher, the Book, and the Student's Private Knowledge,"
       in *The Individual and the System*, W. John Minter, ed. Boulder,
       Colorado: Western Interstate Commission for Higher Education.

EURICH, ALVIN C. (ed.)
  1968 *Campus 1980*. New York: Delacorte Press.

FADER, DANIEL N. AND ELTON B. MCNEIL
  1968 *Hooked on Books: Program and Proof*. New York: Berkeley Pub-
       lishing Corp.

FAHEY, GEORGE L. AND JOE M. BALL
  1960 "Objective Evaluation of a Program in General Education," *Jour-
       nal of Educational Psychology* 51 (June).

FELDMAN, MARVIN J.
  1967 *Public Education and Manpower Development*. New York: Ford
       Foundation, Office of Reports.

FLAUGHER, RONALD L., *et al.*
  1967 *Credit by Examination for College-Level Studies: An Annotated
       Bibliography*. New York: College Entrance Examination Board.

FRIEDMAN, NORMAN L.
  1967 "The Subject Matterist Orientation Toward Field of Academic
       Specialization," *American Scholar* 2 (February).

GAGE, N. L.
  1964 "Toward a Cognitive Theory of Teaching," *Teachers College Rec-
       ord* 65 (February).

GAGNE, ROBERT
  1965 *The Conditions of Learning*. New York: Holt, Rinehart & Winston.

GARDNER, JOHN
  1960 "National Goals in Education," in *Goals for Americans* (U.S.
       President's Commission on National Goals). Englewood Cliffs,
       N.J.: Prentice Hall.
  1963 *Self-Renewal*. New York: Harper & Row.

GARRISON, ROGER
  1967 *Junior College Faculty: Issues and Problems*. Washington: Ameri-
       can Association of Junior Colleges.

GERARD, RALPH W.
  1967 "The New Computerized Shape of Education," in *Inventing Edu-
       cation for the Future*, Werner Z. Hirsch, ed. San Francisco:
       Chandler.

GIDEONSE, HENDRICH
  1967 "The Present, The Future and the Enhancement of the Possible,"
       in *Dialogue on Education*, Richard Kean, *et al.*, eds. Indianapolis:
       Bobbs-Merrill.

GLASER, ROBERT
  1966a "The Design of Instruction," in *The Changing American School*,
       John Goodlad, ed. (65th Yearbook of the National Society for the

Study of Education, Part II). Chicago: University of Chicago Press.

1966b   *The Education of Individuals* (Working Paper No. 12). University of Pittsburgh Learning R & D Center.

GLEAZER, EDMUND J., JR.

1967   "Preparation of Junior College Teachers," *Educational Record* 48 (Spring).

1968a   *This is the Community College.* Boston: Houghton Mifflin.

1968b   "Concerns and Cautions for Community Colleges," *Junior College Journal* 38 (March).

GOODLAD, JOHN I.

1967   "The Future of Teaching and Learning." Address delivered to the National Education Association (October 20).

1968   "Thought, Invention, and Research in the Advancement of Education." Presidential address to the American Educational Research Association (February 8).

GOODMAN, PAUL

1968   "Mini-Schools: A Prescription for the Reading Problem," *New York Review of Books* 9 (January 4).

GRAY, J. GLENN

1968   *The Promise of Wisdom.* Philadelphia: Lippincott.

GROSS, RONALD AND JUDITH MURPHY

1966   *Learning by Television.* New York: Fund for the Advancement of Education.

GUSTAD, JOHN W.

1961   *Policies and Practices in Faculty Evaluation.* Washington, D.C.: American Council on Education.

1964   "On Improving College Teaching," *NEA Journal* 53 (March).

HAEFNER, JOHN H.

1964   "Wanted, Break Through for Better Social Studies Instruction," in *Modern Viewpoints in the Curriculum,* Paul C. Rosenbloom, ed. New York: McGraw-Hill.

HAKANSON, JOHN W.

1967   *Selected Characteristics, Socio-Economic Status, and Levels of Attainment of Students in Public Junior College Occupation-Centered Education* (Final Report, U.S. Office of Education).

HALL, CALVIN S. AND GARDNER LINDZEY

1957   *Theories of Personality.* New York: John Wiley & Sons, Inc.

HALL, LINCOLN H.

1967   *Performances of Average Students in a Junior College and in Four Year Institutions* (Research Brief No. 16). Sacramento: California State Department of Education, Bureau of Pupil Personnel Services (January).

HARLACHER, ERVIN L.
   1968   "New Directions in Community Services," *Junior College Journal,* 38 (March).

HAVIGHURST, ROBERT
   1967   "Social Change and the Community College," *North Central Association Quarterly* 41 (Winter).

HENDERSON, KENNETH B.
   1963   "Research on Teaching Secondary School Mathematics," in *Handbook of Research on Teaching,* N. L. Gage, ed. Chicago: Rand McNally.

HILGARD, ERNEST R. AND GORDON H. BOWER
   1966   *Theories of Learning.* 3rd edition; New York: Appleton-Century-Crofts.

HOLLAND, JOHN L. AND SANDRA W. LUTZ
   1967   *Predicting a Student's Vocational Choice* (American College Testing Program, Report No. 18; March). Iowa City, Iowa.

HOYT, DONALD P.
   1965   *The Relationship Between College Grades and Adult Achievement: A Review of the Literature* (American College Testing Program, Report No. 7; September). Iowa City, Iowa.

HUTCHINS, ROBERT M.
   1966   "Education Fit for a Free Man is the Hardest Thing to Find," *Santa Barbara News Press* (October 30).
   1968   *The Learning Society.* New York: Frederick A. Praeger.

ILLICH, IVAN
   1968   "The Futility of Schooling in Latin America," *Saturday Review* 51 (April 20).

JACOB, PHILIP E.
   1957   *Changing Values in College.* New York: Harper & Row.

JENCKS, CHRISTOPHER AND DAVID RIESMAN
   1968   *The Academic Revolution.* New York: Doubleday.

JENNINGS, FRANK G.
   1966   "The Education of Educators," *Saturday Review* 49 (November 19).

JOHNSON, B. LAMAR
   1952   *General Education in Action.* Washington, D.C.: American Council on Education.
   1964   *Islands of Innovation* (Junior College Leadership Program, Occasional Report No. 6). Los Angeles: University of California.
   1966   "Experimental Junior Colleges: Some Stirrings," *Junior College Journal* 37 (October).
   1969   *Islands of Innovation Expanding.* Beverly Hills: Glencoe Press.

Junior College Research Review.
   1967   1 (February-March).

KAMPF, LOUIS
    1968   "The Scandal of Literary Scholarship," in *The Dissenting Academy*, T. Roszak, ed. New York: Pantheon Books.

KAUFFMAN, JOSEPH F., *et al.*
    1968   *The Student in Higher Education*. New Haven: The Hazen Foundation.

KEAN, RICHARD, *et al.*, eds.
    1967   *Dialogue on Education*. Indianapolis: Bobbs-Merrill.

KEETON, MORRIS
    1968   "Uncertain Future for the Small College," *Saturday Review* 51 (February 17).

KEUSCHER, ROBERT E.
    1968   "An Appraisal of Some Dimensions of Systems Theory as Indicators of the Tendency to Innovate in Selected Public Junior Colleges." Unpublished dissertation, University of California, Los Angeles.

KLAPPER, PAUL
    1949   "The Professional Preparation of the College Teacher," *Journal of General Education* 3 (July).

KNOELL, DOROTHY M.
    1967   "New York Challenges Its Urban Colleges," *Junior College Journal* 37 (March).
    1968   "Are Our Colleges Really Accessible to the Poor?" *Junior College Journal* 39 (October).

KOMISAR, B. PAUL, AND JAMES S. McCLELLAN
    1965   "Professor Arnstine and Programmed Instruction," *Educational Forum* 29 (May).

KRATHWOHL, DAVID, *et al.*
    1964   *Taxonomy of Educational Objectives II: The Affective Domain*. New York: David McKay.

LACY, BILL N. (ed.)
    1962   *Ten Designs, Community Colleges*. Houston, Texas: Rice University, Department of Architecture.

LEGTERS, LYMAN H.
    1968   "The Monolithic Myth," *Saturday Review* 51 (February 3).

LEONARD, GEORGE B.
    1968   *Education and Ecstasy*. New York: Delacorte Press.

LOMBARDI, JOHN
    1969   *Student Activism in Junior Colleges: An Administrator's View*. Washington: American Association of Junior Colleges.

LUMSDAINE, ARTHUR A.
    1968   "Instructional Research: Some Aspects of Its Status," *Journal of Experimental Education* 37 (Fall).

McClellan, James, E.
1968 *Toward An Effective Critique of American Education.* Philadelphia: Lippincott.

McCully, Clyde
1968 "Student Perceptions of Junior College Instructors as Directors of Learning." Unpublished dissertation, University of California, Los Angeles.

McDaniel, J. W.
1968 "Sidewalk College," in *The Experimental Junior College,* B. Lamar Johnson, ed. (Junior College Leadership Program, Occasional Report No. 12). Los Angeles: University of California.

McGrath, Earl J.
1966 Universal Higher Education. New York: McGraw-Hill.

McKeachie, Wilbert J.
1967 "Significant Student and Faculty Characteristics Relevant to Personalizing Higher Education," in *The Individual in the System,* W. John Minter, ed. Boulder, Colorado: Western Interstate Commission for Higher Education.
1968 "Psychology at Age 75: The Psychology Teacher Comes Into His Own," *American Psychologist* 23 (August).

McLuhan, Marshall
1964 *Understanding Media: The Extensions of Man.* New York: McGraw-Hill.

McNeil, John D.
1967 "Concomitants of Using Behavioral Objectives in the Assessment of Teacher Effectiveness," *Journal of Experimental Education* 36 (Fall).

Martin, Marie
1968 President, Los Angeles Pierce College; private communication (January 26).

Martin, Warren B.
1968 *Alternative to Irrelevance.* Nashville: Abingdon Press.

Matteson, Richard V.
1966 *The Junior College Program of Instruction and the Employment Experiences of Graduates* (School of Education Report No. 20). Berkeley: University of California.

Mayhew, Lewis B.
1960 "General Education: A Definition," in *General Education: An Account and Appraisal,* Lewis B. Mayhew, ed. New York: Harper & Brothers.
1966 *The Collegiate Curriculum: An Approach to Analysis* (Research Monograph No. 11). Atlanta: Southern Regional Education Board.

1968a   "Changing the Balance of Power," *Saturday Review* 51 (August 17).

1968b   "The Future Undergraduate Curriculum," in *Campus 1980*, Alvin C. Eurich, ed. New York: Delacorte Press.

MILLER, GEORGE A., *et al.*

1960   *Plans and the Structure of Behavior.* New York: Holt.

MOOD, ALEX M.

1967   "The Operations Analysis Program of the U.S. Office of Education," in *Inventing Education for the Future*, Warner Z. Hirsch, ed. San Francisco: Chandler.

MOUGHAMIAM, HENRY

1967   *A Profile of Chicago City College 1965 Graduates, Follow-Up No. 2.* Chicago: Chicago City College (March).

NATIONAL SCIENCE FOUNDATION

1967   *The Junior College and Education in the Sciences* (Report to Sub-committee on Science Research and Development of the Committee on Astronautics). U.S. House of Representatives, 90th Congress, Session I; Washington, D.C.: U.S. Government Printing Office.

NEILL, A. S.

1968   "Can I Come to Summerhill? I Hate My School," *Psychology Today* 1 (May).

O'CONNELL, THOMAS E.

1968   *Community Colleges: A President's View.* Urbana: University of Illinois Press.

OETTINGER, ANTHONY G.

1968   "The Myths of Educational Technology," *Saturday Review* 51 (May 18).

PACE, C. ROBERT

1966   "Selective Higher Education for Diverse Students," in *Universal Higher Education*, Earl McGrath, ed. New York: McGraw-Hill.

1967   "New Concepts in Institutional Goals for Students." Mimeographed paper; Los Angeles: University of California.

PASCHALL, ELIZABETH

1968   "Organizing for Better Instruction," in *Campus 1980*, Alvin C. Eurich, ed. New York: Delacorte Press.

"PATTERNS FOR CHANGE"

1967   In *New Designs for Liberal Arts Colleges*, George W. Bonham, ed. Yellow Springs, Ohio: Union for Research and Experimentation in Higher Education.

PEARL, ARTHUR AND FRANK RIESSMAN

1965   *New Careers for the Poor.* New York: Free Press.

PETERSON, BASIL H.

1965   "Critical Problems and Needs of California Junior Colleges."

Committee on Institutional Research, California Junior College Association.

POPHAM, W. JAMES
    1965   *The Teacher Empiricist.* Los Angeles: Aegeus Press.
    1967   *Development of a Performance Test of Teaching Proficiency.* Los Angeles: University of California, Graduate School of Education (August).
    1968   "Probing the Validity of Arguments Against Behavioral Goals." Symposium presentation at the American Educational Research Association meeting (February).

POSTLETHWAITE, SAMUEL N.
    1965   *An Integrated Experience Approach to Learning.* Minneapolis: Burgess.

POWELL, HOPE M.
    1966   *Implementing a Curriculum for Provisional Students.* Los Angeles: Los Angeles City College (January).

PRESIDENT'S COMMISSION ON HIGHER LEARNING
    1948   "Report of . . . ," *Higher Education for American Democracy I.* New York: Harper & Brothers.

R & D Perspectives
    1968   "Data on Comparative College Teaching Methods Analyzed by CASEA Researchers," *R & D Perspectives.* (University of Oregon, Center for the Advanced Study of Educational Administration; Fall).

RAMI, RALPH A.
    1967   "Examinations and Grades in College," *AAUP Bulletin* 53 (September).

RATHS, JAMES
    1967   "Another Look at Behavioral Objectives," *Carel Report No. 1* (July).

REES, JACK D.
    1968   "Teachers and Technology," *CTA Journal* 64 (March).

REYNOLDS, JAMES W.
    1966   "Needed Changes in Community Colleges," in *Universal Higher Education,* Earl McGrath, ed. New York: McGraw-Hill.

RICHARDS, JAMES M., JR. AND LARRY A. BRASKAMP
    1967   *Who Goes Where to Junior College?* (American College Testing Program, Report No. 20; July). Iowa City, Iowa.

RICHARDS, JAMES M., JR. AND J. L. HOLLAND
    1966   "Factor Analysis of Student 'Explanations' of Their Choice of a College," *Educational Sciences* 1 (October).

ROSENTHAL, ROBERT
    1968   "Self-fulfilling Prophecy," *Psychology Today* 2 (September).

ROSENTHAL, ROBERT AND LENORE JACOBSON
    1968 *Pygmalion in the Classroom.* New York: Holt, Rinehart and Winston.

ROUECHE, JOHN E.
    1967 "Followups of the Junior College Transfer Student," *Junior College Research Review* 1 (February).
    1968 *Salvage, Redirection or Custody? Remedial Education in the Community Junior College.* Washington: American Association of Junior Colleges.

ROUECHE, JOHN E. AND JOHN R. BOGGS
    1968 *Junior College Institutional Research: The State of the Art.* Washington: American Association of Junior Colleges.

RUDOLPH, FREDERICK
    1965 *The American College and University.* New York: Vintage Books.

SALMON, DAVID
    1904 *Joseph Lancaster.* London: Longmans Green and Company.

SANFORD, NEVITT
    1967 *Where Colleges Fail.* San Francisco: Jossey-Bass, Inc.

The Saturday Review
    1968 51 (April 20).
    1968 "Industries Adopt Schools," *Saturday Review* 51 (June 15).

SCHENZ, ROBERT F.
    1964 "What Is Done for Low Ability Students," *Junior College Journal* 34 (May).

SCHRAG, PETER
    1968a "The Four-Year Generation," *Saturday Review* 51 (June 8).
    1968b "Voices in the Classroom," *Saturday Review* 51 (June 15).

SCHUELER, HERBERT AND GERALD S. LESSER
    1967 *Teacher Education and the New Media.* Washington: American Association of Colleges for Teacher Education.

SIMON, HERBERT A.
    1967 "The Job of a College President," *Educational Record* (Winter).

SINGER, DEREK
    1968 "Do We Need a Community College Institute?" *Junior College Journal* 39 (October).

STECKLEIN, JOHN E.
    1960 "Colleges and Universities — Programs," *Encyclopedia of Educational Research.* New York: Macmillan.

STINNET, T. M.
    1966 *Teachers in Politics: The Larger Roles.* Washington: National Education Association (May).

SWANSON, HERBERT L.
    1965 "An Investigation of Institutional Research in the Junior Colleges

of the United States." Unpublished dissertation, University of California, Los Angeles.

TABA, HILDA AND FRAMAN ELZEY
1964 "Teaching Strategies and Thought Processes," *Teachers College Record* 65 (March).

THOMSON, JACK
1967 "Institutional Studies of Junior College Students," *Junior College Research Review* 1 (May).

THORNTON, JAMES
1966 *The Community Junior College*. 2nd edition; New York: Wiley.

TICKTON, SIDNEY G.
"The Magnitude of American Higher Education in 1980," in *Campus 1980*, Alvin C. Eurich, ed. New York: Delacorte Press.

Time
1967 89 (June 2).

TROW, MARTIN
1968 "Bell, Book, and Berkeley: Reflections Occasioned by a Reading of Daniel Bell's The Reforming of General Education," *Experiment & Innovation* 1 (January).

TROW, WILLIAM C.
1949 "Educational Psychology Charts a Course," *Journal of Educational Research* 40 (May).
1963 *Teacher and Technology: New Designs for Learning*. New York: Appleton-Century Crofts.

TYLER, RALPH W.
1964 "Some Persistent Questions on the Definition of Objectives," in *Defining Educational Objectives*, C. M. Lindvall, ed. Pittsburgh: University of Pittsburgh Press.
1967 "Changing Concepts of Educational Evaluation," in *Perspectives of Curriculum Evaluation*, Ralph W. Tyler, *et al.*, eds. Chicago: Rand McNally.

UNIVERSITY OF CALIFORNIA
1967 "The University as a Major Influence in the State," *Proceedings of the University of California Twenty-Second All-University Faculty Conference*. Santa Barbara: University of California.

VEBLEN, THORSTEIN
1931 *The Theory of the Leisure Class*. New York: Viking Press.

WAITS, MARILYN
1969 "Ivy in the Ghetto," *American Education* 5 (December, 1968-January, 1969).

WALKER, DANIEL G.
1968 "The House Plan at Cypress," *Junior College Journal* 38 (April).

WALTERS, EVERETT
     1967 "Trends Toward a Degree for College Teachers," *Educational Record* 48 (Spring).

WELLMAN, HARRY R.
     1968 Commencement address at University of California, Davis; quoted in *University Bulletin* 17 (July 1).

WERDELL, PHILIP
     1967 "A Student's Aims in Education," in *Dialogue on Education*, Robert Theobald, ed. Indianapolis: Bobbs-Merrill Co., Inc.

WITTROCK, M. C.
     1962 "Set Applied to Student Teaching," *Journal of Educational Psychology* 53 (August).

WOOD, DOROTHY A.
     1967 *Test Construction.* Columbus, Ohio: Charles E. Merrill.

WOODRING, PAUL
     1968 *The Higher Learning in America: A Reassessment.* New York: McGraw-Hill.

WORTHAM, MARY
     1967 "The Case for a Doctor of Arts Degree: A View From Junior College Faculty," *AAUP Bulletin* 53 (December).

WORTHEN, RICHARD
     1967 *Junior College English: Which Way?* Pleasant Hill, California: Diablo Valley College (December).

WRENN, C. GILBERT
     1951 *Student Personnel Work in College.* New York: Ronald Press.

YEO, RICHARD D.
     1968 "If I Could Create Cinderella Junior College," *Junior College Journal* 38 (February).

Index